Mountain Biking Colorado's Front Range

From Fort Collins to Colorado Springs

Stephen Hlawaty

FALCON®

GUILFORD, CONNECTICUT
HELENA, MONTANA
AN IMPRINT OF THE GLOBE PEQUOT PRESS

With much love and gratitude,
I dedicate this book to my parents,
Maria and Hans Hlawaty.
Thank you, Mama and Papa.

A FALCON GUIDE®

Maps created by XNR Productions Inc. © The Globe
Pequot Press
All photos by the author unless otherwise noted.

Library of Congress Cataloging-in-Publication Data
Hlawaty, Stephen.
    Mountain biking Colorado's Front Range : from Fort
Collins to Colorado Springs/by Stephen Hlawaty.—1st ed.
        p. cm.—(A Falcon guide)
    ISBN 0-7627-2555-9
    1. All terrain cycling—Front Range (Colo. and Wyo.)—
    Guidebooks. 2. Front Range (Colo. and Wyo.)—Guide-
    books. I. Title. II. Series.
GV1045.5F6H53 2003
796.6'3'097886—dc21
                                            2003044904

Manufactured in the United States of America
First Edition/First Printing

Contents

The Rides
Fort Collins Region

Boulder Region

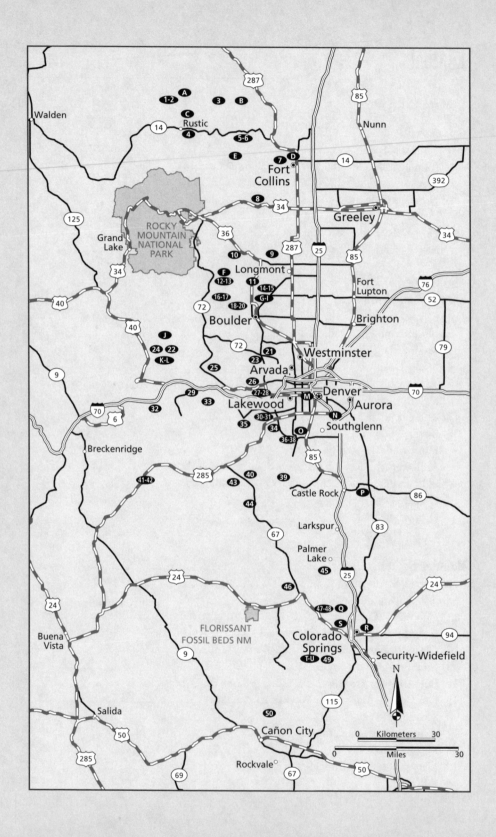

Preface

I first laid tracks in Colorado more than twelve years ago. Armed with a packed duffel bag, a pair of skis, and Muddy Fox's steel-framed "Seeker Mega" bike, I staked my claim in Colorado's Front Range. While Muddy Fox may have been the company to first bring mountain biking to Britain in 1981, it held little presence in Colorado's market share. It seems fitting then, that I, fresh from the paved streets of New York City, as much a newbie to Colorado as one to mountain biking, should start my mountain biking career as a foreigner both in bike and body.

My introduction into mountain biking was most certainly a baptism by fire. On an early spring day in 1993, after portaging our bikes over some boulders in Walker Ranch, my friends and I decided to sit along the banks of the Boulder Creek and enjoy the fierce moving water of the spring runoff. When it came time to continue our ride, I reached for a nearby rock for leverage but pulled it directly onto my leg. The weight of the rock forced me to fall into the creek. Had it not been for the speedy reactions of my friends, I could have taken quite a tumble in that turbulent water. What I remember most of that day isn't the icy cold water of the creek, nor the pain in my leg, but rather the passing of the trees' canopy overhead while being taken out on my back on a stretcher by Rocky Mountain Rescue. This perspective offered me insight into riding the hills surrounding the Front Range. To mountain bike safely requires more than just being safe while on your bike. It demands being safe all the time, always having a certain awareness of your surroundings.

While not attempting to cover all of the rides within the Front Range, I tried to gather a sampling of the variety of rides and terrain in the region, rediscovering old favorites and exploring new possibilities. And so, I present *Mountain Biking Colorado's Front Range* as a kind of trailhead from which to explore new heights, with the understanding that reaching the summit is one thing, but sharing the view—sublime.

Acknowledgments

Grand Master Morihei Ueshiba, the founder of Aikido, once wrote that "the form and beauty that is the world of heaven and earth has become one family." One meaning that we might glean from O Sensei's words is that we all share a kinship with our natural surroundings and each other. And with that, I gratefully acknowledge the participants in this work.

To my parents Hans and Maria Hlawaty, Papa and Mama, thank you for all the love and encouragement that you provide. Your selflessness knows no boundaries and has no equal.

Many thanks go to my younger sister Ingrid and older brother Roland for their continued support. You two have always set the standard by which I judge the quality of my work.

I've had the pleasure to meet a variety of new and interesting people who have all graciously given of their time and talent in preparation for this book.

To Mike Schaub, member of the HandleBar & Grill racing team, thanks for the trail repair efforts on Hayden/Green Mountain Park and for encouraging me to speak with Mike Miller, owner of the HandleBar & Grill. Thank you, Mike Miller, for sitting with me during a busy noonday rush. You weren't yanking mine when you said, "We ain't no chain."

It was great to meet with the entrepreneurial geniuses of Don and Vi O'Connor, Randy Wittmer, and Dan French of Any And All Bikes, Denver's only one-stop mobile bike shop. Thanks again for the Singletrack Club.

The mountain biking community at large owes much to the diligent efforts of the International Mountain Bicycling Association (IMBA). Thank you, Tim Blumenthal, executive director of IMBA, for sharing your thoughts on mountain biking, IMBA, and the environment. It was as much a privilege as it was an education spending time with you. Much appreciation also goes to Judd De Vall, international coordinator for IMBA, for drawing my attention to the "bicycle challenge area" of Eaton Park.

Thank you, Dirk Vinlove, executive director of the Boulder Off-road Alliance (BOA) for clueing me into some of the prospective trail systems for Boulder County. The efforts of you and your staff are greatly appreciated.

Thank you, Pascal Reid of Boulder County Parks and Open Space for providing me with the helpful Heil Valley Ranch information.

Ever mindful that a good time shared makes friends of us all, thanks to all those I met along the trail: Gregg Bromka—Betasso Preserve; Brian Laniel, Wendy

◀ *The Colorado Trail and a bike—a match made in heaven.*

Hedges, Sandy Durkin, and Jeff Curry—Buffalo Creek Area; Chuck Shirk—Kenosha Pass to the Rock Creek Wilderness Area; Brian W. (sorry, I can't read your signature from the Model Photo Release Form)—Bergen Peak; Gerard Finnerty, Judd Warner, and Dami Ashlock—Chimney Gulch; Paul Nugent, Josh Fairchild, his dog Sancho, Jeff Jacobi, and Steve and Danielle Schulte—Argentine Pass; Jon Lenig and Doug Fackelman—Captain Jack's Trail; and Nicole Donathan and Scott Ahrens—HandleBar & Grill (bar side). My thanks to those I've missed.

Thanks to Kim Yactor for pressing on at Reynolds Park. Our hearts were with you during your wiring. Thanks also go to Sara Wade. We don't need no stinking "training" wheels. Steve Garver—Man of Little Words—it was a pleasure riding with you again. Cheers to Lydia Baldwin for setting the precedent. I don't think we ever ended a ride without a beer in hand.

Riding with you, Steve Taylor, was like returning to the Mother Ship for me. Your flat-pedaled, rigid bike riding of Bergen Peak brought me back to our days in Steamboat Springs. I bet you still ski on the "cows."

And now, the Come-Back-Kid Award goes to Jeff Williams. We all winced when you put down your mountain bike for your golf clubs. It's good to see you back on the bike again and better than ever. And to Joanna Williams, the strongest mountain biking novitiate I've seen in a long time, thanks for playing along.

Had it not been for my short stint in Wyoming, I wouldn't have met and ridden with Chad Durr and Aaron Linn. Thanks for heading south to ride. We'll always have the burrito lady.

To my fellow Aikidoka Dante Lividini, a respectful bow to you and the good energy you provide on and off the mat.

Thank you, Scott Adams, my editor, for upgrading the mud, sweat, and gears I offered as a finished manuscript. Now how about upgrading my bike?

Speaking of which, I salute my old Stumpjumper for keeping me rolling. Steel is still real.

To my long-standing friend, spiritual copilot, and soul avenger John Gray, thanks for the music, 'gammon, and good times. Railroad.

Naturally, nothing I do would be complete without the presence of my astonishing wife, Amanda. From the pucker-pinching, back-to-back rides of the Switzerland Trail and Apex Park to dodging lightning bolts atop Rollins Pass, you've shone your smile every step of the way. Were it not for your strength and confidence, the spring and summer of 2001 would have been one huge meltdown. Thank you for sharing with me that smooth singletrack trail to happiness.

And finally thank you, fellow riders, for allowing *Mountain Biking Colorado's Front Range* to be your guide. I hope you enjoy what you see.

Introduction

"In the mountains there is a strange market
where you can barter the vortex of life for boundless bliss . . ."
—*Milarepa, 11th century Tibetan yogi*

The length of Rocky Mountain foothills running south from Fort Collins to Colorado Springs, where amber waves of grain meet the purple mountains' majesty, is generally referred to as the Front Range. It is Colorado's most populated region (home to nearly 80 percent of the state's population). The Front Range's terrain is predominantly semiarid and rocky. Offering cacti, steep grades, and loose rocks, the Front Range delivers some of the most technical riding in the state. Although the views are not as dramatic as the ones found in Colorado's inner Rocky Mountains, the trails here are just as good, albeit somewhat more crowded.

As with the chambers of a heart, Colorado's Front Range is made up of four key communities: Fort Collins, Boulder, Denver, and Colorado Springs. The stellar mountain bike trails in and around these towns have infused Colorado with the pulsating lifeblood that is Front Range mountain biking. And nowhere does the life flow more rapidly than in the more than two million acres that comprise the Arapaho, Roosevelt, and Pike National Forests. These forests rank among the top national forests for year-round recreation use.

The Four Regions

Fort Collins carries with it a certain northern Colorado vibe that is best described as "laid-back authenticity." Not as populated or as diverse as its Front Range counterparts, Fort Collins, nevertheless, includes more than 20 miles of multiuse recreational trails, more than 3,000 acres of open space, and more than 80 miles of designated bikeways, including paved trails, bike lanes, and bike routes. While the Poudre Canyon, Horsetooth Reservoir, and Lory State Park offer the best-known mountain biking trails, there are some gems that require slightly more of an effort getting to but are worth every bit of time it takes getting to them. Some of these trails include those around the Red Feather Lakes area.

Roughly 60 miles southwest of Fort Collins lies Boulder, perhaps the reigning king of recreational mountain towns. With the sheer granite walls of the Flatirons as a backdrop, Boulder provides a dramatic setting for some of mountain biking's best trails. To accommodate the number of bicycle commuters in Boulder (which, incidentally, is seven times greater than the national average), the town boasts more than 60,000 acres of open space and 150 miles of trails. The presence of the International Mountain Bicycling Association's (IMBA) headquarters testifies to Boulder's preeminence as a serious mountain biking town. Hall Ranch, near the small town of

Lyons, provides Boulder County with some of the sweetest and nearest available singletrack riding, while the recent opening of Heil Valley Ranch assures riders that Boulder is committed to the future of mountain biking.

Minutes east of Boulder lies Denver, Colorado's state capital. Denver provides all the art, shopping, and dining that any other city does, but where it differs leaves many other city-dwellers wishing they lived in Colorado. Rated number six by *Bicycling Magazine* in its "Best Bicycling Cities" feature for cities whose populations were greater than 100,000, Denver certainly does its part in contributing to Colorado's healthy lifestyle. Denver's Jefferson County has a particularly enlightened and excellent trail management system, ever keeping in tune with issues surrounding mountain biking. The sinuous Cherry Creek Singletrack that parallels Cherry Creek through downtown Denver passes within minutes of such cityscapes as Neiman Marcus, Saks, and Tiffany's. The lush Hayden/Green Mountain Park trail is another ride destination just minutes from downtown Denver. No wonder, then, that Denver boasts being the thinnest city in the nation, whose residents make up the smallest percentage of overweight adults in the United States.

Just over an hour's drive south of Denver is Colorado Springs, home to Pikes Peak and Colorado's second-largest city. Colorado Springs also does its part in keeping up with Colorado's active lifestyle. Although a major city in its own right, Colorado Springs, nevertheless, is home to USA Cycling (888–405–7223), the national governing body of bicycling, which includes the National Off-Road Biking Association (NORBA), the national governing body for mountain bike racing. Colorado Springs is also home to the U.S. Olympic Training Center. Some of the better rides in the area include Rampart Reservoir Shoreline Loop and Captain Jack's Trail. Each trail features narrow, and oftentimes, technical singletrack. Many of the area trails are lined with Pikes Peak granite. Colorado Springs residents have a love/hate relationship with this geological phenomenon. While riders have likened riding on Pikes Peak granite to riding on ball bearings, it does help absorb water, which keeps trails drier and extends the riding season.

Unlike most major metropolitan areas, Fort Collins, Denver, Boulder, and Colorado Springs are all within an easy thirty minutes' drive of incredible riding. Because trails along the Front Range typically receive a higher volume of use, their routes tend to be considerably easier to follow. That's not to say, however, that Front Range riding is all user-friendly. Front Range trails oftentimes travel through rattlesnake and mountain lion habitats, something to consider if ever riding alone. Moreover, the Front Range's semiarid terrain is an ideal growing environment for the weed commonly referred to as "goathead" or "puncturevine" (*Tribulus terrestris*). The fruits that these weeds produce are also known as goatheads. After these goatheads fall from their host weeds, they harden and dry (with the seed of the weed inside). Becoming a three-pointed, thorn-like enemy on the trail, goatheads have an uncanny ability of finding their way into your tires. Their pervasion throughout the

Front Range demands that riders ride with thicker and/or spare tubes, pump, and stocked patch kit.

Because the Front Range abuts the Continental Divide, riding here includes the rigors of routinely negotiating up and down steep, sandy, and rocky slopes. Added to this is the dustier, hotter, and more exposed terrain of the Front Range at large. Moreover, while riding in Colorado's more interior Rockies may require more sustained lung and leg power, Front Range riding requires that you have enough stored energy for short bursts and tight switchbacks. Rhythms are broken very easily and quite frequently. These characteristics make Front Range riding a challenge. To us is left the fortunate task of surpassing these challenges.

Mountain Biking Guidelines

If every mountain biker always yielded the right-of-way, stayed on the trail, avoided wet or muddy trails, never cut switchbacks, always rode in control, showed respect for other trail users, and carried out every last scrap of what was carried in (candy wrappers and bike-part debris included)—in short, if we all did the right things—we wouldn't need a list of rules governing our behavior.

The fact is, most mountain bikers are conscientious and are trying to do the right thing; however, thousands of miles of dirt trails have been closed due to the irresponsible habits of a few riders.

Here are some basic guidelines adapted from the International Mountain Bicycling Association Rules of the Trail. These guidelines can help prevent damage to land, water, plants, and wildlife; maintain trail access; and avoid conflicts with other backcountry visitors and trail users.

1. **Only ride on trails that are open.** Don't trespass on private land, and be sure to obtain any necessary permits. If you're not sure if a trail is closed or if you need a permit, don't hesitate to ask.

2. **Keep your bicycle under control.** Watch the condition of the trail at all times, and follow the appropriate speed regulations and recommendations.

3. **Yield to others on the trail.** Make your approach well known in advance, either with a friendly greeting or a bell. When approaching a corner, junction, or blind spot, expect to encounter other trail users. When passing others, show your respect by slowing to a walking pace.

4. **Don't startle animals.** Animals may be easily scared by sudden approaches or loud noises. For your safety—and the safety of others in the area as well as the animals themselves—give all wildlife a wide berth. When encountering horses, defer to the horseback riders' directions.

5. **Zero impact.** Be aware of the impact you're making on the trail beneath you. You should not ride under conditions in which you will leave evidence of your passing, such as on certain soils after rain. If a ride features optional side hikes

into wilderness areas, be a zero-impact hiker, too. Whether you're on bike or on foot, stick to existing trails, leave gates as you found them, and carry out everything you brought in.

6. **Be prepared.** Know the equipment you are using, the area where you'll be riding, and your cycling abilities and limitations. Avoid unnecessary breakdowns by keeping your equipment in good shape. When you head out, bring spare parts and supplies for weather changes. Be sure to wear appropriate safety gear, including a helmet, and learn how to be self-sufficient.

How to Use This Guide

Mountain Biking Colorado's Front Range features 50 mapped and cued rides and 21 honorable mentions. The book has been divided into four regions: Fort Collins, Boulder, Denver, and Colorado Springs. Each region features an introduction in which you're given a sweeping look at the lay of the land.

Every ride description follows the same format. Here's an explanation of some of the information you'll find:

Start: What the sign at the trailhead says, what the locals call it, or the name of the place surrounding it.

Distance: Miles traveled from start to finish and if the ride is a loop, point-to-point, or out-and-back trip. Because one ride is never exactly the same as the one before, this is a ballpark figure so you'll know approximately what you're in for when you leave the trailhead behind.

Approximate riding time: The time it took to move from the starting point to the ending point, not including time spent during any major deviations from the route described. The times of these rides are gauged for both advanced and intermediate riders.

Aerobic level: The amount of "hurt" a trail will put on your heart and lungs, rated easy, moderate, challenging, or strenuous. Distance, overall elevation gains, trail surface, and steepness of pitch were all considered when rating the aerobic level of each trail, but perhaps the biggest factor in this category will be the speed and consistency with which you greet each ride. Your best bet is to ride at a pace where you feel most comfortable. With a few notable exceptions, the trails in this book should be accessible to most people with a bit of off-road biking experience.

Technical difficulty: The level of bike-handling skills required to ride a trail. These skills include climbing loose surfaces, climbing steep grades, descending both of these, dropping off rock ledges, and managing small obstacles such as rocks, roots, logs, and any of the other things that can come at you during the course of a ride.

Terrain: The trail's surface, whether it's singletrack, doubletrack, jeep road, gravel path, and so on. There are no rides here with a majority of paved surface, though some do have paved sections. Singletrack is the first and foremost in desirability for any mountain biker, but plenty of trails in this book have doubletrack and jeep road that offer some great riding.

You'll also find information about when the ride is open, the nearest town, other trail users you might encounter, and whether the trail is dog-friendly, as well as a detailed and honest description of the ride.

Elevation Profiles

An elevation profile accompanies each ride description. Here the ups and downs of the route are graphed on a grid of elevation, with *feet above sea level* on the sides, and *miles pedaled* across the top. Note that these graphs are compressed (squeezed) to fit on the page. The actual slopes you will ride are not as steep as the lines drawn on the graphs (it just feels that way). Also, some extremely short dips and climbs are too small to show up on the graphs. All such abrupt changes in gradient are, however, mentioned in the mile-by-mile ride description.

Honorable Mentions

The Honorable Mentions at the end of each region in the book detail all of the rides that didn't make the cut as a full-featured route. In many cases it's not because they aren't great rides, but because they're overcrowded or environmentally sensitive to heavy traffic.

How to Read the Maps

The individual route map is your primary guide to each ride. It shows all of the accessible roads and trails, points of interest, water, towns, landmarks, and geographical features. It also distinguishes trails from roads and paved roads from unpaved roads. The selected route is highlighted, and directional arrows point the way.

We don't want anyone, by any means, to feel restricted to just the routes and trails that are mapped here. We hope you will have an adventurous spirit and use this guide as a platform to dive into the Front Range backcountry and discover new routes for yourself. One of the simplest ways to do this is to ride a course in reverse. The change in perspective is fantastic, and the ride should feel quite different. With this in mind, it will be like getting two distinctly different rides on each map. Not to mention that if you ride the same trails in the dark, the rides become completely different. Like night and day! Pun intended!

Map Legend

=**84**=	Limited access highway
-**97**-	U.S. highway
-**35**-	State highway
———	Paved road
═══	Gravel road
= = = = =	Unimproved road
- - - - -	Singletrack trail
▬ ▬ ▬ ▬	Featured trail
··············	Doubletrack
▬▬▬▬▬	Featured doubletrack
+++++++	Railroad
)———(	Tunnel
•——•——•	Powerline
⌒	Bridge
▲	Campground
†	Cemetery
🧗	Climbing
🏇	Horse trail
•—•	Gate
◘	Overlook/viewpoint
🅿	Parking
)(	Pass
▲	Peak
🌲	Picnic area
★	Point of interest/other trailhead
▌	Ranger station
🚻	Rest room
∘~	Spring
≡	Stairs
START 🚴	Start of featured trail
⫽	Waterfall

● Easy   ■ Moderate   ◆ Difficult   ◆◆ Very Difficult

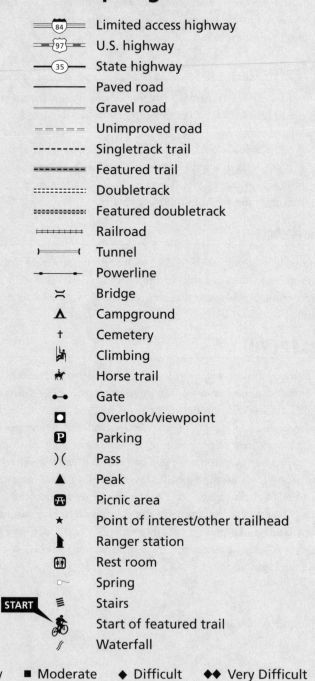

Fort Collins Region

Instead of "I'm going to Disneyland," the likes of Orel Hershiser, Michael Jordan, and John Elway could easily have said "I'm going to Fort Collins" when asked "What's next?" after their respective wins in the 1988 World Series, the 1991 NBA Championships, and the 1998 Superbowl XXXII. It's true. In fact, if you were to say that Fort Collins was the inspiration behind Disneyland, you wouldn't be too far from the truth. Originally from Fort Collins, Harper Goff designed the main street in Disneyland after the buildings found in Fort Collins's Old Town. But that's as close to Disneyland as you are going to get.

Situated in northern Colorado at the foot of the Rocky Mountains, Fort Collins lies in the Cache la Poudre River Valley. The Cache la Poudre River begins in Rocky Mountain National Park and flows through the Poudre Canyon to meet the South Platte River east of Greeley. From its headwaters to the confluence with the South Platte, the Poudre drops roughly 7,000 feet. Sitting at an elevation of 4,984 feet and boasting more than 300 days of annual sunshine, Fort Collins offers mountain bikers a great access point to the foothills and the higher mountains to the west.

In 1862 Camp Collins was established and served as a fortification for travelers and settlers along the Colorado branch of the Overland Trail. On August 20, 1864, Lieutenant Colonel William O. Collins of the Eleventh Ohio Volunteer Cavalry established a new and permanent post to replace Camp Collins. This post became what is now known as Fort Collins and served to protect a strategic trading post. By 1867 the area around Fort Collins was deemed safe from Native tribes, and the fort was abandoned.

By the 1870s and 1880s construction of irrigation canals was complete and led the development of the area's long-standing agricultural industry. The newly irrigated and the semiarid lands around Fort Collins proved to be a perfect blend for growing wheat, oats, and barley; no wonder that Fort Collins is noted for having the most microbreweries per capita in Colorado. Fort Collins owes much of its initial growth explosion to these early agricultural years. In fact, many of the elegant and showcase houses (many of which are listed on the National Register of Historic

Places) in Fort Collins today were built during the growth years of the 1880s.

Today, Fort Collins has grown into a thriving community of more than 100,000 and boasts an expanding technology sector as well as a healthy tourism industry. With Horsetooth Mountain Park, Lory State Park, and Roosevelt National Park all lying within minutes west of Fort Collins, the town offers an impressive display of outdoor opportunities. The foothills west of Fort Collins are riddled with several trail networks that are managed and maintained by the City Natural Areas and Larimer County Parks. Comprising 5,545 acres of foothills, wetlands, prairies, riparian areas, and urban sites, the city of Fort Collins maintains thirty-nine natural areas. These natural areas provide habitat to wildlife and native plants. The Larimer County Parks and Open Lands manages open space and outdoor recreational areas in Larimer County. Thanks to the ¼-cent open-space sales tax, more than 12,000 acres of land have been preserved in Larimer County alone. But Fort Collins's commitment to riding isn't only found in the foothills. Transfort, the Fort Collins municipal bus service, equips all its buses with bike racks that can carry two bikes. Available on a first-come, first-serve basis, there is no extra charge for using the bike racks.

For more information on Fort Collins, contact the Fort Collins Chamber of Commerce at (970) 482–3746, the Colorado Welcome Center at (970) 491–3583, or the Fort Collins Convention and Visitors Bureau, (970) 491–3388.

1 Killpecker Trail

Hmmmm, you wonder why the trail is named "Killpecker." You'll find out. The Killpecker Trail travels from the North Fork Poudre Campground to Forest Road 517 (Elkhorn Baldy Road). The route described here follows Deadman Road, Forest Road 300 (Killpecker Road), and FR 517, which accesses a variety of other motorized trails, such as Bald Mountain and Green Ridge trails, before reaching Middle Bald Mountain, the second highest of the three bald peaks in the area, at 10,700 feet. Two-thirds of this route involves climbing steadily along these three roads for a total of roughly 10 miles. While the road riding seems long in comparison to the time on the singletrack—and it is—there's good reason for that. The singletrack burns a direct and steep line from the top, at the base of Middle Bald Mountain, to the bottom, south of the North Fork Poudre Campground. Between top and bottom, riders are offered rock- and root-filled singletrack, along sometimes narrow, and otherwise, killpecker terrain.

Start: The Killpecker trailhead
Distance: 14.5-mile loop
Approximate riding time: Advanced riders, 2 hours; intermediate riders, 3 hours
Aerobic level: Physically moderate to challenging due to extended periods of climbing at high elevations
Technical difficulty: Technically moderate with some more-technically challenging sections of steep grades and large rocks
Terrain: Dirt road and singletrack that reaches elevations in excess of 10,000 feet. While most of the trail runs its course through thick forest, the top of the trail climbs through a very exposed and open meadow, so be aware of any inclement weather that might be rolling in as you near 10,000 feet.
Schedule: June–October
Maps: DeLorme *Colorado Atlas & Gazetteer*, page 19; USGS: South Bald Mountain, CO; Trails Illustrated: #111, Red Feather Lakes, Glendevey, CO
Nearest town: Red Feather Lakes
Other trail users: Hikers, motorcyclists, horseback riders, campers
Canine compatibility: Dog-friendly, but be advised that vehicular traffic can occur throughout the entire route
Trail contact: Arapaho and Roosevelt National Forests, Canyon Lakes Ranger District, Fort Collins; (970) 498-2770

Finding the Trailhead: From Fort Collins, drive north on U.S. Highway 287. After passing Ted's Place and the intersection with Colorado Highway 14, continue driving north on US 287 for 11 miles before turning left onto Red Feather Lakes Road (Larimer County Road 74E) by the Forks Restaurant. Drive west on Red Feather Lakes Road for 24.6 miles before the road turns to dirt and becomes Deadman Road. Drive on Deadman Road for another 7 miles before bearing left (south) into the Killpecker Trail pullout on the left, across from the North Fork Poudre Campground.

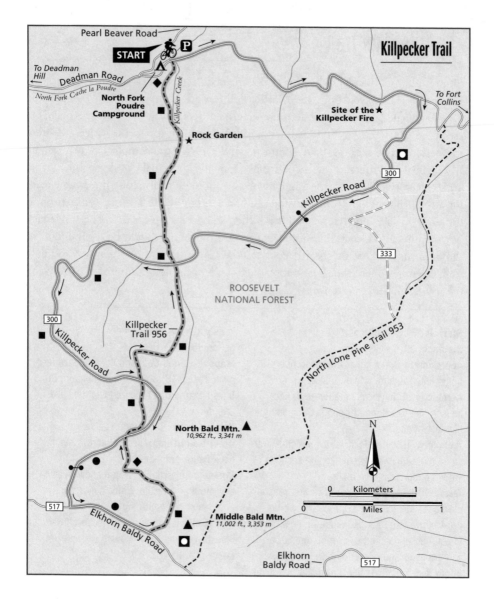

Pearl Beaver Road

START

To Deadman Hill

Deadman Road

North Fork Cache la Poudre

North Fork Poudre Campground

Killpecker Creek

To Fort Collins

Site of the ★ Killpecker Fire

300

Rock Garden

Killpecker Road

333

ROOSEVELT NATIONAL FOREST

300

Killpecker Road

Killpecker Trail 956

North Lone Pine Trail 953

North Bald Mtn. ▲
10,962 ft., 3,341 m

N

517

Elkhorn Baldy Road

Middle Bald Mtn.
11,002 ft., 3,353 m

0   Kilometers   1

0   Miles   1

Elkhorn Baldy Road

517

The Ride

Riders begin by climbing up Deadman Road, heading in a northeasterly direction. Deadman Road is named after the Deadman Lookout Tower. The original wooden tower was built by the Civil Conservation Corps (CCC) in 1937 to spot area forest fires. The tower was one of eight fire lookouts in the Front Range, extending from southern Wyoming south to Denver. The wooden tower was replaced by the existing metal structure in 1961. By 1963 there was nothing remaining of the original wooden tower. In service for more than 35 years, the Deadman Lookout Tower was the last of the eight Front Range towers to retire, as spotter planes took on the responsibility of locating fires.

On April 1, 1991, the National Historic Lookout Register recognized the Deadman Lookout Tower as one of historic and cultural significance. Today, Roosevelt National Forest volunteers oversee the Tower. Visitors can still climb to the top of the tower to enjoy 360-degree unobstructed views that extend north into Wyoming and south to the Mummy Range and the Rawah Wilderness Area.

With the thought of fire in mind, the climb up Deadman Road makes for a good warm-up to the rest of the day. Within 2 miles of beginning your ride, you pass through what was once the Killpecker Fire. The Killpecker Fire began on June 12, 1978, and burned more than 1,200 acres. The cause of the fire was determined to be careless campers. The effects of their carelessness are still very noticeable today.

Once intersecting with FR 300, you're offered stellar views of West Lake and the Red Feather Lakes area. This section of trail follows the same route as the North Lone Pine Trail. After roughly 5 miles of riding, FR 300 will come to its first intersection with the Killpecker Trail. From this first intersection, the climbing becomes more physically challenging, as you make your way into the route's higher elevations. After 6.5 miles, the trail levels off a bit and will intersect with the Killpecker Trail two more times. Many area riders will access the Killpecker Trail at its third intersection with FR 300 because from here you begin to lose elevation before having to climb again.

At 10 miles you connect with the Killpecker Trail at a brown trail-marker sign identifying it as a multiple-use trail. Once connecting onto this singletrack, the trail is both technically and physically challenging, as it makes its way over rocky and steep terrain to the base of Middle Bald Mountain. You'll eventually come out of the forest into a clearing as you near Middle Bald Mountain. The trail climbs alongside the western edge of the clearing, passing a large cairn with a stick stuck in the middle of it on your left. To your right will be Middle Bald Mountain.

The climb to the top of Middle Bald Mountain is well worth the effort, as it offers 360-degree Rocky Mountain views of Red Feather Lakes to the east, Wyoming to

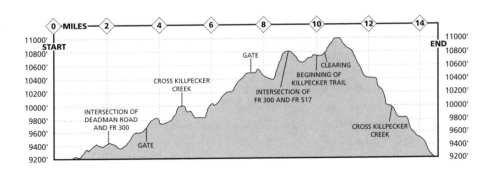

A successful crossing of the Killpecker Creek.

the north, the Rawah Wilderness and Medicine Bow Range to the west, and the Mummy Range to the south. The Mummy Range lies in the northeast corner of Rocky Mountain National Park. Early prospectors to the area noticed that the range resembled a mummy lying on its back with its hands folded across its chest. The Mummy Range comprises seven prominent peaks: Mt. Dunraven (12,571 feet); Mt. Chiquita (13,069 feet); Mt. Chapin, the mummy's head (12,454 feet); Mummy Mountain (13,425 feet); Mt. Fairchild (13,502 feet); Ypsilon Mountain (13,514 feet); and Hague's Peak (13,562 feet). Not to be diminished by its 13,000-foot neighbors, Middle Bald Mountain stands proudly at 10,700 feet and marks the Killpecker Trail's highest point. After climbing through the clearing, you'll reenter the forest and negotiate over rocky terrain, before intersecting with FR 300.

The descent along the singletrack from its first intersection with FR 300 is fast and moderately technical, providing a variety of more rutted and rockier sections along the way. The middle section of singletrack offers a fast run through a mixed conifer forest and delivers some tighter terrain. Tight rocks, big drop-offs, and steep terrain greet you as you begin the final section of singletrack. Once beyond this section, however, the Killpecker Trail descends to meet Killpecker Creek. The rest of the route is fast and furious, as the trail weaves alongside, as well as crosses, the creek from time to time. After roughly 13.5 miles, you arrive at a rock garden where you will have to hike-your-bike. Once crossing the creek again at 13.9 miles, the trail delivers one last technical section, replete with rocks and steep grades, before returning you to your vehicle.

Miles and Directions

0.0 Start from the Killpecker trailhead and begin climbing in a northeasterly direction on the dirt Deadman Road.

1.7 Pass through the area burned by the Killpecker Fire.

2.1 Deadman Road intersects with FR 300 (Killpecker Road) on your right. Bear right onto FR 300.

3.5 Pass through a gate and continue riding on FR 300.

4.9 FR 300 will cross Killpecker Creek and intersect with the singletrack of the Killpecker Trail. Continue riding on FR 300.

7.5 FR 300 will once again intersect with the singletrack of the Killpecker Trail. Continue riding on FR 300.

7.6 Pass through a gate and continue on FR 300.

8.6 FR 300 will intersect with the singletrack of the Killpecker Trail (956) for the third time. Continue riding on FR 300.

9.3 FR 300 intersects with FR 517 (Elkhorn Baldy Road). Bear left onto FR 517.

10.0 FR 517 passes a foot-travel-only trail on your left. Just past that on your left will be your connection with the Killpecker Trail (956), marked by a brown, multiple-use trail sign. Bear left onto the Killpecker Trail (956).

10.3 Arrive at a clearing, as you near Middle Bald Mountain, and continue climbing along the clearing's western side. Middle Bald Mountain will be on your right.

11.0 The Killpecker Trail intersects with FR 300. Cross FR 300 and continue descending on the singletrack Killpecker Trail.

11.7 Intersect with FR 300. Cross the road and continue descending on the trail on the other side of the road.

12.7 Intersect with FR 300 again. Bear left on FR 300 for roughly 30 feet and connect with the singletrack again on the other side of FR 300.

13.0 Cross Killpecker Creek.

13.9 Cross Killpecker Creek again.

14.5 Arrive at your vehicle.

Ride Information

Trail Information

Diamond Peaks Mountain Bike Patrol, Timnath; (970) 482-6006 ext. 22; e-mail DPMBP@aol.com

Local Information

Poudre River/Red Feather Lakes Tourist Council, 31635 Poudre Canyon, Bellvue 80512; (970) 881-2142

Local Events and Attractions

Creedmore Lakes, north of Red Feather Lakes Road, off County Road 180, via County Road 73C

Deadman Lookout Fire Tower, west of Killpecker Trail on Deadman Road

Red Feather Lakes, off Red Feather Lakes Road (County Road 74E)

Restaurants

The Forks Mercantile, Livermore; (970) 221-2080

Pot Belly Restaurant and Lounge, Red Feather Lakes; (970) 881-2984

2 North Lone Pine Trail

The North Lone Pine Trail is predominantly used by hikers and horseback riders. But owing to the trail's relatively smooth singletrack, which runs underneath a thick canopy of green for its entire length, North Lone Pine offers us "velocipedestrians" one sweet ride. While the entire North Lone Pine Trail continues along the east side of Middle Bald Mountain, at 10,700 feet the second highest of the three bald peaks in the area, this trail description concerns itself only with the lower half of the North Lone Pine Trail. The upper half isn't particularly suited for mountain biking, as there are a number of places where you would have to hike-a-bike. While mostly hidden by dense, lodgepole pine and aspen forests, the trail does open up near its end to offer easterly views of Red Feather Lakes village. Recreational campers, four-wheelers, and hunters regularly use all the Forest Service roads listed in this description, so be careful as you ride.

Start: The North Lone Pine trailhead
Distance: 4.8-mile loop
Approximate riding time: Advanced riders, 30–45 minutes; intermediate riders, 1–1.5 hours
Aerobic level: Physically easy to moderate, due to the lack of any significant climbing
Technical difficulty: Technically easy to moderate, due to a few rockier and steeper sections
Terrain: Dirt road and singletrack. The singletrack runs over mostly smooth terrain under a dense evergreen canopy and alongside North Lone Pine Creek. While most of the trail is smooth and wide singletrack, there are some exposed root sections with which you will have to contend.
Schedule: June–October
Maps: DeLorme *Colorado Atlas & Gazetteer*, page 19; USGS: South Bald Mountain, CO; Trails Illustrated: #111, Red Feather Lakes, Glendevey, CO
Nearest town: Red Feather Lakes
Other trail users: Hikers, horseback riders, campers, and hunters (in season)
Canine compatibility: Dog-friendly
Trail contact: Arapaho and Roosevelt National Forests, Canyon Lakes Ranger District, Fort Collins; (970) 498-2770

Finding the Trailhead: From Fort Collins, drive north on U.S. Highway 287. After passing Ted's Place and the intersection with Colorado Highway 14, continue driving north on US 287 for roughly 11 miles before turning left onto Red Feather Lakes Road (Larimer County Road 74E) by the Forks Restaurant. Drive west on Red Feather Lakes Road for 24.6 miles before the road turns to dirt and becomes Deadman Road. Drive on Deadman Road for another 4.5 miles before bearing left into the North Lone Pine overlook and trailhead parking lot area.

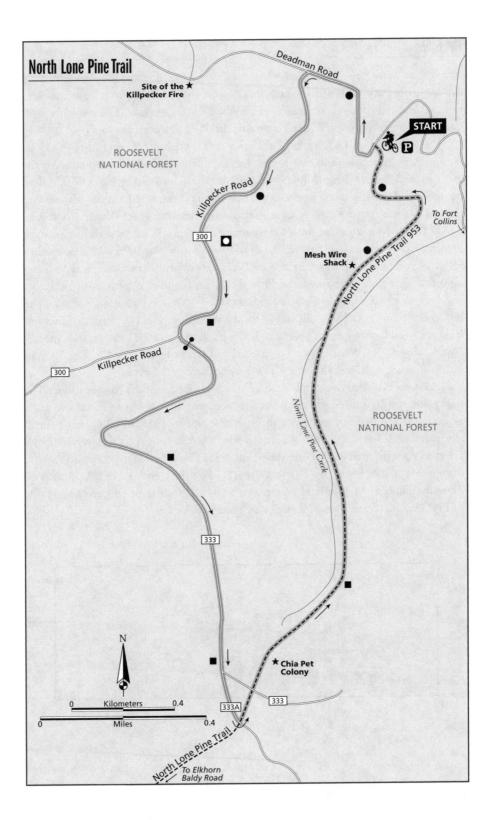

North Lone Pine Trail

**Site of the ★
Killpecker Fire**

ROOSEVELT
NATIONAL FOREST

Killpecker Road

300

Killpecker Road

300

333

Deadman Road

START

P

To Fort
Collins

**Mesh Wire
Shack** ★

North Lone Pine Trail 953

North Lone Pine Creek

ROOSEVELT
NATIONAL FOREST

★ **Chia Pet
Colony**

333A   333

N

0   Kilometers   0.4

0   Miles   0.4

North Lone Pine Trail

To Elkhorn
Baldy Road

The Ride

From your vehicle, bear left onto Deadman Road (a dirt road) and climb in a southerly direction to Forest Road 300 (Killpecker Road). FR 300 follows the same route as the Killpecker Trail, a longer, more technical area trail. Once on FR 300, you'll be offered beautiful easterly views of the Red Feather Lakes area.

The area around Red Feather Lakes was first settled as a mining camp in 1871. Although no minerals were ever found, local residents turned their attention to the area's natural beauty. Originally called Westlake, the Red Feather Lakes would then be developed as a mountain resort. Local developers constructed a series of dams and ditches to form the area's many lakes in hopes of attracting Front Range city folk in need of high country diversions. As expected, the city folk came with not as many leaving. Indeed, the town's first school district was formed in 1895 with a post office following only a year later at the nearby Percy ranch. With an education system and a post office firmly established, the little mountain community was evolving into a full-fledged town. The town's first cabin, built by Nettie Poore along the banks of the smooth Ramona Lake, still stands today. Aside from this one, many of the area lakes are named after Native American lexicon: Hiawatha, Red Feather, and Apache. By the early 1900s, Westlake was renamed Red Feather Lakes after "Princess" Tsian-ini Redfeather, a singer who was part Cherokee and part Creek.

Once on FR 333, you climb gradually in and out of mixed conifer forests. The trail passes through some old clear-cut fire lines, presumably cut to battle the man-made forest fire that ran its course through this area in 1978. FR 300 will eventually meet with FR 333A. You'll ride on FR 333A for a very short while before intersecting with the North Lone Pine Trail (953). You'll notice that the trail extends from either side of FR 333A. The section of trail on the right side of FR 333A continues to climb to Middle Bald Mountain, while the section of trail on the left side of FR 333A descends along North Lone Pine Creek.

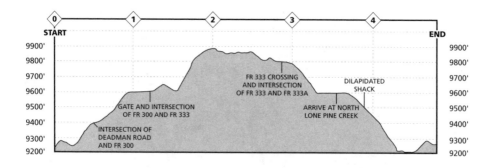

The gate across FR 333.

The North Lone Pine Trail was once a stock driveway, which was reconstructed as a hiking trail during 1979 and acquired as a mountain biking trail some time between then and now. Once bearing left onto the North Lone Pine Trail, you'll enjoy a fast cruise over smooth singletrack. Almost immediately, you'll notice the low-standing grass to the left and right of the trail, reminiscent of a small colony of Chia Pets, those handmade pottery planters that come with Chia seeds that, when planted, grow green, leafy sprouts.

After 3.5 miles into your ride, the trail runs down a moderately steep and technical hill to meet North Lone Pine Creek. This section of the trail makes for a great watering hole for you, your friends, or some other such faithful companion. You'll cross the creek a couple of times before arriving at a dilapidated shack made of mesh wire. The shack is probably a remnant of when this trail was used as a stock drive for resident ranchers. Nowadays, it's more familiar to see stock drives along Red Feather Lakes Road than on nearby area trails. After 4 miles into your ride, the forest will open up briefly to offer glimpses of the Red Feather Lakes area. From here, it's a short and fast trip to your vehicle and the end of your ride.

Miles and Directions

0.0 Start by riding out of the parking lot and bearing left onto Deadman Road.

0.5 Deadman Road intersects with FR 300 (Killpecker Road). Bear left onto FR 300, riding in a southerly direction.

1.3 FR 300 intersects with FR 333. Bear left onto FR 333, pass through the iron gate, and continue riding in a southeasterly direction.

2.8 FR 333 bears left and intersects with FR 333A. Continue riding straight on FR 333A and intersect the singletrack trail of the North Lone Pine Trail (953). Bear left onto the cairn-marked singletrack of the North Lone Pine Trail.

2.9 Cross FR 333 and continue riding on the North Lone Pine Trail.

3.6 Arrive at North Lone Pine Creek and continue descending on the trail.

3.9 Pass a dilapidated shack of mesh wire on your left and continue descending on the trail.

4.8 Arrive at your vehicle.

Ride Information

Trail Information

Diamond Peaks Mountain Bike Patrol, Timnath; (970) 482-6006 ext. 22; e-mail DPMBP@aol.com

Local Information

Poudre River/Red Feather Lakes Tourist Council, 31635 Poudre Canyon, Bellvue 80512; (970) 881-2142

Local Events and Attractions

Creedmore Lakes, north of Red Feather Lakes Road, off County Road 180, via County Road 73C

Deadman Lookout Fire Tower, west of Killpecker Trail on Deadman Road

Red Feather Lakes, off Red Feather Lakes Road (County Road 74E)

Restaurants

The Forks Mercantile, Livermore; (970) 221-2080

Pot Belly Restaurant and Lounge, Red Feather Lakes; (970) 881-2984

3 Mount Margaret Trail

The Mount Margaret Trail is widely used by horseback riders, hikers, and mountain bikers. Its fairly level terrain is well suited for those new to mountain biking. The trail passes by a number of campsites and through a variety of open meadows and quiet stands of aspen and ponderosa pine on its way to the top of Mount Margaret, which overlooks the North Lone Pine Creek drainage. The huge giant rock walls that stand alongside parts of the Mount Margaret Trail offer mountain bikers ample amounts of rock scrambling diversion. Except for the last leg of the trail, which is tight single-track, the trail follows an old roadbed. Several side trails lead to Dowdy Lake and make loops with the main trail.

Start: The Mount Margaret trailhead
Distance: 7.8-mile out-and-back, with several side trails that make loops with the main trail
Approximate riding time: Advanced riders, 45 minutes; intermediate riders, 1 hour
Aerobic level: Physically easy due to a lack of any significant elevation gain
Technical difficulty: Technically easy with a couple of moderately technical sections of tight singletrack and rockier terrain
Terrain: Singletrack and doubletrack delivers wider and smoother terrain for most of the trail's length, as it passes through open meadows and mixed stands of ponderosa pine and aspen. Tighter and rockier terrain toward the end of the trail.
Schedule: April–November
Maps: DeLorme *Colorado Atlas & Gazetteer*, page 19; USGS: Red Feather Lakes, CO; Trails Illustrated: #111, Red Feather Lakes, Glendevey, CO
Nearest town: Red Feather Lakes
Other trail users: Hikers, horseback riders, and campers
Canine compatibility: Dog-friendly
Trail contact: Arapaho and Roosevelt National Forests, Canyon Lakes Ranger District, Fort Collins; (970) 498-2770

Finding the Trailhead: From Fort Collins, drive north on U.S. Highway 287. After passing Ted's Place and the intersection with Colorado Highway 14, continue driving north on US 287 for roughly 11 miles before turning left onto Red Feather Lakes Road (Larimer County Road 74E) by the Forks Restaurant. Drive west on Red Feather Lakes Road for 20.5 miles before bearing right into the Mount Margaret Trail parking lot on the north side of the road.

The Ride

The trail begins as a rough-looking doubletrack, which crosses a grassy area on its way to the South Lone Pine Creek drainage. Upon coming to South Lone Pine Creek, riders can wade through it, ride through it, or cross it via a split-log foot-bridge roughly 50 feet downstream. After crossing the creek, the trail is more apparently wide doubletrack, which follows an old roadbed used for fuelwood-cutting in an area once infested with pine beetle. The doubletrack is predominately smooth, save for a few rocky and sandy sections that come up from time to time.

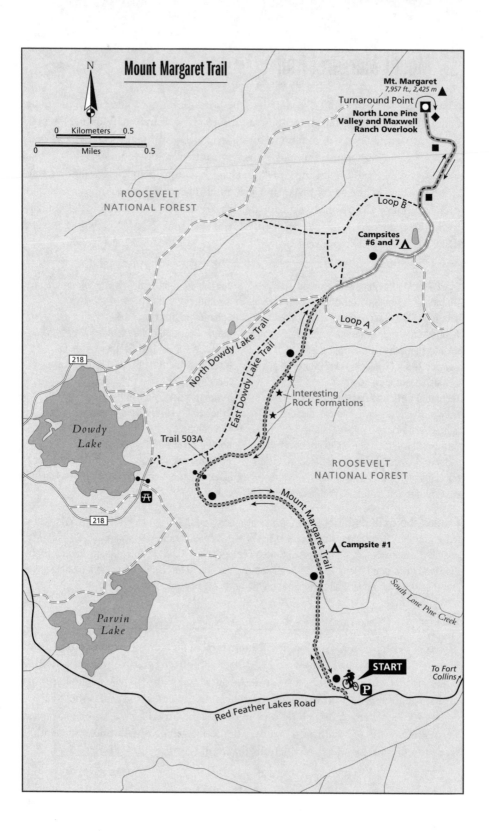

Once you pass through the gate at 1.6 miles, the Mount Margaret Trail intersects with Trail 503A on your left. From this intersection, continue riding in a northerly direction on the wide doubletrack of the Mount Margaret Trail, as it descends moderately over rockier terrain and through a thick patch of aspen. Soon after passing through the aspen, riders can take a break to check out the awesome granite rock formations that stand on either side of the trail. From here riders will pass a variety of campsites and other side trails.

Local Livermore ranchers lease this area for cattle grazing, so it isn't unlikely to pass a few cattle, as well as their droppings, along the way. Due courtesy should be given to the cattle, as their ancestors could well have been the first Livermore residents. Adolphus Livernash and Stephen Moore founded the town of Livermore in 1863 when the two of them built a one-room cabin and started prospecting for minerals. With the search for minerals not panning out as Livernash and Moore would have hoped, Livermore soon started growing its ranching roots.

After roughly 2.5 miles, the Mount Margaret Trail intersects with three other trails. The East Dowdy Lake Trail lies to your immediate left and cuts back toward the direction from which you came and heads southwest toward Dowdy Lake. The North Dowdy Lake Trail is also on your left and heads in a northwesterly direction toward Dowdy Lake. At 120 acres, with a shoreline of roughly 3 miles and a maximum depth of 28 feet, Dowdy Lake is the largest of all the lakes in the Red Feather Lakes area. Sitting at an elevation of 8,365 feet, Dowdy Lake makes for a great camping, fishing, and boating spot. The Loop A Trail lies to your immediate right and heads in an easterly direction through quiet stands of aspen before reuniting with the Mount Margaret Trail after 1.25 miles. Loop A is a well-worth-it diversion from the main trail.

After roughly 3 miles the ride will pass along the eastern flank of a meadow with a small pond at its center. Following the intersection with Loop B, riders begin descending on singletrack through a mixed conifer forest. This last leg of the trail offers more rocks and tighter sections, making it moderately challenging. The singletrack will begin to climb, as it makes its way to the top of Mount Margaret over tight and moderately technical terrain.

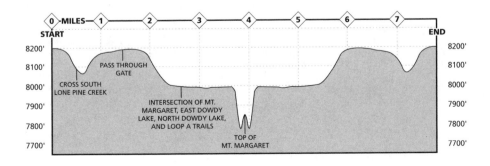

Weaving through a rocky singletrack section, returning from the top of Mount Margaret.
PHOTO: AMANDA HLAWATY

From here, riders can see the Maxwell Ranch below in the North Lone Pine Valley. Looking into the North Lone Pine Valley from atop Mount Margaret, riders can see the U-shaped formation of the valley created by Earth's last major glacial period. The Pleistocene or Ice Age began about two million years ago. During this period, large glacial ice sheets covered much of North America, Europe, and Asia. In North America the higher altitudes of the Rocky Mountains were the site of the Pleistocene glaciers' first formations. The glaciation that appears before you is a result of the Pleistocene glaciers retreating (interglacial) and advancing (glacial) due to warmer and colder temperatures of Earth's surface. Today's glacial retreat started some 14,000 years ago and is known as the Holocene epoch.

That should give you something worth pondering as you scramble on the variety of rock formations atop Mount Margaret. After taking in the sights, it's time to make a retreat of your own. The initial descent from the top of Mount Margaret is fast and moderately technical with rock, sand, and tighter sections. Be aware of upcoming hikers and horseback riders as you return to your vehicle.

Miles and Directions

0.0 Begin riding on the Mount Margaret Trail in a northerly direction on doubletrack, through stands of ponderosa pine and open meadows.

0.5 Cross South Lone Pine Creek.

0.7 Pass campsite #1 on your right.

1.6 Pass through the gate, closing it behind you, and continue riding in a northerly direction on the wide doubletrack. Here, the Mount Margaret Trail intersects with Trail 503A on your left.

2.6 The Mount Margaret Trail intersects with the East Dowdy Lake Trail, North Dowdy Lake Trail, and Loop A Trail. From here, continue riding in a northerly direction on the Mount Margaret Trail following the sign on your right that reads MOUNT MARGARET—1.5 MILES.

2.7 The Mount Margaret Trail again intersects with the North Dowdy Lake Trail on your left. Continue riding on the Mount Margaret Trail.

3.1–3.2 The Mount Margaret Trail again intersects with the Loop A Trail on your right and will also intersect with the Loop B trail on your left. Continue riding on the Mount Margaret Trail.

3.9 Reach the top of Mount Margaret then return the way you came.

7.8 Arrive at your vehicle.

Ride Information

Trail Information

Diamond Peaks Mountain Bike Patrol, Timnath; (970) 482-6006 ext. 22; e-mail DPMBP@aol.com

Local Information

Poudre River/Red Feather Lakes Tourist Council, 31635 Poudre Canyon, Bellvue 80512; (970) 881-2142

Local Events and Attractions

Creedmore Lakes, north of Red Feather Lakes Road, off County Road 180, via County Road 73C

Deadman Lookout Fire Tower, west of Killpecker Trail on Deadman Road

Red Feather Lakes, off Red Feather Lakes Road (County Road 74E)

Restaurants

The Forks Mercantile, Livermore; (970) 221-2080

Pot Belly Restaurant and Lounge, Red Feather Lakes; (970) 881-2984

4 Lower Dadd Gulch Trail

The Lower Dadd Gulch Trail is becoming more and more popular among mountain bikers, particularly since the trail received much-needed maintenance during the summers of 1995, 1996, and 1997. From Colorado Highway 14 to Salt Cabin Road, this trail winds through Dadd Gulch as it follows a stream through thick forests of juniper, ponderosa pine, aspen, and Douglas fir trees. The shade provided by the heavily wooded terrain of Dadd Gulch and a plentitude of creek crossings make this trail a winner of a ride during one of those savagely hot Front Range days. Upon reaching Dadd Gulch Road, riders have the option of either returning to their vehicles the way they came or continuing into Salt Cabin Park to make a loop.

Start: The Lower Dadd Gulch trailhead
Distance: 11.2-mile lariat with an option for a 7-mile out-and-back
Approximate riding time: Advanced riders, 1 hour; intermediate riders, 1.5 hours
Aerobic level: Physically easy to moderate, due to a moderate gain in elevation
Technical difficulty: Technically easy to moderate, due to some rockier and steeper sections
Terrain: Singletrack, doubletrack, and dirt road, which follows a stream in the bottom of a gulch through a heavily wooded mixed conifer forest. The terrain is mostly hard-pack singletrack, with a variety of rockier sections.
Schedule: April–November
Maps: DeLorme *Colorado Atlas & Gazetteer*, page 19; USGS: Rustic, CO; Trails Illustrated: #112, Poudre River, Cameron Pass, CO; Arapaho and Roosevelt National Forests map.
Nearest town: Rustic
Other trail users: Hikers and horseback riders
Canine compatibility: Dog-friendly
Trail contact: Arapaho and Roosevelt National Forests, Canyon Lakes Ranger District, Fort Collins; (970) 498-2770

Finding the Trailhead: From Fort Collins, drive north on U.S. Highway 287. Turn left onto CO 14 at Ted's Place, following signs for the Poudre Canyon, and drive west on CO 14 for 29.5 miles before turning left into the Lower Dadd Gulch trailhead parking lot, just after passing the trailhead to Indian Meadows. A wooden and wired gate marks the beginning of the trail. After entering the gate, please be sure to close it behind you.

The Ride

The Lower Dadd Gulch Trail winds its way through a mixed conifer forest following the old Dadd Gulch Stock Drive up and out of the Poudre Canyon toward the southwest. The first half-mile of the trail requires a variety of creek crossings over moderately ascending terrain. You'll follow alongside the creek for the first mile before having to climb steeply uphill, away from the creek. After roughly 1.5 miles the trail becomes increasingly tighter, as it courses its way through thick, leafy vegetation. By 2 miles you're facing a physically challenging climb, which

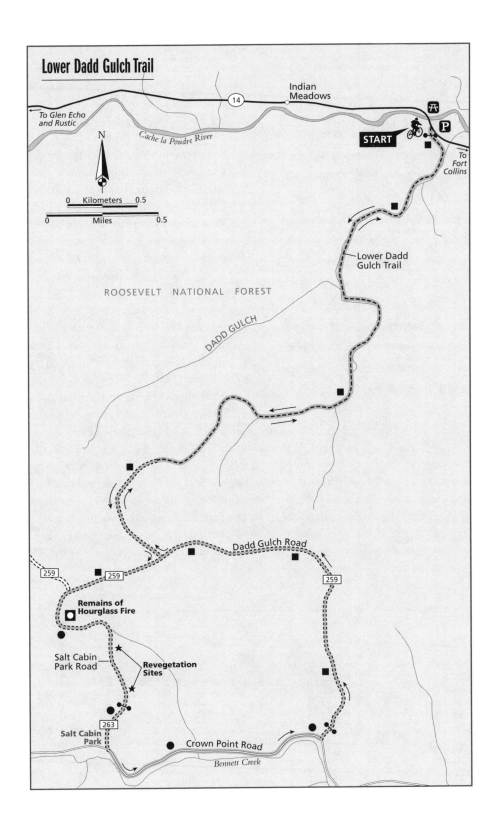

Lower Dadd Gulch Trail

Indian Meadows

14

To Glen Echo
and Rustic

Cache la Poudre River

START

P

To
Fort
Collins

N

0   Kilometers   0.5

0   Miles   0.5

Lower Dadd
Gulch Trail

ROOSEVELT NATIONAL FOREST

DADD GULCH

Dadd Gulch Road

259

259

259

Remains of
Hourglass Fire

Salt Cabin
Park Road

Revegetation
Sites

263

Salt Cabin
Park

Crown Point Road

Bennett Creek

soon levels off into a grassy meadow with large boulders off to your right. From here the trail climbs more moderately over smooth singletrack, then it will begin to level off through an open area. Once beyond the barbed wire fence, you'll pass through a pine forest clear-cut before intersecting with Dadd Gulch Road.

LONG LIVE THE LODGEPOLE Interestingly, the lodgepole pine has developed its own natural defense against forest fires. Lodgepole pine have both closed (serotinous) and open (nonserotinous) cones. Closed cones require the intense heat of a forest fire to melt resins and expose the seeds within, allowing for natural revegetation of the lodgepole pine in the wake of a forest fire. In periods of little to no forest fire activity, nonserotinous lodgepole pine regenerate the species. Thus, the lodgepole pine species of tree, the dominant tree species in the forests surrounding Dadd Gulch, will survive with or without fire.

The climb on Dadd Gulch Road to Salt Cabin Park Road is moderate, a welcome relief from the singletrack climb through lower Dadd Gulch. As you connect with the Salt Cabin Park Road, you'll find the descent is fast over large rocks and loose sand. Burned trees recall the Hourglass Fire of July 1, 1994. The National Weather Service in Denver had issued a Haines Index of 6 for that day. On a scale of 2–6, the Haines Index indicates wildfire growth potential based on humidity and temperature differences between different elevations in the atmosphere. Owing to localized convective storm activity, a lightning strike was the culprit behind the fire that started at 1:45 A.M. in Pingree Park, southwest of Dadd Gulch. Following the conventional naming strategies for wildfires, the Hourglass Fire took its name from a local topographical feature. In this case, the fire was named after the Hourglass Reservoir, just north of the fire's origin and south of Salt Cabin Park. By midday, the fire, fueled by winds in excess of 50 mph, raged through the Pingree Park campus of Colorado State University, destroying three faculty cabins, the North Residence Hall, a staff housing facility, six conference center residence buildings, and a staff duplex cabin near the conference center. Luckily, no

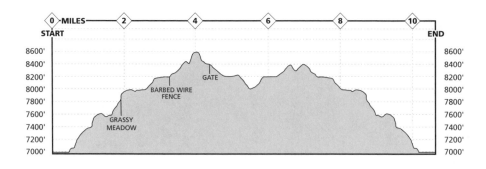

Salt Cabin Park Road.

one was injured during the four-day blaze that consumed 1,275 acres and cost $10.5 million to fight.

In an effort to curb future wildfire hazards, nearby forests have been thinned, while grass seeding and tree planting have aided in erosion-control efforts. Evidence of reseeding and planting can now be seen as you pass through a variety of revegetation sites around Salt Cabin Park. Bear in mind that there is vehicular traffic on Salt Cabin Park Road once you pass through the iron gate at 4.4 miles.

After descending to Salt Cabin Park and connecting with the much-improved, dirt Crown Point Road, you make a smooth, speedy descent, with Bennett Creek to your right, before reconnecting with Dadd Gulch Road. Riders should watch their mileage, as there are no real identifying signs for this part of Dadd Gulch Road. There is, however, a large dirt pullout at the intersection of Crown Point Road and Dadd Gulch Road for which riders can look out. Be sure to stay on the main Dadd Gulch Road, as there are many crisscrossing roads throughout your climb to the Lower Dadd Gulch Trail. Once you've reconnected with the Lower Dadd Gulch Trail, the descent is fast, with many tight turns and a number of whoop-di-doos off which to catch air (should you be so inclined).

Miles and Directions

0.0 Begin riding on the Lower Dadd Gulch Trail, heading in a southwesterly direction.

1.9 After a short grunt of a climb, arrive at a grassy meadow, and continue riding in a south-westerly direction toward Dadd Gulch Road.

2.6 Arrive at another meadow, with a row of aspen trees off to your left. Continue riding in a southwesterly direction on the Lower Dadd Gulch Trail.

3.3 Pass through a barbed wire fence, and continue riding toward Dadd Gulch Road on a wide doubletrack.

3.5 The southern terminus of the Lower Dadd Gulch Trail intersects with Dadd Gulch Road (FR 259). Bear right onto Dadd Gulch Road, and climb moderately in a westerly direction. **Option:** Where Dadd Gulch Road (FR 259) and the southern terminus of the Lower Dadd Gulch Trail intersect, riders can choose to turn around and retrace the route to their vehicles.

4.0 Dadd Gulch Road (FR 259) intersects with Salt Cabin Park Road (FR 263). Bear left onto Salt Cabin Park Road (FR 263), heading in a southeasterly direction, and descend toward Salt Cabin Park.

4.4 Pass through the iron gate and continue descending on Salt Cabin Park Road (FR 263) toward Salt Cabin Park.

4.6 Salt Cabin Park Road (FR 263) will come to a fork at a clearing. Bear left, descending on the road in a southeasterly direction.

4.9 Salt Cabin Park Road (FR 263) intersects with Crown Point Road at Salt Cabin Park. Bear left onto the much-improved, dirt Crown Point Road, and descend in an easterly direction with Bennett Creek to your right. Beware of vehicular traffic.

6.0 Crown Point Road intersects with Dadd Gulch Road. Bear left onto Dadd Gulch Road (FR 259), passing through the iron gate, and begin climbing in a northerly direction.

7.7 Dadd Gulch Road (FR 259) completes the loop and intersects with the Lower Dadd Gulch Trail. Bear right onto the Lower Dadd Gulch Trail and return to your vehicle.

11.2 Arrive at your vehicle.

Ride Information

Trail Information

Diamond Peaks Mountain Bike Patrol, Timnath; (970) 482–6006 ext. 22; e-mail DPMBP@aol.com

Local Information

Poudre River/Red Feather Lakes Tourist Council, 31635 Poudre Canyon, Bellvue 80512; (970) 881-2142

Local Events and Attractions

Mishawaka Amphitheater, Fort Collins; (970) 482-4420

5 Young Gulch

Young Gulch is a great ride for those who like to get wet. During the spring thaw the trail crosses a number of larger creeks. Since this ride travels through mixed conifer forests and under thick canopies, the trail remains quite cool, so don't expect to be warm or to dry too quickly. In fact, it's best that you bring a towel and an extra pair of shoes and socks. There are a few rocky and steep technical sections, but for the most part, this out-and-back is well suited for the beginner and intermediate rider. The advanced rider will find some of these steeper, rockier sections a challenge and the descent back to his or her vehicle, a riot.

Start: On the south side of Colorado Highway 14, at milepost 109, 3.2 miles west of Poudre Park

Distance: 10.3-mile out-and-back

Approximate riding time: Advanced riders, 1.5 hours; intermediate riders, 2.5 hours

Aerobic level: Physically moderate due to its mellower elevation gain: 5,800-7,040 feet

Technical difficulty: Technically moderate to challenging due to its rocky, but short climbs and descents

Terrain: Singletrack, traveling through a gulch, with many creek-crossings under forest cover

Schedule: April–November

Maps: DeLorme *Colorado Atlas & Gazetteer*, page 19; USGS: Poudre Park, CO; Trails Illustrated #101, Cache La Poudre & Big Thompson, CO; Arapaho and Roosevelt National Forests map

Nearest town: Poudre Park

Other trail users: Campers, hikers, and horseback riders

Canine compatibility: Dog-friendly

Trail contact: Arapaho and Roosevelt National Forests and Pawnee National Grassland, Forest Supervisor Office, Fort Collins; (970) 498-1100

Finding the Trailhead: From Fort Collins, head north on U.S. Highway 287. Turn left onto CO 14, following signs for the Poudre Canyon. Drive on CO 14 for 13 miles. The dirt road turnoff to Young Gulch is 3.2 miles past the tiny town of Poudre Park and will be on the left, at milepost 109. Drive up the dirt road to the parking area and trailhead. A wooden and wired gate marks the beginning of the trail. After entering the gate, please be sure to close it behind you.

The Ride

The Young Gulch Trail is located in Roosevelt National Forest's Poudre Canyon. In 1918 the Forest Service granted the town of Fort Collins permission to develop Young Gulch as a place where people could picnic, camp, and hike. Three years later Young Gulch was opened. Today it stands as a reminder of Colorado's early commitment to mountain recreation.

Convict labor built the original road leading to Young Gulch—now Colorado 14. The Poudre Valley Good Roads Association constructed a masonry fireplace to

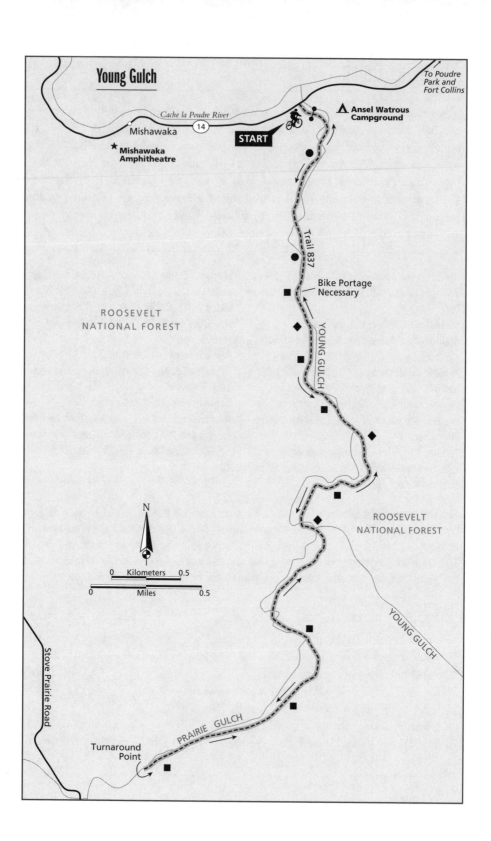

Young Gulch

To Poudre Park and Fort Collins

Cache la Poudre River

Mishawaka

14

△ Ansel Watrous Campground

★ Mishawaka Amphitheatre

START

Trail 837

ROOSEVELT NATIONAL FOREST

Bike Portage Necessary

YOUNG GULCH

N

0 Kilometers 0.5

0 Miles 0.5

ROOSEVELT NATIONAL FOREST

YOUNG GULCH

Stove Prairie Road

PRAIRIE GULCH

Turnaround Point

celebrate the completion of the road to that point. Located just beyond the turnoff for Young Gulch, the fireplace was left for others to use in the future.

Just before the old fireplace, a Forest Service sign marks the Cache la Poudre River as a "Wild and Scenic River System." The Poudre is the only river in Colorado to receive protection under the National Wild and Scenic River Act. Covering an estimated 150 miles, the Poudre River originates from Poudre Lake (an alpine lake located high in the mountains of Rocky Mountain National Park) and extends to the South Platte River just east of the town of Greeley.

The Poudre Canyon is dedicated to a variety of outdoor activities: mountain biking, hiking, camping, rock climbing, four-wheeling, kayaking, and rafting. Local citizens groups, like Friends of the Poudre, are currently working together

CHECK THE ADDRESS FIRST As a point of reference if you're traveling the Poudre Canyon, the first digit of a four-digit address (or the first two digits of a five-digit address) marks the distance from the start of the canyon to the residence. For instance, Mishawaka Amphitheater, at 13714 Poudre Canyon, is 13 miles up the canyon.

to develop boat chutes at diversion structures on the river so kayakers and rafters can run the entire river in the lower canyon without having to portage their crafts. These chutes are estimated to cost between $200,000 and $300,000 each—further evidence of Colorado's commitment to recreation and healthy living.

Just 3 miles up CO 14 from the Young Gulch trailhead stands the Mishawaka Inn, a laid-back, riverside complex including an inn, amphitheater, and restaurant serving locally brewed beer. The property is a summer venue for the likes of Merle Saunders, The Radiators, Arlo Guthrie, The Ugly Americans, Robert Bradley's Blackwater Surprise, Bella Fleck and the Flecktones, and the David Grisman Quintet—to name but a few. In February of 1916, Walter S. Thompson, a musician from Fort Collins, purchased the surrounding land with the intent of operating a self-supporting home. Within three years, Thompson had built himself a very comfortable house, several cabins, a general store, and a dance hall. More than eighty years later, the music continues to play throughout the Poudre Canyon, keeping time with the rocking and rolling of our bikes through Young Gulch.

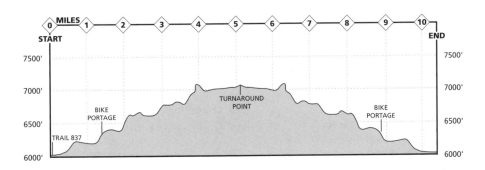

Rocking and rolling do well to describe this trail. Young Gulch offers a vast array of terrain for any level mountain biker. Its steep-sided, narrow, and rocky terrain offers challenges for even the best riders, while its many creek-crossings allow the novice mountain biker many chilling thrills. The creek-crossings, along with dense forests, make this trail ideal for those hot summer days. Unfortunately, the heavy forest cover causes the snow at Young Gulch to melt late, creating a potentially cold and wet environment late into the spring. These spring conditions can be tricky to ride in. Deep creek crossings, wet rocks, and slippery roots can all cause loss of significant braking power.

The last 3 miles of Young Gulch are smoother and wider, making for a fast descent on your way back. Take care on your return, as rocky approaches into creeks come up on you fast. The rocky downhills can be hairy if not approached carefully—but oh! the fun.

Miles and Directions

0.0 Start from the gate at the trailhead. Begin riding through the thickly forested gulch.

0.6 Arrive at a sweet, shaded spot, just to your right—ideal for a quick rest or snack. Blooming cacti abound, creekside.

1.3 Reach one of two short, but technical climbs. Climb this section with thoughts of your returning descent. Picking the line to your right on your return is probably best.

1.4 A rocky impasse requires a bike portage.

3.5 Pick up the trail by walking upcreek for approximately 50 feet. From here the gulch widens out with fewer rocks and roots.

5.0 The trail merges with a four-wheel-drive road heading up the hillside to your left. Climb for another 0.2 mile to reach the turnaround point.

5.2 As the top of this climb levels out, bear an immediate right for a short grind to the top of a knob of stone. From here, there is a good view of the gulch and Stove Prairie Road. Private property begins beyond the gate. Do not cross without permission. After resting, backtrack and enjoy the fast and rocky descent.

10.3 Arrive back at your vehicle.

Ride Information

Trail Information

Diamond Peaks Mountain Bike Patrol, Timnath; (970) 482-6006 ext. 22; e-mail DPMBP@aol.com

Forest to Grassland Information Center, Fort Collins; (970) 498-2770

Local Information

Poudre River/Red Feather Lakes Tourist Council, 31635 Poudre Canyon, Bellvue 80512; (970) 881-2142

Local Events and Attractions

Mishawaka Amphitheater, Fort Collins; (970) 482-4420

Restaurants

CooperSmith's Pub & Brewing, Fort Collins; (970) 498-0483

Rio Grande (the best margaritas you'll ever drink), Fort Collins; (970) 224-5428

6 Hewlett Gulch

Hewlett Gulch is a favorite among mountain bikers in and around Fort Collins. Its fast singletrack, big drop-offs, creek-crossings, killer climbs, and one very rocky descent will satisfy any mountain biker's idea of a good ride. Although technically and physically moderate to challenging, the ride serves first-time mountain bikers well as it can be ridden at any pace. For those who like to grab air, there's a great spot at the 2.3-mile mark where the trail dips into a small gully. With enough speed, you'd swear you were flying.

Start: Just past Poudre Park in the Poudre Canyon

Distance: 8.5-mile loop (with an additional 4 miles if one opts for the 4-mile out-and-back)

Approximate riding time: 2 hours

Aerobic level: Physically moderate to challenging due to an extended climb midway through the ride

Technical difficulty: Technically challenging, due to a very rocky and steep descent on the return

Terrain: Rough doubletrack and singletrack. This trail has many creek crossings and weaves in and out of mixed conifer forests before climbing up through a meadow. Although most of this ride is manageable by the intermediate rider, there are big drop-off sections, as well as one of the rockiest single-track descents in all of the Front Range.

Schedule: April–November

Maps: DeLorme *Colorado Atlas & Gazetteer*, page 19; USGS: Poudre Park, CO; Trails Illustrated: #101, Cache La Poudre & Big Thompson, CO; Arapaho and Roosevelt National Forests map

Nearest town: Poudre Park

Other trail users: Campers, hikers, hunters, and horseback riders

Canine compatibility: Dog-friendly

Trail contact: Arapaho and Roosevelt National Forests and Pawnee National Grassland, Forest Supervisor Office, Fort Collins; (970) 498-1100

Finding the Trailhead: From Fort Collins, head north on U.S. Highway 287. Turn left onto Colorado Highway 14 following signs for the Poudre Canyon. Drive on CO 14 for 10 miles. After passing the tiny town of Poudre Park, you'll spot a bridge to the north crossing the Cache la Poudre River. The bridge is blocked by an iron bar, but biking is allowed. Park on either side of CO 14; additional parking is located 100 yards down the road on the right. Respect residents of the Poudre Canyon by not parking in front of their driveways or mailboxes.

The Ride

As the waves of the Cache la Poudre River crash through the Poudre Canyon in Roosevelt National Forest, the echoes of a distant pioneering past resound from its granite walls. The very name of the canyon (and more specifically the river) recalls the struggles that the early pioneers had to endure in order to come to terms with this western wilderness.

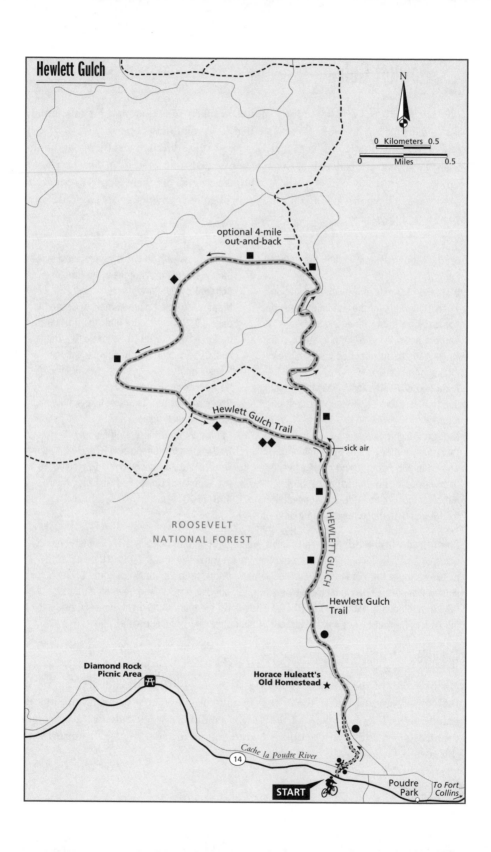

Hewlett Gulch

N

0 Kilometers 0.5

0   Miles   0.5

optional 4-mile
out-and-back

Hewlett Gulch Trail

sick air

ROOSEVELT
NATIONAL FOREST

HEWLETT GULCH

Hewlett Gulch
Trail

Diamond Rock
Picnic Area

Horace Huleatt's
Old Homestead

Cache la Poudre River

14

START

Poudre
Park

To Fort
Collins

The story goes that a party of French-Canadian trappers and traders, led by Antoine Janis of John Jacob Astor's American Fur Company, was en route to a prescribed rendezvous on the Green River when bad weather hit. It was November of 1836. The snowstorm made it impossible for the company to safely ford the Poudre Canyon's river, so Janis gave the order to lighten the wagons' loads. The men dug a large pit, lined it with pine boughs and animal skins, and filled it with what could be spared from each wagon. After backfilling the pit, the trappers burned a large fire on top of the pit to disguise the site. They feared the supplies would be taken by the native Arapaho and Cheyenne Indians. Included in the buried supplies were several hundred pounds of gunpowder. The French-speaking trappers called this place *cache la poudre* ("the hiding place of the powder"). Some months later, the party returned to the Poudre Canyon and recovered all of their supplies. The name stuck.

Typical of the mountain biking trails of Colorado's Front Range, Hewlett Gulch delivers smooth, fast-riding singletrack; rocky, uncompromising climbs and descents; and a dizzying array of creek-crossings. The trail begins as an overgrown double-track, which soon turns to singletrack within half a mile. There are four creek-crossings within the first mile of the trail. To slow erosion, waterbars lie across the trail for the first 2 to 3 miles, making for some steep drop-offs and tough, "taco-bending hill hops" (jumps that can bend, or "taco," your front wheel). The waterbars have effectively made Hewlett Gulch more technical than ever before.

Within the first mile, you encounter the remnants of Horace Huleatt's old homestead. Huleatt settled the gulch in 1870 on land he later found out was sacred Ute Indian land. When Horace realized this, he quickly moved on, leaving his homestead as a parting gift. Today a stone chimney and a concrete foundation are all we have of old Horace Huleatt, but his name lives on, though slightly corrupted, in Hewlett Gulch. After the homestead the trail leads into a lush pine-covered sanctuary awash with thousands of wildflowers.

The trail continues through intermittent fields and groves of cedar and pine. The canyon narrows here. Sheer granite walls climb the sides of the canyon in a vain

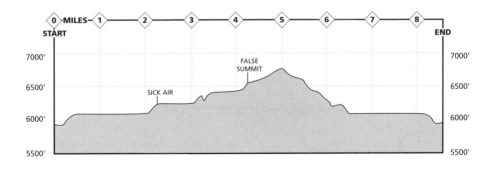

attempt to pierce the sky. The surroundings become more rugged, save the yellow flowering cacti—a bittersweet reminder of the agony and ecstasy through which we mountain bikers put ourselves.

After about 2 miles into the ride, the trail comes to a T before a big gully, offering the opportunity for "sick air" or a long jump. Bear left and climb the side of the hill. The hit or jump is on the right side of the trail as you scream up the other side of the gully. From there the trail meanders through alternating stands of lodgepole pine and spruce, offering occasional short, rocky, and steep climbs. After one such climb the trail lets out onto a broad grassy hill completely devoid of trees. A half-mile to the north of this hill stands a beautiful house boasting an even better southerly view. Turn around and enjoy an inspiring view of the canyon through which you've just ridden.

The 2-mile climb to the top of this hill is deceiving, as there is a false summit at mile 4.2. This false summit does, however, offer a great opportunity to dismount and take in the views. Although Hewlett Gulch does have its challenging, short, steep climbs, it rewards the persistent rider with incredible, rocky singletrack descents. After arriving at the second gully, the trail once again comes to a T. Here you have the option to bear right for a rugged 4-mile out-and-back or simply bear left and continue on the main trail.

The descent from this point is famed for its technical riding. Complete with steep grades and loose, football-size rocks and lined with thorny cacti and thistle, this downgrade has some of the sickest singletrack descents on Colorado's Front Range. Once you arrive at the bottom, bear right and backtrack for the remaining 2.3 miles.

Miles and Directions

- **0.0** Start from CO 14. Cross the gated, wooden-planked bridge. The Cache la Poudre River will be below you. Ride up the road.
- **0.1** Bear left onto a rough doubletrack, and enter Roosevelt National Forest. (A right will take you to private homes.)
- **0.4** The singletrack begins.
- **1.1** The trail crosses the creek for the fourth time and leads into a lush pine forest carpeted with wild poppies. A great place for a picnic or resting spot.
- **2.3** Sick air. The trail Ts. Bear right.
- **3.3** An extremely difficult and rocky descent delivers you to a broad and grassy 2-mile hill climb.
- **4.2** Don't be fooled. This is a false summit, albeit an ideal resting spot for those in need.
- **4.3** A short, but fast stretch of singletrack highlighted by a couple of rocky sections rewards the patient hill climber.
- **5.3** The trail leads into a deep gully. You'll need your speed getting out of it, as the trail continues up a steep, but short ascent. At the top of this short climb, you'll once again come to

a T in the trail. Bearing right offers a 4-mile out-and-back option, while bearing left contin-ues on the main trail. Bear left here, toward your eventual descent.

5.4 Beginning of a rugged, sick descent.

6.2 You arrive at the bottom where you caught the sick air. Bear right and backtrack the first part of Hewlett Gulch Trail.

8.5 Arrive at your vehicle.

Ride Information

Trail Information

Diamond Peaks Mountain Bike Patrol, Tim-nath; (970) 482-6006 ext. 22; e-mail DPMBP@aol.com

Forest to Grassland Information Center, Fort Collins; (970) 498-2770

Local Information

Poudre River/Red Feather Lakes Tourist Council, 31635 Poudre Canyon, Bellvue 80512; (970) 881-2142

Local Events and Attractions

Mishawaka Amphitheater, Fort Collins; (970) 482-4420

Restaurants

CooperSmith's Pub & Brewing, Fort Collins; (970) 498-0483

Rio Grande (the best margaritas you'll ever drink), Fort Collins; (970) 224-5428

7 Mill Creek Trail

Lory State Park/Horsetooth Mountain Park is prime real estate for some of the area's best mountain biking. The Mill Creek Trail is arguably one of the most technically and physically challenging rides in all of Fort Collins. With gorgeous views of Colorado's great plains and Horsetooth Reservoir to the east, riders climb into the semi-arid woodlands of Colorado's Front Range, the first step into the Rocky Mountains. This route offers rolling terrain alongside Horsetooth Reservoir, a burly climb to Horsetooth Mountain, and a steep and rocky descent down the Mill Creek Trail. An experience reaching biblical proportions, the Mill Creek Trail is David to the Goliath-like trails of the giant Rocky Mountains.

Start: Entrance to Lory State Park, at the guard station, just beyond the stop sign
Distance: 13.3-mile lariat
Approximate riding time: 1.5–2 hours for advanced riders; 2.5–3 hours for intermediate riders
Aerobic level: Physically moderate to challenging. Three miles of rolling singletrack run south along Horsetooth Reservoir, while three miles of steep and arduous hill climbing takes you to the top of Horsetooth Mountain and the trailhead of Mill Creek.
Technical difficulty: Technically moderate to challenging due to its rocky and steep singletrack descents—a trademark of Front Range mountain biking
Terrain: Rocky and rolling terrain on both singletrack and dirt road surfaces

Fees and permits: $2.00 individual park pass must be purchased (price subject to change)
Schedule: April–November
Maps: DeLorme *Colorado Atlas & Gazetteer*, page 20; USGS: Horsetooth Reservoir, CO; Colorado State Parks Maps: Lory State Park; Larimer County Parks Department Map: Horsetooth Mountain Park
Nearest town: Fort Collins
Other trail users: Hikers, campers, horseback riders, and those enjoying various forms of water recreation.
Canine compatibility: Dog-friendly, but beware the horseback riders
Trail contact: Larimer County Parks and Open Lands Department, Loveland; (970) 679-4570

Finding the Trailhead: From downtown Fort Collins at the junction of College Avenue and Mountain Road, drive north on College Avenue out of Fort Collins for 6.3 miles, heading toward La Porte and Lory State Park. Having driven through La Porte, veer left onto Route 52E. Drive on 52E for approximately 1 mile before making a left onto Route 23, by the red flagstone Bellvue Senior Center. At 8.7 miles, turn right onto Route 25G and follow signs to Lory State Park. Drive another 1.6 miles to the entrance of Charles A. Lory State Park. Leave your vehicle outside of the park, as you will begin your ride by the guard station.

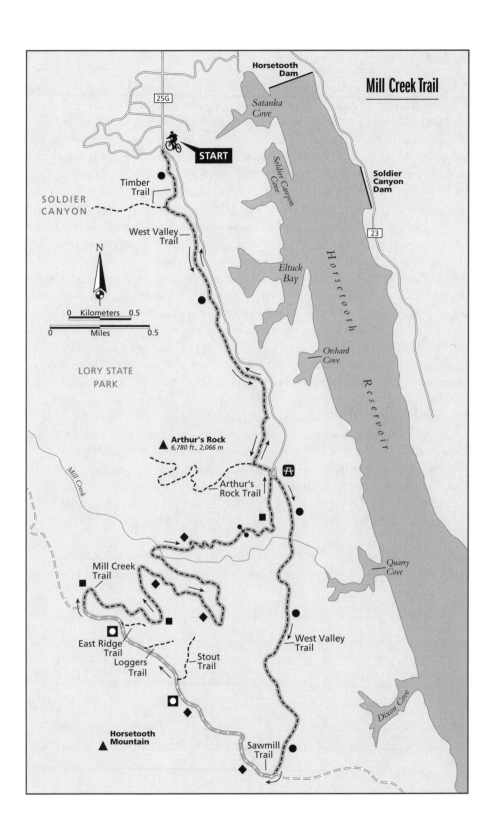

Mill Creek Trail

Horsetooth Dam

Satanka Cove

Soldier Canyon Cove

Soldier Canyon Dam

23

SOLDIER CANYON

Timber Trail

West Valley Trail

N

Eltuck Bay

Horsetooth

0 Kilometers 0.5

0 Miles 0.5

LORY STATE PARK

Orchard Cove

Reservoir

Arthur's Rock
6,780 ft., 2,066 m

Arthur's Rock Trail

Quarry Cove

Mill Creek Trail

Mill Creek

West Valley Trail

East Ridge Trail

Loggers Trail

Stout Trail

Dixon Cove

Horsetooth Mountain

Sawmill Trail

START

The Ride

The 4,500 acres that comprise Lory State Park and Horsetooth Mountain Park boast a venous network of trails. This network, running along the transitional ecology of the Rocky Mountain foothills, weaves its way through a variety of terrain and vegetation: unique rock outcroppings, sandstone hogbacks, grassy open meadows, cacti-laden hillsides, and ponderosa pine forests. To the northwest, Arthur's Rock (6,780 feet) marks the high point in Lory State Park and overlooks the city of Fort Collins. Its jutting granite foundation stands as a testament to the strength of will and the indomitable character of the people of Fort Collins.

On July 29, 1997, Fort Collins's local newspaper, the *Coloradoan,* ran the headline "Torrential Rain Floods City." That same morning, City Manager John Fischbach declared Fort Collins under a state of local emergency. In a five-hour span, Fort Collins received 8.41 inches of rain. The ensuing flood washed trains off their tracks. Ninety-two mobile homes were destroyed; 145 houses and 116 apartments were damaged; and five lives were lost. The city suffered millions of dollars in damages. It was Fort Collins's worst natural disaster to date.

The deluge dropped in excess of 10 inches of rain on nearby Lory State Park, wreaking havoc on the park's trails. By September of 1997 a massive reconstruction effort of the park's trails was under way, involving the efforts of the Diamond Peaks Mountain Bike Patrol, trail design professionals from the International Mountain Biking Association (IMBA), and local residents and riders.

Prior to becoming a state park in 1967, this area was primarily ranch land. The trails most likely started as game trails. Over the years, and after much use, they've evolved into mountain bike trails. Unfortunately, the trails had never received proper attention, not in the way of erosion-proofing or trail system design. And so, when the flood of '97 hit, Lory State Park's trail system sustained substantial damage. Since the flood, a concerted effort has been devoted to redesigning and preserving these natural trails.

At this point, much of the damage has been rectified. The lower stretches of trail—those hardest hit by the flood—which lie just west of Horsetooth Reservoir

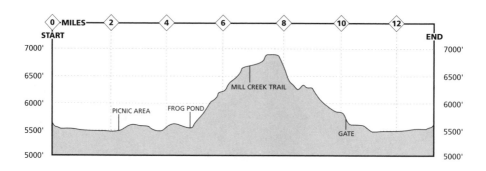

in Lory State Park's valley, offer ideal riding conditions for beginners practicing their techniques. Advanced riders wanting to increase their heart rates will enjoy them as well. The first 4.7 miles of West Valley Trail meander through rolling, open meadows and past a number of Horsetooth Reservoir's coves and bays. There's Santanka Cove, named for the red sedimentary formations in the area, and Soldier Cove, located at the base of Soldier Canyon—so-called because a skeleton and three U.S. Army buttons were found there. Eltuck Bay was named after Elton Collins, who with the help of Tuck (J. Morris) Howell helped build the reservoir as part of the Colorado–Big Thompson Irrigation Project in the late 1940s. Before the waters of the reservoir swept in to cover them, Quarry Cove was a sandstone quarry and Orchard Cove, a cherry orchard. Dixon Cove gets its name from a local landowner of the mid-1900s.

Once you arrive at the service road in Horsetooth Mountain Park (a.k.a. Sawmill Trail), you begin your 2.4-mile climb to the top of Horsetooth Mountain—the Front Range's answer to those lung-busting climbs of the Colorado high-country interior. While climbing, you pass beneath Horsetooth Rock, from which the mountain receives its name. According to an Arapaho Indian legend, Horsetooth Rock is the heart of the Great Red Warrior who was killed by the Great Black Warrior in a long and bitter struggle in the heavens. The blood shed in the battle is said to have stained the rock red. So how did it get its name? Even a cursory inspection will reveal its striking resemblance to a horse's molar.

With the grind of capping this tooth accomplished, it's time for a sick ride down the singletrack of the Mill Creek Trail. The trail begins through a dense ponderosa pine forest. Heading south, as you hug the east face of Horsetooth Mountain, you'll have to negotiate your line through some steep and rocky sections, all within the first mile of starting the Mill Creek Trail. Remember, the straightest line is always your strongest line. At mile 9.6, you cross Mill Creek—so-called because the Latham Mill once operated on it, behind Horsetooth Reservoir. The mill provided lumber for bridges in the early history of Larimer County. Nothing of the mill remains.

As you cross the creek and begin your climb out, notice the small wading pond to your left. If you don't cool off here, the next leg of the trail may toss you. Just 0.2 mile ahead is the tight switchback section of the trail. Although the approaches to each switchback can be ridden quickly, check your speed, as the switchbacks come up quickly. The remaining descent through Lory State Park to your vehicle comes complete with short, rocky sections and smooth-running singletrack.

Miles and Directions

0.0 Start on the singletrack by the visitor center and entrance to the park, just beyond the stop sign. Daily park passes must be purchased before entering the park. Follow the singletrack to the group picnic area.

0.3 Ride right into the Timber Trail group area and pick up the singletrack of the Timber Trail to the left of the sign. Within 0.2 mile from where Timber Trail started, the singletrack will Y.

Bear left at the Y onto West Valley Trail (Timber Trail continues to the right where bikes are not allowed). Note that West Valley Trail will cross a number of other trails leading into the hills. Do not veer right on any offshoots.

2.3 Reach group picnic area. From here, there are a number of routes that branch left to coves at Horsetooth Reservoir. Following the rolling terrain of West Valley Trail, continue through the meadow, paralleling the sandstone hogbacks of Horsetooth Reservoir to your left.

4.7 Reach the junction of West Valley Trail and Sawmill Trail. Look for a frog pond to your right. Head right, climbing up Sawmill Trail. Note that Sawmill Trail is a rough service road and marks your entrance into Horsetooth Mountain Park.

7.1 Having climbed for 2.4 miles, passing the tempting singletracks of the Stout, Loggers, and East Ridge Trails, the trailhead to Mill Creek Trail will be on your right. Note that there are a number of offshoots to your left, leading down the west side of Horsetooth Mountain. Reserve taking any of these trails for another day.

9.1 Reach the junction of Loggers Trail and Mill Creek Trail. Veer left, continuing on Mill Creek Trail.

10.2 You arrive at a red gate, marking your reentrance into Lory State Park. Close the gate behind you, and enjoy the views of Fort Collins and Horsetooth Reservoir to the East. Ride for 0.1 mile to the sign for Arthur's Rock, Horsetooth Mountain, and Parking Area. Ride straight ahead, past sign.

10.8 Arrive at the sign that marks the trailheads for Bridal and Arthur's Rock Trails. From here, either return via the road or via the singletrack to your vehicle.

13.3 Reach the entrance of Lory State Park and the ranger station.

Ride Information

Trail Information

Diamond Peaks Mountain Bike Patrol, Timnath; (970) 482-6006 ext. 22; e-mail DPMBP@aol.com

Local Information

Fort Collins Convention and Visitors Bureau, 3745 East Prospect Road, #200, Fort Collins 80525; (970) 491-3388 or (800) 274-FORT

Local Events and Attractions

Horsetooth Mountain Park, 4 miles from Fort Collins; contact Larimer County Parks and Open Lands Department at (970) 679-4570
Lory State Park, Bellevue; (970) 493-1623

Restaurants

CooperSmith's Pub & Brewing, Fort Collins; (970) 498-0483
Rio Grande (the best margaritas you'll ever drink), Fort Collins; (970) 224-5428

8 Devil's Backbone

It wasn't until a few years ago that one of Larimer County's most impressive and striking geological landmarks was opened to mountain bikers. The Devil's Backbone had originally been opened to hikers; indeed, there is still a "hiking only" trail that leads hikers to the base of the backbone. Aside from offering views of an interesting geological formation, as well as swirling raptors overhead, the aptly named Devil's Backbone delivers mountain bikers a technically challenging trail in exposed and rocky terrain. Due to the trail's exposure, be sure to drink enough water, wear plenty of sunscreen, and try to complete the ride before or after the hottest hours of the day. This trail runs along the lower eastern flank of the Backbone and includes two possible loops. This description covers both loops.

Start: The Devil's Backbone trailhead
Distance: 6.5-mile double lariat
Approximate riding time: Advanced riders, 1 hour; intermediate riders, 1.5–2 hours
Aerobic level: Physically moderate due to its exposed terrain and steep climbing sections
Technical difficulty: Technically moderate to challenging due to some steeper ascents and descents over large rocks, big drop-offs, and loose sand
Terrain: Dirt road and singletrack, which runs over intermittent hard-packed and rockier terrain. The trail is very exposed with little to no shade, so temperatures can get quite hot in the summer months.

Schedule: Seasonal wildlife closures in effect, March 1–June 15
Maps: DeLorme *Colorado Atlas & Gazetteer*, page 30; USGS: Masonville, CO; Devil's Backbone Open Space trail map; Larimer County Parks and Open Lands map
Nearest town: Loveland
Other trail users: Hikers and horseback riders
Canine compatibility: Dog-unfriendly—there is little to no water or shade available on the route. Rattlesnakes have also been spotted in this area.
Trail contact: Larimer County Parks and Open Lands Department, Loveland; (970) 679-4570

Finding the Trailhead: From Fort Collins, drive south on Interstate 25 for roughly 12 miles and exit at 257B and U.S. Highway 34 in Loveland. Bear right and drive west on US 34 for 8.5 miles before bearing right onto Wild Lane (Larimer County Road 22B), marked by the large, cement, Loveland water tank on your right. Drive on Wild Lane for 0.2 mile, crossing a creek, and bear right into Pete-O-Day Lane and the Devil's Backbone parking lot.

The Ride

In 1998 Larimer County acquired the Devil's Backbone Open Space through the Help Preserve Open Space sales tax, passed by Larimer County voters to help protect important area natural resources. It's good to know that Larimer County residents ride mountain bikes and that they vote.

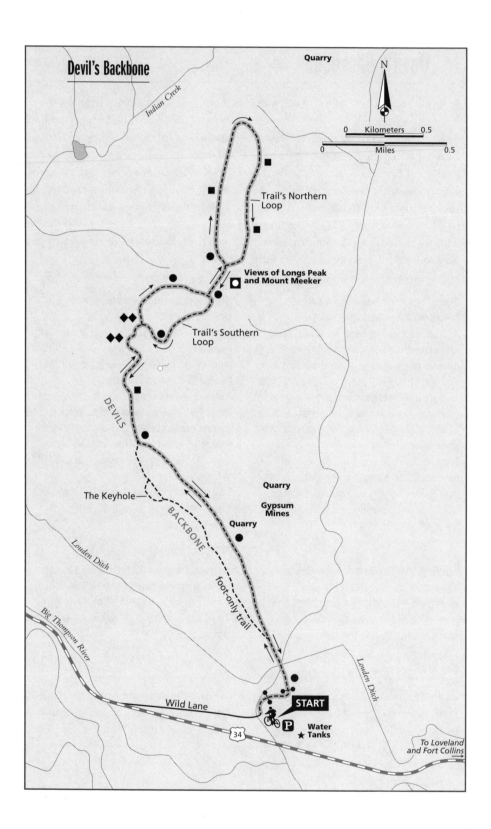

Devil's Backbone

Indian Creek

Quarry

N

Kilometers
0   0.5

Miles
0   0.5

Trail's Northern
Loop

Views of Longs Peak
and Mount Meeker

Trail's Southern
Loop

DEVILS

The Keyhole

Quarry

Gypsum
Mines

Quarry

BACKBONE

foot-only trail

Louden Ditch

Big Thompson River

Wild Lane

Louden Ditch

START

P

Water
★ Tanks

34

*To Loveland
and Fort Collins*

The beginning of the Devil's Backbone Trail rolls over smooth and wide single-track as it parallels a fence and crosses a couple of footbridges. One such footbridge, which crosses the southern end of the Devil's Backbone, spans the Louden Ditch. A native of Louden, Iowa, Aaron Benson settled in the Big Thompson Valley in 1878. Benson built the ditch to carry water from the Big Thompson River, through the Devil's Backbone, to irrigate 12,000-plus acres of area farmland. While constructing the ditch, workers unearthed a soft, white material that absorbed much of the water passing through it. The material turned out to be high-quality gypsum ($CaSO_4$), the same material used in the manufacture of plaster of paris, drywall, and fertilizers.

As you ride from the ditch, you can still notice the abandoned gypsum mines to the east. These mines also bore several mammal fossils, including a prehistoric elephant with 5-foot long tusks and a jawbone with seven teeth. While these remains were of mammals of the Cenozoic era, much of the Devil's Backbone rock is from the Morrison Formation, which dates back more than 150 million years. By touching the gray rock of the Backbone, you may well be touching the same stones once trod upon by dinosaurs. But due to the extremely fragile and unstable nature of the Devil's Backbone, do not climb on the rocks.

Once past the first, short climb, the trail bears north and runs alongside the eastern flank of the Devil's Backbone, over relatively smooth singletrack, through a low-lying valley of Morrison and Entrada rock outcroppings, as well as mountain mahogany shrublands and needle grasslands. After 0.5 mile of riding, the "multiuse" trail intersects with the foot-only portion of the Devil's Backbone Trail. Taking the left fork, this hiking trail climbs steeply and travels north along the base of the Backbone before descending and returning to the multiuse portion of the trail.

Shortly after intersecting with the northern terminus of the Devil's Backbone's Foot-Only Trail, you begin a medium-length climb over rocky and steep terrain. The climb is physically challenging over technically moderate terrain of sand and loose rock. Just before reaching the 2-mile mark of your ride, you come to the trail's most technical section, which combines a steep climb with loose rock.

Continuing from the intersection with the trail's southern loop, you ride over moderately rolling terrain, heading in a northerly direction. From here, the trail

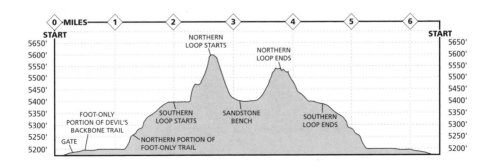

Enjoying the fast descent, with the Devil's Backbone in the background. PHOTO: AMANDA HLAWATY

becomes increasingly rockier. Upon connecting with the trail's northern loop, you'll begin climbing in a westerly direction over imbedded rock and narrow singletrack. This is an enjoyable section of the trail for a number of reasons. Not only does it present technically moderate terrain, but it also runs along the rim of a small plateau, offering westerly views of the Devil's Backbone rock formation. The erosive forces of wind and water have produced openings in the formation, such as the Keyhole.

From these views and roughly 3 miles into your ride, you descend over rocky terrain that delivers a variety of bigger drop-offs. The trail eventually veers to the south, offering some technically challenging terrain over tight, imbedded rock and returns to where you began this northernmost loop. After finishing this loop, you're offered views of Longs Peak and Mount Meeker to the west, as you race toward the trail's southern loop.

The second loop is short but sweet. Upon intersecting with the main trail again, take care in descending. The terrain offers loose rock and sand over steeper slopes before letting out to the more moderate terrain below the Backbone. With the Backbone to your right, it's a fast cruise back to your vehicle.

Miles and Directions

0.0 From the parking lot, begin riding up the dirt road underneath the cottonwood trees in a northerly direction. Shortly thereafter, bear right onto the Devil's Backbone singletrack, following signs to the Devil's Backbone Trail.

0.1 Pass through a wooden gate and continue on the singletrack heading in a northerly direction.

0.3 Pass through an iron gate and begin a short climb in a northwesterly direction over moderately steep terrain.

0.5 Arrive at the intersection of the Foot-Only portion on your left and the multiuse portion of the Devil's Backbone Trail on your right. Bear right, continuing on the multiuse portion of the Devil's Backbone Trail.

1.3 The Devil's Backbone multiuse trail intersects with the northern terminus of its Foot-Only Trail on the left. Continue right on the multiuse singletrack.

2.0 Arrive at the trail's southern loop. (This will be the second loop you complete). Bear left here, continuing in a northerly direction.

2.3 Arrive at the second intersection of the trail's southern loop on your right. Bear left here.

2.6 Arrive at another trail intersection: the beginning of the trail's northern loop. Bear left here and begin riding the loop in a clockwise direction.

3.1 Pass a sandstone bench off to your right.

3.8 Arrive at the intersection and end of the trail's northern loop. Bear left here and return from where you came to the next loop.

4.1 Arrive at the intersection with the next loop. Bear left and begin climbing in a southerly direction.

4.5 Arrive at the intersection and end of the trail's southern loop. Bear left here and return the way you came.

6.5 Arrive at your vehicle.

Ride Information

Local Information

Loveland Chamber of Commerce, 5400 Stone Creek Circle, Suite 200, Loveland 80538; (970) 667–6311

Local Events and Attractions

Estes Park and Rocky Mountain National Forest, west through the Big Thompson Canyon Rocky Mountain National Forest: recorded message, (970) 586–1333; general information, (970) 586–1206. For additional information or correspondence, write to Rocky Mountain National Forest, Superintendent, Estes Park 80517. Backcountry permits in the summer months cost $10; reservations are recommended. For reservations or bivouac permits, call (970) 586–1242.

Honorable Mentions

Fort Collins Region

Five more rides in the Fort Collins area deserve mention, even though they didn't make the "A" list. They may be a bit out of the way or more heavily traveled, but they still deserve your consideration when choosing a destination.

A Beaver Meadows

Beaver Meadows is a little-known resort ranch situated roughly 4.5 miles northwest of the town of Red Feather Lakes. Surrounded by the Roosevelt National Forest, Beaver Meadows offers outdoor enthusiasts plenty of recreation. Although privately owned, the proprietors of Beaver Meadows allow mountain bikers to ride their trails without having to stay at the ranch. Maps of the area are located at the ranch's small bike shop.

Some of Roosevelt National Forest's best and relatively unknown trails can be accessed from Beaver Meadows Resort Ranch. Riders can make the day trip from Fort Collins to enjoy some of northern Colorado's greatest and least traveled mountain biking trails.

To get to Beaver Meadows Resort Ranch from Fort Collins, drive north on U.S. Highway 287. After passing Ted's Place and the intersection with Colorado Highway 14, continue driving north on US 287 for roughly 11 miles before turning left onto Red Feather Lakes Road (Larimer County Road 74E) by the Forks Restaurant. Drive west on Red Feather Lakes Road for 24.5 miles before making a right onto County Road 73C, by the Pot Belly Restaurant. Drive on CR 73C for roughly 4.5 miles before bearing left into the Beaver Meadows Resort Ranch entryway. There will be a log sign with red and white lettering. Follow the entryway to the main parking lot, and check in at the Beaver Shop or the restaurant.

B Lone Pine Trail

Located 8 miles west of US 287 along Red Feather Lakes Road, the Lone Pine Trail is a popular equestrian trail. While mountain bikers do use the trail, they are certainly in the minority. Managed by the Colorado Division of Wildlife, the Lone Pine Trail is only open to mountain bikers, horseback riders, and hikers from May 1 to September 1. Throughout the rest of the year, the area serves as a winter migratory route for resident elk. However, the area is open to hunters during regular hunting seasons. With this short riding season, it's easy to see why mountain bikers tend to overlook the riding here. But to overlook the Lone Pine Trail is a mistake.

The trail offers some stellar singletrack, both ascending and descending, before meeting with the wider doubletrack of an old ranch road that runs along the North Lone Pine Creek. The doubletrack leads in a northwesterly direction through a series of small valleys and open meadows and crosses the creek a number of times before ending at the Colorado Division of Wildlife boundary. From there riders return the way they came.

To get to the Lone Pine Trail from Fort Collins, drive north on US 287. After passing Ted's Place and the intersection with CO 14, continue driving north on US 287 for roughly 11 miles before turning left onto Red Feather Lakes Road (Larimer County Road 74E) by the Forks Restaurant. Drive west on Red Feather Lakes Road for roughly 8 miles and bear right into the Lone Pine Trail parking lot.

C Kelly Flats Trail

This four-by-four road/trail can be ridden in any number of ways—as a loop, a point-to-point, or an out-and-back. In any way, the trail offers a tough climb of sometimes very technical and always challenging terrain.

The Kelly Flats Trail climbs out of the Poudre Canyon and descends to the Boy Scout Camp Road near the town of Rustic and the Goodell Corner. Riders can access the trail from either the Poudre Canyon or the Boy Scout Camp Road. Either option delivers a physically challenging climb to the top where riders are rewarded with stunning views of Rocky Mountain National Park's Mummy Range.

The initial climb north out of the Poudre Canyon is extremely strenuous. The trail will veer left near its high point and pass Lonetree Mountain to the north. Heading west, riders will eventually pass through Wintersteen Park before descending to the Boy Scout Camp Road, near the Goodell Corner.

The Goodell Corner pays tribute to the area's earliest pioneers. Ermine Robinson and Clark Goodell homesteaded the area in 1886. A year later Fort Collins businessmen named the area Manhattan, as they settled upon mining for gold. The gold mining never proved profitable, so Manhattan was abandoned in 1915.

To reach Kelly Flats from Fort Collins, drive north on US 287. Turn left at Ted's Place onto CO 14, following signs for the Poudre Canyon, and drive west on CO 14 for roughly 27 miles before turning right into the Kelly Flats trailhead parking lot.

D Foothills Trail

The Fort Collins Foothills Trail is a popular and easily accessible trail for mountain bikers and hikers. Upon reaching Road 23 atop Horsetooth Reservoir, there are a variety of other riding options. The Foothills Trail, then, offers willing riders a portal through which to explore other area trails.

Beginning on Fort Collins's western flank, the Foothills Trail extends from the flats of Fort Collins into the foothills to the west. The trail combines wide single-track with rocky terrain and climbs moderately to Horsetooth Reservoir and its northern dam. From here, riders can cross Road 23 and intersect the singletrack to the right of the Skyline Picnic Area. From here it's a steep and rugged descent to Soldier Canyon Dam. Much of the trail that follows the waterline is eroded, so take caution if proceeding. From here the trail leads south to County Road 42C and Dixon Reservoir. Dixon Reservoir also offers a number of networked trails and is worth exploring.

To reach the Fort Collins Foothills Trail, drive west from Fort Collins to the Overland Trail. Drive or ride north on Overland Trail. After passing Lee Lake on the right, Overland Trail curves sharply to the west for 0.1 mile before heading north again. Where Overland Trail again bears north (right), continue driving or riding west (straight) and intersect with Michaud Lane (RD 50). Drive or ride west on Michaud Lane to its end and the trailhead of the Foothills Trail.

E Old Flowers Road

Old Flowers Road is a long-standing, popular ride that offers incredible views of the Rawah Wilderness Area. While many mountain bikers may have an aversion to riding roads, paved or otherwise, this old wagon road is not to be missed. Old Flowers Road delivers one of the best descents in the area and includes 360-degree Rocky Mountain views. Old Flowers Road can be ridden as either an out-and-back or as a point-to-point.

Old Flowers Road takes its name from Jacob Flowers, the founding father of the nearby town of Bellvue. The town's first general store, also built by Flowers from local red sandstone, still stands today. Old Flowers Road was originally a wagon road that serviced the onetime silver-mining towns of Lulu and Teller Cities, west of Cameron Pass, at the headwaters of the Colorado River. One story recalls Flowers's habit of nailing tin cans packed with wildflowers to the trees along the road as a way to set his road apart from all the others.

You can reach Old Flowers Road by driving north on US 287, following signs to Laporte. US 287 will bear right and travel in a more northerly direction. When US 287 bears right, continue driving straight on Road 54G through Laporte. By Vern's Restaurant, bear left (west) onto Road 52E and drive through Rist Canyon to Stove Prairie Road 27. Park your vehicle by the old schoolhouse and start riding.

Boulder Region

There's good reason why Boulder earned the title of "America's Number One Sports Town" from *Outside Magazine*. The town's almost over-the-top enthusiasm for healthy living and recreation, along with its prime location, sets it apart from other outdoor towns.

While some believe Boulder to be swaddled by a broad valley whose towering granite Flatiron formations lean against the eastern flanks of the central Rocky Mountains and the Continental Divide, others still hold to the old-standing claim that Boulder lies "somewhere between the mountains and reality." While this is open to some debate, there's no denying that wherever the town lies, it does so for good reason.

The Southern Arapaho Indians first occupied the Boulder Valley, living near Haystack Mountain because of its favorable climate and its abundance of elk, bison, and deer. The prospect of gold would later lure nonnative settlers to set up camp near the entrance of Boulder Canyon on October 17, 1858. Known originally as Deadwood Diggings and developing as a supply center for area mining camps, Boulder grew increasingly larger and became an officially incorporated city on November 4, 1871. Today, Boulder's central industries include education, research and technology, and tourism, the latter of which, quite possibly, standing above the rest.

To its credit, Boulder had the foresight to grow responsibly. While definitely embracing the call from wealth and opportunity, Boulder has remained true to its natural riches and has developed programs to safeguard these riches. After purchasing thousands of acres of open space in 1967, Boulder implemented the Boulder Valley Comprehensive Plan three years later, which serves to manage proper land use and development in the Boulder Valley. In 1972 Boulder passed a height restriction ordinance for any newly built structures. These actions, along with several others, have to a large part been the impetus behind the town's continued commitment to its outdoor lifestyle, not the least of which is its commitment to cycling.

Raising the bicycle to anthropomorphic status, all of Boulder's city bus and shuttle services accept bikes in their racks or cargo compartments, accommodating the 93,000 bicycles—more than one per person—that reside in the town. Moreover, the city offers its cyclists nearly 100 miles of bike paths, lanes, and routes, and that's just within the roughly 25-square-mile city limits of the surrounding 1.5 million-acre Arapaho and National Forests, along with the 37,823 acres of Open Space and Mountain Parks, all provide excellent biking opportunities. The fact that bicycles are not allowed in the Boulder Mountain Parks system, however, hasn't swayed Boulderites from adopting the bicycle as their main mode of transportation.

For more information on Boulder, contact the Boulder Convention and Visitors Bureau at (303) 442–2911 or (800) 444–0447 or the Boulder Chamber of Commerce at (303) 442–1044.

9 Rabbit Mountain

Rabbit Mountain offers riders a short and accessible network of trails that deliver rocky singletrack, short but steep climbs, and incredible views of the Front Range and Longs Peak. While suited more for beginner to intermediate riders, Rabbit Mountain can easily be enjoyed by more advanced riders who appreciate a variety of terrain within a small amount of space. Rest rooms are located in the parking lot. Because this area is quite exposed to the elements, make sure to bring enough water for you as well as for any pets that are with you.

Start: The Rabbit Mountain trailhead

Distance: 5.8-mile lariat with out-and-back spur

Approximate riding time: Advanced riders, 30 minutes; intermediate riders, 45–60 minutes

Aerobic level: Physically easy to moderate due to some shorter, but steeper climbs, particularly when ascending on the Little Thompson Overlook Trail

Technical difficulty: Technically easy to moderate due to some rockier and sandier singletrack, particularly on the Eagle Wind and Little Thompson Overlook Trails

Terrain: Dirt road and singletrack that weave through stands of evergreen and over imbedded granite, other loose rock, and sand

Schedule: March–October; although seasonal closures span from February 1 through July 31 in the critical wildlife habitat found alongside the Eagle Wind Trail. The route described here, however, never enters the critical wildlife habitat.

Maps: DeLorme *Colorado Atlas & Gazetteer*, pages 29–30; USGS: Carter Lake Reservoir and Hygiene, CO; ZIA Maps: *Boulder County Mountain Bike Map*

Nearest town: Lyons

Other trail users: Hikers and horseback riders

Canine compatibility: Dog-friendly

Trail contact: Boulder County Parks and Open Space, Boulder; (303) 441-3950

Finding the Trailhead: From Boulder, drive on U.S. Highway 36 west (North Foothills Highway) for roughly 13.3 miles heading north toward the town of Lyons. At a stoplight, US 36 comes to a T and intersects with Colorado Highway 66. Bear right onto CO 66 and drive east for roughly 1 mile before bearing left onto Fifty-third Street, just after passing a brown Rabbit Mountain Open Space sign. Drive north on Fifty-third Street for 2.8 miles before bearing right into the trailhead. Parking spaces are provided at the trailhead.

The Ride

Residents of Boulder County have been visiting Rabbit Mountain Open Space since 1983, but records indicate that humans have inhabited the Rabbit Mountain area for the last 5,000 years. Arapaho Indians favored Rabbit Mountain as an ideal wintering ground, while miners who didn't strike it rich opted to farm in the area.

The first couple of miles along the Little Thompson Overlook Trail and the Eagle Wind Trail climb gradually over rocky and sandy singletrack. As you head up

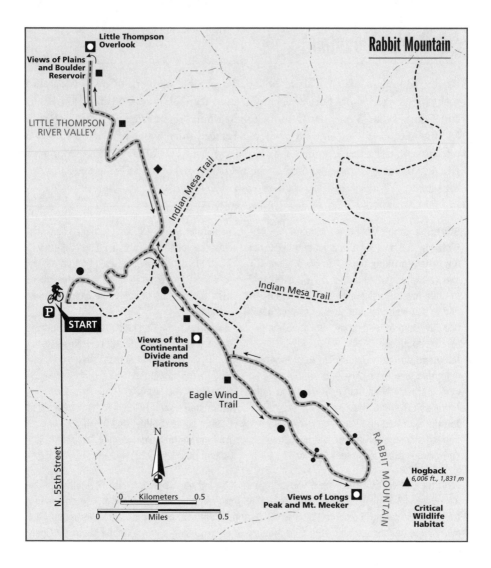

the Eagle Wind Trail, there are beautiful views of the Continental Divide and the Flatirons before you plunge into a dense ponderosa pine forest. Here the trail levels and becomes rockier with imbedded granite and sandstone. This healthy forest remains so due, in part, to controlled burns, which took place nearby in 1996 and 1997. You might still be able to glimpse the remains of the burns, which help to thin crowded forests and leave a natural mix of trees and plants, thereby maintaining a healthy ecosystem.

Once through the first gate, it's a short ride to the top of Rabbit Mountain where you're offered magnetic views of Longs Peak (14,255) and Mount Meeker.

The name Rabbit Mountain may provide riders with a false sense of security as the mountain was once called Rattlesnake Mountain for good reason. This is rattlesnake country. Some stories report that area developers found "Rattlesnake" to be too much of a PR problem when luring settlers. So they changed the name to "Rabbit" because some say the mountain resembles a crouching rabbit with lowered ears when seen from the east.

Once the Eagle Wind Trail levels atop Rabbit Mountain, riders ride alongside a critical wildlife habitat area before making their northerly descent. This critical wildlife habitat marks the park's transitional zone ecosystem, where prairie and foothill montane ecosystems meet. This seasonally closed (February 1–July 31) area protects wildlife's hunting, eating, sleeping, and breeding grounds. A sign reading ONLY BY OUR COLLECTIVE STEWARDSHIP CAN WE PRESERVE THE INTEGRITY OF THIS PARK stands before the protected area and speaks the truth.

From the Eagle Wind Trail, riders descend to the Indian Mesa Trail. Riders who wish to extend their trip can opt to ride on the Indian Mesa Trail that leads to the eastern portion of the Open Space. Crossing the Indian Mesa Trail, however, riders connect with the Little Thompson Overlook Trail.

The Little Thompson Overlook Trail was named after David Thompson (1770–1857), an English fur trapper with the Northwest Fur Company. This trail's initial climb is steep and rocky over broken shale and slabs of sandstone, but it offers panoramic easterly views of the Great Plains and the Boulder Reservoir. While riding, you may notice caves carved by erosion in the mountainside. These caves provide shelter for mountain lions. Nearing 4 miles, the more technical terrain levels off as the trail descends moderately, past a barrier that reads STOP. THIS IS NOT A DESIGNATED TRAIL. Stay on the main trail and follow the other sign that points in the direction of the Little Thompson Overlook.

After arriving at the Little Thompson Overlook, take in the beautiful views of the Little Thompson River Valley and the surrounding geological terrain. Sadly, the Little Thompson River has run dry in both 2000 and 2001. This is unfortunate when you consider that the small town of Pinewood Springs, lying directly west of Rabbit Mountain on Interstate 36, depends upon the Little Thompson River for roughly

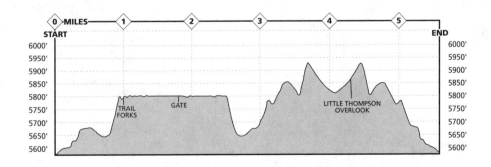

80 percent of its water. In recent years, the town has had to ship in water to fill the shortage left by the drying Little Thompson.

From the overlook, descend on the Little Thompson Overlook Trail along technically challenging terrain to your vehicle.

Miles and Directions

0.0 From the Rabbit Mountain trailhead, begin climbing on the upper singletrack of the Little Thompson Overlook Trail, heading in a northeasterly direction.

0.5 The Little Thompson Overlook Trail intersects with the Indian Mesa Trail (the gravel dirt road) and the Eagle Wind Trail. Bear right onto the Eagle Wind Trail, crossing the Indian Mesa Trail, and continue on the Eagle Wind Trail, heading in a southeasterly direction.

1.0 The Eagle Wind Trail forks. Bear right at the fork, riding in a counterclockwise direction. **Option:** You can opt to bear left here and ride the loop in a clockwise direction, thereby descending through a thick ponderosa pine forest.

1.8 Pass through a gate, as the trail starts veering east.

2.3 Pass through another gate and continue descending to the Indian Mesa Trail.

3.5 The Eagle Wind Trail intersects with the Indian Mesa Trail. Cross the Indian Mesa Trail, continuing up the singletrack you had previously ridden down, and connect with the Little Thompson Overlook Trail. Bearing right onto the Little Thompson Overlook Trail, you begin to climb in a northeasterly direction, turning shortly toward the northwest.

4.3 Arrive at the Little Thompson Overlook. Turn around and descend on the Little Thompson Overlook Trail toward your vehicle.

5.3 Reach the intersection of the Little Thompson Overlook, Eagle Wind Trail, and the Indian Mesa Trail. Continue descending along the Little Thompson Overlook Trail.

5.8 Arrive at your vehicle.

Ride Information

Local Information
Lyons Chamber of Commerce, P.O. Box 426, Lyons 80540; (303) 823-5215

Local Events and Attractions
Good Old Days, June, Lyons; (303) 823-5215

Planet Bluegrass, July, Lyons; (303) 823-0848

Rocky Mountain National Park, (303) 586-2371

Lodging
Kumpfenberg Manor, Lyons; (303) 823-0708

Lyons Den Bed and Breakfast, Lyons; (303) 823-6071

Restaurants
Calvin Huss Inn, Lyons; (303) 823-6362

Oskar Blues, Lyons's oldest brewery; (303) 823-6685

◀ *The unique and fun imbedded granite of the Eagle Wind Trail.*

10 Hall Ranch

Opened in 1997, Hall Ranch is one of Boulder County's newer trails. As part of the North Foothills Open Space, Hall Ranch has become a favorite among Boulder area mountain bikers and deservedly so. Its smooth and wide singletrack leads mountain bikers through varying terrain of open meadow and higher mixed conifer forests. Dramatic hogbacks, exposed sandstone granite domes, and distant cliffs are all to be seen by the curious rider. At one point, riders are offered an incredible view of Longs Peak (14,255 feet) and Mount Meeker. A great ride for both the beginner and advanced rider, Hall Ranch offers a short, moderately easy to technical trail system close to Boulder.

Start: The Hall Ranch trailhead along Colorado Highway 7

Distance: 10.2-mile lariat

Approximate riding time: Advanced riders, 1 hour; intermediate riders, 1.5–2 hours

Aerobic level: Physically easy to moderate due to moderate climbing

Technical difficulty: Technically easy to moderate due to wide and smooth singletrack. There is a short rocky and steeper section that requires more advanced bike handling skills.

Terrain: Mostly wide and hard-packed singletrack. There are some rockier sections, as well as some sandy patches, as the trail winds through grasslands, shrublands, woodlands, forests, cliffs, and canyons.

Schedule: March–October. Open sunrise to sunset.

Maps: DeLorme *Colorado Atlas & Gazetteer,* pages 29–30; USGS: Lyons, CO; Boulder County Parks and Open Space Hall Ranch trail map; ZIA Maps: *Boulder County Mountain Bike Map*

Nearest town: Lyons

Other trail users: Hikers and horseback riders

Canine compatibility: Dogs are not permitted at the North Foothills Open Space, including Hall Ranch, for wildlife habitat protection purposes.

Trail contact: Boulder County Parks and Open Space, Boulder; (303) 441-3950

Finding the Trailhead: From Boulder, drive on U.S. Highway 36 west (North Foothills Highway) for roughly 13.3 miles heading north toward the town of Lyons. At a stoplight, US 36 comes to a T at its intersection with Colorado Highway 66. Bear left at the stoplight, continuing west on US 36 for 1.6 miles through the town of Lyons before bearing left onto CO 7 (South St. Vrain Drive). Drive south on CO 7 for roughly 1.2 miles before bearing right into the Hall Ranch parking lot.

The Ride

With more than 3,200 acres to its credit, Hall Ranch is part of a large block of undeveloped land that includes the North St. Vrain Canyon, the USDA Forest Service's Coffintop Gulch area, and the City of Longmont's Button Rock Reservoir. Combined, these three large parcels of public land are nearly equal in size to Rocky Mountain National Park.

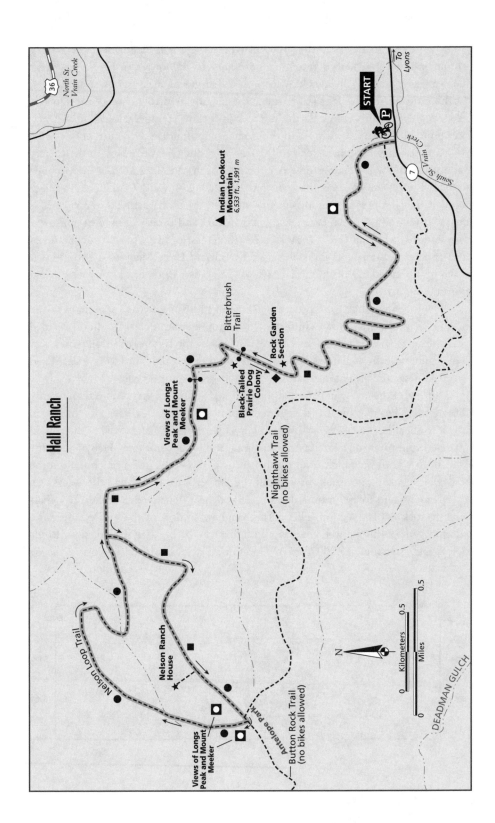

Hall Ranch

START

To Lyons

North St. Vrain Creek

36

South St. Vrain Creek

7

▲ **Indian Lookout Mountain**
6,533 ft., 1,991 m

Bitterbrush Trail

Rock Garden Section

Black-Tailed Prairie Dog Colony

Nighthawk Trail
(no bikes allowed)

Views of Longs Peak and Mount Meeker

Nelson Loop Trail

Nelson Ranch House

Antelope Park

Views of Longs Peak and Mount Meeker

Button Rock Trail
(no bikes allowed)

N

Kilometers
0   0.5

Miles
0   0.5

DEADMAN GULCH

Because the ranch lies at the junction where the Great Plains meet the Rocky Mountains, rock formations dating back roughly 1.7 billion years can be seen near the western side of Hall Ranch. After upward surges of magma powered through Earth's crust during the Precambrian era, the magma gradually cooled into igneous rock roughly 15 miles below Earth's surface. Over time, continental shifting and erosion brought this cooled magma to the surface, exposing large granite shelves.

But what may best characterize the meeting of the Great Plains with the Rocky Mountains are the tilted sandstone rock formations that jut skyward near the entrance to Hall Ranch. As the seas that covered Boulder County 260 million years ago receded, they left behind windblown sand dunes that later hardened into quartz. This quartz sandstone is known as the Lyons Formation and is heavily used in construction. Indeed, the sandstone quarry located to the east of Hall Ranch is made up of fifty-two small quarry pits and was started by Edward Lyon. Many of the stones that make up the buildings of the University of Colorado's Boulder campus were taken from these quarries.

As you begin riding, you'll see Hat Rock and Indian Lookout Mountain to the north—they offer the best examples of these prehistoric rock formations. Named after the area's abundant antelope bitterbrush bushes, the Bitterbrush Trail passes over wide and smooth singletrack. As the trail weaves through meadows and mixed conifer forests, the area's great natural variety becomes quite clear.

Although Edward Lyon patented the land in 1885, there were more than twenty different families that lived and operated businesses in the area. This area had been home to sugar beet farmers who settled here after World War I, as well as those who quarried sandstone and logged ponderosa pine and Douglas fir trees. Hallyn and June Hall, from whom the ranch takes its present name, also operated a ranch here in the mid-1940s, grazing livestock throughout the property for more than fifty years.

Meadows and forests soon fade away as you near your second mile and a challenging rock garden section. This is the toughest section of the entire ride. After climbing out of this section, you pass through a gate before arriving at one of Boulder County's highest (6,200 feet in elevation) black-tailed prairie dog (*Cynomys*

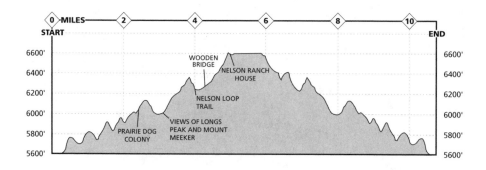

Enjoying Hall Ranch's technical side. PHOTO: AMANDA HLAWATY

ludovicianus) colonies. Specifically built to minimize impact to this area, the Bitter-brush Trail circumvents this one-of-a-kind colony.

After passing the prairie dog colony, you'll descend quickly through the meadow before the trail turns upward again on its way to the Nelson Loop Trail. Ponderosa pines are the most abundant trees in the area. Once you intersect with the Nelson Loop Trail, continue to climb in a southwesterly direction through fairly heavily wooded terrain. The trail switches back through mixed conifer forests over rock-imbedded singletrack before delivering you to Antelope Park, a beautiful meadow offering incredible views of Longs Peak and Mount Meeker.

Originally homesteaded in 1890 by Richard Clark, the land known as Antelope Park was purchased from Clark in 1922 by the Nelson family, who operated a successful ranch here. A short trail leads to the Nelson Ranch House. The ranch once consisted of a standing house, root cellar, and cement silo.

As you pass through Antelope Park, you begin your speedy descent along the Nelson Loop Trail, heading in a northeasterly direction. The descent passes through mixed conifer forests over relatively smooth singletrack before intersecting with the

Bitterbrush Trail. Once you reconnect to the Bitterbrush Trail, it's a fast and wild ride over moderately rocky terrain to your vehicle.

Miles and Directions

0.0 Begin riding in a westerly direction on the wide singletrack of the Bitterbrush Trail.

0.2 The Bitterbrush Trail intersects with the Nighthawk Trail to the left—no bikes are allowed on the Nighthawk Trail. Bear right here, continuing on the Bitterbrush Trail.

2.2 Pass through a gate and continue riding in a northerly direction toward the Nelson Loop.

2.3 Pass a large prairie dog colony on your left.

2.6 Pass through another gate, and ride through a speedy smooth descent through a meadow.

3.6 Views of Longs Peak and Mount Meeker.

4.0 The Bitterbrush Trail intersects with the Nelson Loop Trail. Bear left onto the Nelson Loop Trail, traveling the loop in a clockwise direction.

4.2 Cross a small, wooden bridge.

4.8 Arrive at the Nelson Ranch House in Antelope Park. Caution: The foundation of the ranch house is unstable, so keep out.

5.0 The Nelson Loop Trail intersects with the Nighthawk Trail to the left. Bear right to continue riding on the Nelson Loop Trail, with views of Longs Peak and Mount Meeker directly in front of you.

6.3 The Nelson Loop Trail intersects with the Bitterbrush Trail. Veer left onto the Bitterbrush Trail, and retrace your path back to the start.

10.2 Return to your vehicle.

Ride Information

Trail Information

Division of Wildlife Headquarters, Denver; (303) 297-1192

Local Information

Lyons Chamber of Commerce, P.O. Box 426, Lyons 80540; (303) 823-5215

Local Events and Attractions

Good Old Days, June, Lyons; (303) 823-5215
Planet Bluegrass, July, Lyons; (303) 823-0848

Rocky Mountain National Park, (303) 586-2371

Lodging

Kumpfenberg Manor, Lyons; (303) 823-0708
Lyons Den Bed and Breakfast, Lyons; (303) 823-6071

Restaurants

Calvin Huss Inn, Lyons; (303) 823-6362
Oskar Blues, Lyons's oldest brewery; (303) 823-6685

11 Heil Valley Ranch

As one of Boulder County's newest Open Space Parks, Heil Valley Ranch includes all the furnishings of a carefully constructed trail system. Its wide and smooth single-track climbs moderately through ponderosa pine forests to incredible views of Longs Peak and Mount Meeker, as well as to an overlook of Hall Ranch and the ruddy sandstone hogbacks near Lyons. The ranch's technically tame terrain makes it ideally suited for riders who haven't yet mastered the big drops and rocky trails for which the Front Range is famous. More advanced riders will appreciate Heil Valley Ranch as a spinner's playground, offering ample opportunities for spinning both up and down its smooth-running course.

Start: The Heil Valley Ranch Open Space trailhead

Distance: 8.1-mile lariat

Approximate riding time: Advanced riders, 45 minutes; intermediate riders, 1 hour

Aerobic level: Physically easy to moderate due to the lack of any significant steep climbing

Technical difficulty: Technically easy due to the smooth riding surface of the trail's wide singletrack

Terrain: Singletrack and dirt road, delivering a smooth-riding and wide surface that courses in and out of ponderosa pine forests and meadows

Schedule: March–October; open sunrise to sunset

Maps: DeLorme *Colorado Atlas & Gazetteer,* page 30; USGS: Lyons, CO; Boulder County Parks and Open Space Heil Valley Ranch trail map

Nearest town: Boulder

Other trail users: Hikers and horseback riders

Canine compatibility: Dogs are not permitted at the North Foothills Open Space, including Heil Valley Ranch, for wildlife habitat protection purposes

Trail contact: Boulder County Parks and Open Space, Boulder; (303) 441-4559

Finding the Trailhead: From Boulder, drive north on U.S. Highway 36 to Left Hand Canyon Drive. Make a left onto Left Hand Canyon Drive, and drive west for 0.7 mile. Turn right onto the dirt Geer Canyon Drive and drive 1.25 miles before bearing right into Heil Valley Ranch Open Space. Park in the designated area at the trailhead.

The Ride

It's been a long time coming for many eager outdoor enthusiasts, but what took several years finally came on a cold and blustery autumn afternoon.

The ribbon was cut at roughly 3:00 P.M. on October 5, 2001, and the long-awaited Heil Valley Ranch officially opened for mountain biking. The mountain bike trails within the ranch are Sweeco cut—created by a small bulldozer device

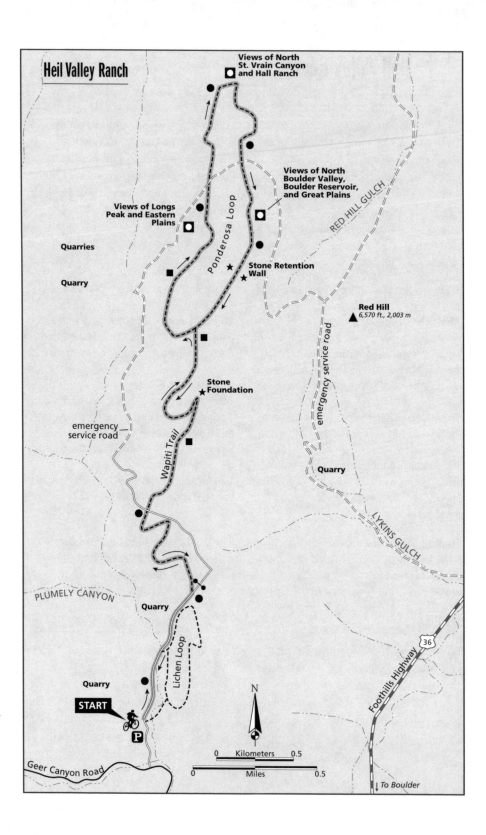

adopted by land managers and trail groups nationwide for the construction of multi-use trail systems. As such, Heil Valley Ranch's trails are roughly 3 feet wide. This almost highway-wide singletrack makes for a great spin in the saddle.

Nestled among the hogbacks of Geer Canyon, the area surrounding Heil Valley Ranch was originally settled by Solomon Geer in 1888. Bought by the Heil family in 1949, the land grew into a successful ranching business. Now, however, the Heil Valley Ranch Open Space comprises 4,923 acres of land and presents a network of trails that includes the Lichen Loop, Wapiti Trail, and Ponderosa Loop. As part of the North Foothills Open Space, Heil Valley Ranch is among a large parcel of undeveloped land that includes the North St. Vrain Canyon, the Roosevelt National Forest, and the Trevarton Conservation Easement.

Although Boulder County Parks and Open Space purchased Heil Valley Ranch in 1996, the North Foothills Open Space Management Plan conducted a variety of studies that weighed future resource protection against recreational activities at the ranch before opening it to the public. Its findings allowed for the opening of the 1.3-mile hikers-only Lichen Loop Trail in March of 2000.

Fittingly, riders begin their route on the dirt road of the Lichen Loop Trail's west edge (the only portion of this trail where bikes are allowed). As the first trail to be opened in Heil Valley Ranch, the Lichen Loop Trail marked the conclusion of Phase 1 in Heil Valley Ranch's long-term, three-phase plan. The ease of the Lichen Loop Trail along with the ranch's new picnic shelter, which can accommodate up to 75 people, make this area of the ranch ideally suited for mellow family outings. (To reserve the large, covered picnic area, complete with barbecue grill, call the Boulder County Parks and Open Space at 303–441–3950.)

After connecting with the wide and smooth singletrack of the Wapiti Trail, riders climb moderately in a northwesterly direction. Part of aligning the Wapiti Trail within the greater Heil Valley Ranch involved tracking the migratory animal from which the trail takes its name. *Wapiti,* a Shawnee Indian word meaning "white rump," is commonly identified with the North American elk (*Cervus canadensis*).

The Wapiti Trail also passes through a winter range for elk migrating down from the Indian Peaks Wilderness. This altitudinal migration represents the only one of its

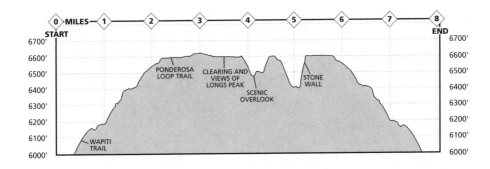

kind in which Front Range elk migrate from the Continental Divide to the Great Plains. That's good news when one considers that elk were once nearly extinct. Prized for sport, clothing, food, and medicinal value—their canine teeth were once used as charms—elk were nearly eradicated throughout North America, disappearing from 90 percent of their range by 1900. In fact, to this day, elk are no longer present in the eastern United States. Even Boulder County witnessed the elimination of all of its elk population by the turn of the twentieth century. Fortunately, elk were reintroduced into the area from 1913 to 1917.

Nearing a mile into your ride, the trail levels off a bit but continues to climb through a ponderosa pine forest. To its credit, the Wapiti Trail's few switchbacks are well constructed and secured by tight-fitting granite. Two miles into the ride, riders pass the foundation of an old building on the right, most likely left over from the area's rich ranching and quarrying history. Contrasting the architectural fortitude of the building's foundation is a natural shelter that appears on the left soon thereafter. Hung in the balance between structural integrity and structural wilderness, riders continue their moderate climb toward the Ponderosa Loop Trail.

The intersection of the Wapiti Trail and the Ponderosa Loop Trail marks the completion of Phase 2 of Heil Valley Ranch's long-term goals, which included construction of an 8-mile multiuse, stacked loop trail system. With the few exceptions that offer riders views of Longs Peak and Hall Ranch to the north, almost all of the Ponderosa Loop is contained under a thick cover of forest. Once riders reach the scenic overlook, they are rewarded with sweeping views of the red sandstone walls of the North St. Vrain Canyon and Hall Ranch. For the future, local land administrators hope to extend Heil Valley Ranch's trail system to Colorado 7, connecting Heil Valley Ranch with Hall Ranch (see Ride 10). This phase is a long way from being completed, however, as there are some private property issues that would need to be worked out first.

From the scenic overlook, riders climb gradually through a thick ponderosa pine forest before engaging in a speedy descent nearing 5 miles into the ride. The descent courses through a hillside whose trees are more widely spread apart, offering ample views of the North Boulder Valley, Boulder Reservoir, and Great Plains.

Once reconnecting with the Wapiti Trail, riders are delivered a fast descent over smooth singletrack. But while the smooth and wide singletrack invites a speedy descent, the trail's closely flanking evergreens, along with its sinuous path, require attention from riders with a need for speed. That said, the descent is simply awesome. However, as always, be aware of other trail users as you make your swift return to your vehicle.

◀ *Returning from the open views of Longs Peak and Mount Meeker.*

Miles and Directions

0.0 Begin riding north on the dirt road of the multiuse portion of the Lichen Loop. (Bikes are not permitted on the Lichen Loop's singletrack trail, which veers off to the right of the road.)

0.5 The multiuse portion of the Lichen Loop intersects with the Wapiti Trail on the left. Before the iron gate bear left onto the singletrack Wapiti Trail, then cross a bridge and climb gradually in a northwesterly direction.

1.3 Cross an emergency service road and continue riding straight ahead on the Wapiti Trail.

2.6 The Wapiti Trail intersects with the Ponderosa Loop Trail. Bear left onto the Ponderosa Loop Trail, riding the loop in a clockwise direction.

3.5 Reach a clearing in the Ponderosa Loop Trail with views of Longs Peak and the eastern plains.

3.8 Cross an emergency service road, and continue riding straight ahead on the Ponderosa Loop Trail.

4.1 Reach the Scenic Overlook off to your left.

4.5 Cross the emergency service road, and continue riding straight ahead on the Ponderosa Loop Trail.

5.2 Pass through a stone retention wall before a moderate climb to the Ponderosa Loop Trail's intersection with the Wapiti Trail.

5.4 Reach the intersection of the Ponderosa Loop Trail and the Wapiti Trail. Veer left onto the Wapiti Trail and retrace your path toward the trailhead.

8.1 Arrive at your vehicle.

Ride Information

Trail Information
Division of Wildlife Headquarters, Denver; (303) 297-1192

Local Information
Boulder Chamber of Commerce, 2440 Pearl Street, Boulder 80302; (303) 442-1044

Local Events and Attractions
Good Old Days, June, Lyons; (303) 823-5215
Planet Bluegrass, July, Lyons; (303) 823-0848

Organizations
Boulder Area Trails Coalition (BATCO), Boulder; (303) 485-2162

Boulder Off-Road Alliance (BOA), Boulder; (303) 667-2467

Front Range Mountain Bike Association, Boulder; (303) 674-4862

In Addition

International Mountain Bicycling Association (IMBA)

The International Mountain Bicycling Association (IMBA) grew from five California advocacy clubs that had banded together to appease widespread mountain bike trail closures under consideration by the California State Parks. Hearing of crowded trails and trail-user tensions worldwide, the newly formed group decided to adopt a global perspective. And on what certainly must have been a sunny California day in 1988, the International Mountain Bicycling Association was born.

Combining mountain bike advocacy with environmental and social considerations, IMBA includes a network of roughly 32,000 individual members in all fifty states, in most Canadian provinces, and in thirty other countries. With more than 400 bicycle clubs and 100 corporate partners, IMBA continues to add new local, national, and international affiliates. Some of IMBA's ongoing projects include the Subaru/IMBA Trail Care Crew, the National Mountain Bike Patrol, IMBA Trailbuilding Schools, Federal Agency Mountain Bike Partnerships, and IMBA Epic Rides. "In some ways," IMBA executive director Tim Blumenthal admits, "we've grown into our name."

In the beginning, IMBA was a completely volunteer-run organization. Faced with ever-increasing population growth and development, it became clear that both IMBA and mountain biking needed professional leadership.

As the editor-in-chief for *Mountain Bike Magazine,* Tim Blumenthal occupied a seat on IMBA's board of directors in 1989. He offered to become executive director if IMBA would relocate its headquarters to Colorado, the home to major offices of the USDA Forest Service, the Bureau of Land Management, and the National Parks Service. Perhaps more important, according to Tim, "So much of the energy and the enthusiasm for the sport of mountain biking was based in the Rocky Mountains." Thus, IMBA moved to Boulder, Colorado, in the summer of 1994.

By "blending national and international leadership with grassroots support," IMBA strikes a balance between its local and international constituency. IMBA works with the Bureau of Land Management (BLM) and the Forest Service to promote and manage mountain biking on public lands. The Wilderness Society regularly consults IMBA during the shaping of new Wilderness Area proposals. Along with the National Parks Service, IMBA works to get people out of their cars and onto their bikes to improve the quality of air and visitor experience in national recreation areas. IMBA also speaks at the National Bike Summit, a gathering for all bicycling advocacy groups in the country, to discuss federal leadership projects.

Some members of IMBA include (front, from left) advocacy coordinator Dan Vardamis, membership and events coordinator Heather Szabo, and finance director Erik Esborg; (back, from left) executive director Tim Blumenthal, national mountain patrol coordinator Kevin Stein, senior national policy advisor Gary Sprung, and Subaru/IMBA trail care crew coordinator Jon Alegranti.

Moreover, IMBA offers strategic advice to local groups with sensitive mountain bike issues, gives cash grants to its member clubs, and donates thousands of trailwork tools for construction and maintenance of trails worldwide. IMBA regularly conducts trail-building schools and provides information on how to build sustainable, heavy-use trails, how to obtain 501c3 nonprofit status for local groups, how to address liability concerns, how to work with other trail user groups, and how to educate new mountain bikers. In short, says Tim, "IMBA is a marvelous blend of cycling, environmental conservation, [and] education."

It's no wonder that the Forest Service and the Bureau of Land Management have partnered with IMBA. This partnership may well have best been represented in recent years by the BLM's campaign to include mountain biking in its draft Off-Highway Vehicle (OHV) Strategy released December 4, 2000.

BLM proposed that mountain bikes be considered OHVs and subject to the same kind of regulations and restrictions. Managing 264 million acres of U.S. public land, the BLM was poised to dramatically affect mountain biking as we know it.

Tim visited with the BLM in Washington, D.C., in January 2001 to convince the agency to remove mountain biking from the plan. Coupled with roughly 14,000 letters in support of mountain biking, IMBA persuaded the BLM to remove mountain bikers from OHV designation.

On a more local level, Tim agrees that there's mostly good things happening for Front Range mountain biking. Heil Valley Ranch opened a new 8-mile trail in the fall of 2001. There are discussions of creating a trail leading from Eldorado Canyon State Park to Walker Ranch. There is also work being done on the Front Range Backdrop Project. This project would include a shared-use trail along the hills of the Front Range that would extend from the Wyoming border south to Colorado Springs. There have been discussions regarding the creation of a new singletrack trail near the Boulder Reservoir. Also, work is being done to the Winniger Ridge Dot Trail System (Dot Trail), a trail system that would stretch from Nederland to Boulder. (See Honorable Mention J: Winniger Ridge Dot Trail System in the Boulder Region.)

International Mountain Bicycling Association (IMBA)
P.O. Box 7578
Boulder, CO 80306
Phone (303) 545–9011 or (888) 442–4622
Fax (303) 545–9026
Web site www.imba.com
E-mail info@imba.com

12 Ceran St. Vrain Trail

The Ceran St. Vrain Trail has long been a Boulder favorite. Locals enjoy its proximity to Boulder and drool over the pristine singletrack that leads through a mixed conifer forest and along the South St. Vrain Creek. The trail follows the west bank of the South St. Vrain Creek to Miller Rock Road. The creek offers additional amenities for anglers, as well as for those who like to camp out to the sounds of rushing waters nearby. Once arriving at Miller Rock Road, the trail's high point, riders can take in the incredible views of the Indian Peaks Wilderness Area and Pleasant Valley. Take care when riding this area, as there is a vast network of trails that can disorient an unfamiliar rider.

Start: The Ceran St. Vrain trailhead
Distance: 6.4-mile lariat
Approximate riding time: Advanced riders, 45 minutes–1 hour; intermediate riders, 1.5–2 hours
Aerobic level: Physically moderate due to the steeper sections and higher elevations of the trail
Technical difficulty: Technically moderate due to some steeper, rocky climbs and descents. There are sections of this trail where the route passes over precipitously sloping terrain.
Terrain: Doubletrack and singletrack along sometimes rocky, sandy, and rooted trail. The trail follows the South St. Vrain River through mixed conifer forests.

Schedule: May–October
Maps: DeLorme *Colorado Atlas & Gazetteer,* page 29; USGS: Raymond, CO; ZIA Maps: *Boulder County Mountain Bike Map;* Trails Illustrated: #102, Indian Peaks–Gold Hill, CO
Nearest town: Jamestown
Other trail users: Hikers, anglers (fishing in the South St. Vrain Creek is catch-and-release only), and ATVs
Canine compatibility: Dog-friendly
Trail contact: Roosevelt and Arapaho National Forests, Boulder Ranger District, Boulder; (303) 444–6600

Finding the Trailhead: From Boulder, drive north on U.S. Highway 36 to Left Hand Canyon Drive (CR 81) and make a left onto Left Hand Canyon Drive. Left Hand Canyon Drive and the Overland Road (CR 94) share the same route for roughly 5 miles before Left Hand Canyon Drive forks sharply to the left on its way to the town of Ward. At this fork, bear right, continuing on Overland Road (CR 94), and follow it for roughly 3 more miles to the town of Jamestown. Drive for another 4.7 miles past Jamestown on the paved Overland Road (CR 94) and past the point where the road turns into dirt to the St. Vrain Trail sign on the right (north) side of CR 94. Park at the trailhead.

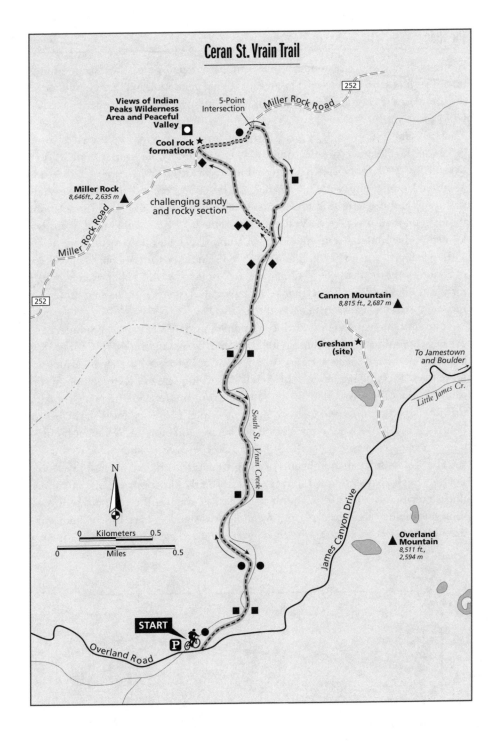

The Ride

Along this ride, you'll pass under a thick canopy of aspen, pine, and firs and through underbrush of currant, wild rose bushes, aster, wild geranium, and yarrow. Add to this the sound of the crashing South St. Vrain River, and you have one winner of a trail—Colorado-style.

The Ceran St. Vrain Trail takes its name from a fur trader with an illustrious career on the Colorado frontier. Born in St. Louis County, Missouri, Ceran St. Vrain (May 5, 1802–October 28, 1870) arrived in Colorado in 1824. Between 1830 and 1840, St. Vrain, along with his partner Charles Bent, created the Bent–St. Vrain Company and began setting up a number of forts on the Colorado plains. Among those established was Fort St. Vrain, near present-day Platteville. Fort St. Vrain was located at the confluence of the South St. Vrain Creek and the North Platte River and operated as a major trading post until 1845. Another fort was built entirely out of adobe along the Santa Fe Trail of eastern Colorado. As the only privately owned fortification in the West, this elaborate adobe fort was the premier trading center and meeting place for many traveling to the frontier.

Through fur trapping and fortification building, St. Vrain gained prominence in business, the military, and political circles. Indeed, his partnership with Charles Bent became one of the greatest enterprises in frontier history with annual earnings of more than $40,000. In a letter to his family describing one of his expeditions to the Boulder area, Ceran St. Vrain wrote, "I equipt sum men to goe trapping, thinking that it will be the most profitable for me . . . the men I have equipt is all the best of hunters, if they make a good hunt, I will doe verey good business." Whether he, himself, ever trapped beaver along the St. Vrain River remains unknown.

The Ceran St. Vrain Trail begins heading through a dark evergreen forest alongside the creek. As you follow the creek in a northerly direction, the trail oftentimes slopes precipitously toward it. Within the first half-mile of the trail, you're thrown some moderately technical terrain, including rocks and steeper hits or jumps and drop-offs. After descending to the creek level, the narrow trail continues as a mellow

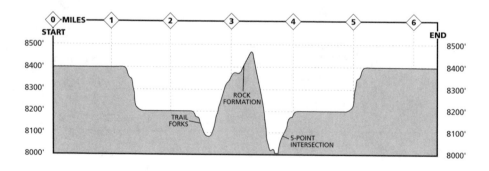

cruise through the forest with the creek to your right. But don't let this mellow meander fool you into believing that this trail is all made up of soft places to fall. On the contrary, technical hits appear without warning, so you really need to be aware of where the sinuous trail leads.

One such technical section arrives at roughly 2 miles. Riders need to grind up a challenging sandy and rocky section. Upon reaching the trail's high point atop Miller Rock Road, the trail levels out as riders are offered views of the Indian Peaks Wilderness Area and Peaceful Valley.

Lured by available land, John and Mildred Roberts arrived near what was then known as "Wildcat Gulch" in 1907. Reportedly, Mildred's reaction upon seeing their new home for the first time included the exclamation, "Oh, what a peaceful valley." And within a sentence breadth, Wildcat Gulch was renamed.

From the rock formations atop Miller Rock Road and the distant views of Miller Rock to the southwest, it's easy to see how a body can get lost up here. And, indeed, one did—intentionally. Word in the west has it that a crook by the name of Miller once took refuge among these rocks to successfully evade impending capture by the authorities.

As you descend from Miller Rock Road, you ride over an assortment of imbedded granite sections. Nearing 4 miles into your ride, you'll come to what is known as the 5-Point Intersection. Should you continue straight on the leftmost trail, you will eventually run into private property in the town of Raymond. Rather, take the trail that is immediately to the right of it. This route falls over rocky and root-filled sections.

Upon reconnecting with the trail intersection that you encountered at 2.2 miles, take care in your final descent to your vehicle and enjoy avoiding the sheer drop-offs that come within inches of the trail.

Miles and Directions

0.0 Cross a footbridge of the South St. Vrain Creek and begin riding in a northeasterly direction.

0.9 Descend to the creek, where you are offered the chance to soak your bum in a small waterfall runoff.

2.0 The singletrack opens up to a grunt of a climb over sandy and rocky doubletrack as it heads in a northerly direction.

2.2 The trail forks, with one trail leading in a northwesterly direction to your left, the other continuing straight ahead in a northerly direction. Bear left here and climb steeply out of the drainage. You will eventually return to this point after descending from Miller Rock Road.

2.5 The trail arrives at another intersection. Veer left here, heading in a westerly direction and continuing your climb over a challenging sandy and rocky section, toward Miller Rock Road.

2.7 Pass through a dilapidated fence over wide and sandy singletrack.

3.0 The singletrack intersects with Miller Rock Road. Bear right onto Miller Rock Road.

3.2 Pass a rock formation on your left as you continue riding in a northeasterly direction. Climbing these rocks will offer views of the real Miller Rock to the southwest.

3.6 Arrive at another trail intersection. A singletrack trail veers off to the right and heads in a southerly direction, which, if taken, will eventually return to the point where you originally connected with the Miller Rock Road. At this point, however, ride straight ahead, continuing your descent in a northeasterly direction.

3.7 Arrive at an intersection with two dirt roads. One road leads to the left, the other leads to the right. Bear right here, continuing on the main trail, and pass a cairn with a stick in it. The trail now leads in an easterly direction.

3.8 Arrive at the 5-Point Intersection. Do not continue straight on the leftmost trail. Instead, take the trail that is immediately to the right of it.

4.2 Arrive at the intersection where you previously turned toward Miller Rock at 2.2 miles. Now retrace your path to the trailhead.

6.4 Arrive at your vehicle.

Ride Information

Local Information

Boulder Convention and Visitors Bureau, 1850 Table Mesa Drive, Boulder 80305; (303) 442–2911

Local Events and Attractions

Jamestown Loop Trail (Ride 13)

◀ *Pristine singletrack through the woods.*

13 Jamestown Loop

The Jamestown Loop is only one option in this funky old mining community. Harking to its mining roots, the area boasts myriad choices of interconnecting routes and trails. For this reason, it's important that riders are familiar with the route and have sufficient map reading skills. The Jamestown Loop climbs through the James Creek drainage where it tops out offering views of the Indian Peaks. From its high point, the trail descends rapidly over quite technical terrain. The final descent travels over incredibly rocky and rutted terrain, as it falls steeply back to Jamestown.

Start: Start riding away from town on Ward Street in a southeasterly direction

Distance: 9.2-mile loop

Approximate riding time: Advanced riders, 1.5 hours; intermediate riders, 2–3 hours

Aerobic level: Physically moderate with some more challenging sections. The final push to the trail's high point climbs along very steep and rocky terrain.

Technical difficulty: Technically challenging due to the particularly rocky descent over the rutted and root-filled terrain of extreme Gillespie Gulch

Terrain: Paved and four-by-four roads through quiet streets in Jamestown, and up the steep James Creek drainage over rocky terrain. Most of the trail is covered by trees.

Schedule: May–October

Maps: DeLorme *Colorado Atlas & Gazetteer*, page 29; USGS: Gold Hill, CO; ZIA Maps: *Boulder County Mountain Bike Map;* Trails Illustrated: #102, Indian Peaks–Gold Hill, CO

Nearest town: Jamestown

Other trail users: Hikers, anglers, and four-by-four vehicles

Canine compatibility: Dog-friendly

Trail contact: Roosevelt and Arapaho National Forests, Boulder Ranger District, Boulder; (303) 444–6600

Finding the Trailhead: From Boulder, drive north on U.S. Highway 36 to Left Hand Canyon Drive (CR 81) and make a left onto Left Hand Canyon Drive. Left Hand Canyon Drive and the Overland Road (CR 94) share the same route for roughly 5 miles before Left Hand Canyon Drive forks sharply to the left on its way to the town of Ward. At this fork, bear right, continuing on Overland Road (CR 94) and follow it for roughly 3 more miles to the town of Jamestown. Drive through Jamestown for roughly 0.3 mile before bearing left onto Ward Street. The Jamestown post office will be on your left. Park your vehicle alongside Ward Street.

The Ride

Riders begin by riding up the quietly quaint Ward Street, leaving behind the town of Jamestown. At first glance, Jamestown appears to offer the kind of quality of life that many associate with living in the Colorado mountains: quiet, solitude, quaintness, scenery, and the unmistakable roaring sounds of James Creek. But we'll soon

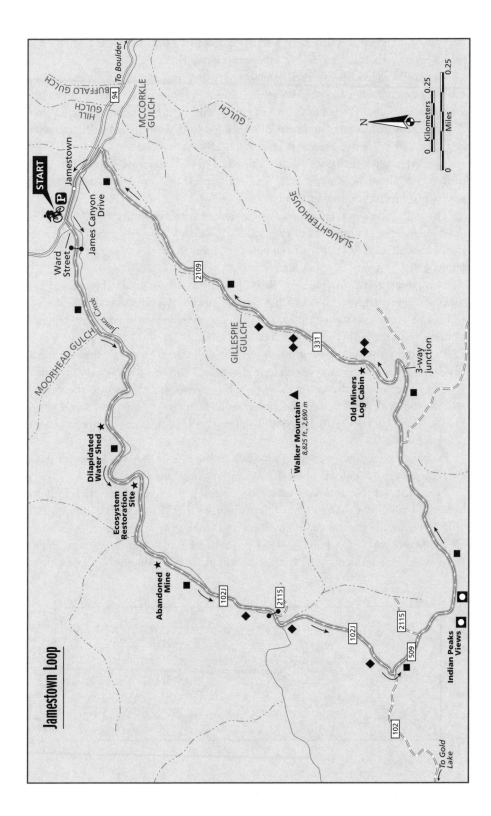

Jamestown Loop

START

Jamestown

To Boulder

BUFFALO GULCH

HILL GULCH

MCCORKLE GULCH

94

SLAUGHTERHOUSE GULCH

James Canyon Drive

Ward Street

MOORHEAD GULCH

James Creek

2109

GILLESPIE GULCH

331

3-way junction

Walker Mountain
8,825 ft., 2,690 m

Old Miners Log Cabin ★

Dilapidated Water Shed

Ecosystem Restoration Site

Abandoned Mine ★

1021

2115

2115

1021

509

102

Indian Peaks Views

To Gold Lake

N

0 Kilometers 0.25
0 Miles 0.25

discover that this quality has been a struggle to obtain throughout the town's history, a struggle that will repeat itself throughout this ride.

Originally called Elysian Park, Jamestown is one of Colorado's original mining camps. A rancher from Longmont, George Zweck was one of the area's original residents, as he would often graze his cattle here during the summer months. When Zweck discovered galena, the principal mineral in lead, word spread that Jamestown might be harboring other more precious minerals and metals.

In 1864 silver was discovered and a flood of miners filled the valley. With more than 400 residents now populating the area, the U.S. government established the town's first post office, calling it Jamestown.

Once the ride connects with CR 102J, however, the quaint town all but disappears as riders begin their climb alongside James Creek. The quiet stays around for riders, though, as CR 102J has been closed to motorized vehicles in an attempt to improve water quality in James Creek.

Now riders must struggle up CR 102J, as it becomes considerably steeper and rockier. After roughly 2 miles of solid climbing, riders pass through an aspen stand and onto a more level stretch of trail with an ecosystem restoration site, also designed to improve water quality in James Creek.

From the ecosystem restoration project, the trail opens up a bit. Climbing moderately, riders pass an abandoned mine to the right as they near 3 miles into the ride. Careful inspection of the area will reveal a bumper sticker attached to the driver's side door of a derelict orange truck that reads THIS LAND IS YOUR LAND. KEEP IT CLEAN, dating back to 1970. It's good to know that great ideas, no matter how old, never die.

Although Jamestown struggled for years to hit the mother lode, it never quite did. The James Creek flood of 1894 destroyed much of the town.

Now, you venture into that same flood plain as you cross James Creek. From here, the trail climbs sharply to its intersection with FS 2115. Continuing on CR 102J, however, the trail becomes physically and technically challenging.

As devastating as the flood of 1894 proved to be, it would not be the end of Jamestown. The residents rebuilt their community, and although a second flood

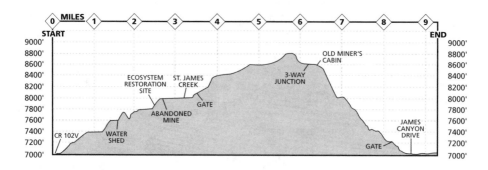

An abandoned truck by an old mine on CR 102J.

would hit the area in 1913, it wouldn't dampen their spirits. By now Jamestown had begun producing fluorspar, a mineral containing calcium fluoride. The mineral was in wide demand after America entered into World War I and II, as it was used to temper steel and make high-octane aviation fuel.

Once connecting with FS 509, the trail meanders through aspen glens and mixed conifer forests. This section provides a welcome relief from the grueling climbing it took to get here. After roughly 4.5 miles, riders may notice some singletrack trails off to the left. Unless you are familiar with this area and the routes these trails follow, it's best to keep on the main trail; although, the Siren's-song lure of prime singletrack can oftentimes take command over reason.

Those that stay the course described here are offered compelling views of the Indian Peaks. Be aware, however, these views will be behind you, so you'll have to get off your bike to check them out. Just to the north of here stands Porphyry Mountain.

The Southern Arapaho Indians considered Porphyry Mountain a sacred place. In fact, in the 1860s two miners from Jamestown uncovered a grave in which Native American bodies were found, facing Porphyry Mountain. Hikers still venture to the top of the mountain to scout for arrowheads.

After passing the second intersection with FS 2115, riders shoot through a fine rocky singletrack descent to a three-way junction. Taking the leftmost trail, which is the unmarked FS 331 (Trails Illustrated map #102 lists this road as FS 2109), riders descend through Gillespie Gulch, passing Walker Mountain to the left. This gulch is enough to make even the toughest riders dizzy. Although with its steep descent, rutted and rock-filled terrain, this section delivers far more Hendrix rock than Gillespie jazz.

Upon arriving in Jamestown, it's a mellow cruise back to your vehicle.

Miles and Directions

0.0 Begin riding away from town on Ward Street, heading in a southeasterly direction.

0.1 Pass through the gate and connect with CR 102J.

1.6 Pass a dilapidated water shed on your right.

2.3 Arrive at an ecosystem restoration site. Continue riding on the road.

2.8 Pass an abandoned mine off to your right.

3.1 Cross James Creek and continue climbing in a southerly direction.

3.5 Pass through an iron gate. Here CR 102J intersects with FS 2115. After passing through the gate, bear right, continuing your very steep and rutted climb on CR 102J.

4.1 CR 102J intersects with FS 102 and FS 509. Bear left here onto FS 509, riding in an easterly direction.

5.7 FS 509 intersects with FS 2115 again. Continue straight here on FS 509.

6.2 Arrive at the 3-way junction. Bear left onto the unmarked FS 331, the leftmost trail of the three, and continue descending, at first, in an easterly direction, but then switching back to descend in a northerly direction. Bear in mind that FS 331 is open to motorized vehicular traffic.

6.4 Pass an old miner's log cabin off to your left.

6.6 Cross a stream and pass rusted mining equipment.

8.2 Pass through a wooden gate.

8.3 FS 331 intersects with a maintained dirt road. Bear right onto the maintained dirt road.

8.8 Cross James Creek and intersect James Canyon Drive by the Jamestown Fire Department. Bear left onto the paved James Canyon Drive.

9.1 James Canyon Drive intersects with Ward Street. Bear left onto Ward Street.

9.2 Arrive at your vehicle.

Ride Information

Local Information

Boulder Convention and Visitors Bureau, 1850 Table Mesa Drive, Boulder 80305; (303) 442-2911

Local Events and Attractions

Ceran St. Vrain Trail (Ride 12)

Restaurants

Jamestown Mercantile Company Cafe, Jamestown; (303) 442-5847

14 Boulder Valley Ranch

Still a working cattle ranch, the Boulder Valley Ranch offers a trail system that weaves atop mesas and through rich agricultural fields. Along the route you'll find views of the Flatirons to the west, the Boulder Valley to the north and south, and the Great Plains to the east. Throughout the route a variety of migratory waterfowl can be seen in the many nearby ponds, that is, if not chased by the many dogs out strolling with their families. This is a great beginner's ride, as it meanders casually, save for one trickier singletrack section, through the northern lowlands of the Boulder Valley.

Start: Start riding on the Eagle Trail from the Foothills trailhead off U.S. Highway 36

Distance: 7.6-mile lariat

Approximate riding time: Advanced riders, 30–45 minutes; intermediate riders, 1–1.5 hours

Aerobic level: Physically easy due to the lack of any significant elevation gains. A technical section does challenge one's aerobic levels, but it is a short-lived challenge.

Technical difficulty: Technically easy due to the route's smooth surfaces. There is, however, one rockier singletrack section that descends precipitously down a slope.

Terrain: Farm-access dirt roads, doubletrack, and singletrack that roll over relatively smooth terrain atop plateau-like mesas on its way to the Boulder Reservoir

Schedule: Open year-round from 5 A.M. to midnight

Maps: DeLorme *Colorado Atlas & Gazetteer*, page 30; USGS: Boulder and Niwot, CO; ZIA Maps: *Boulder County Mountain Bike Map*

Nearest town: Boulder

Other trail users: Hikers and horseback riders

Canine compatibility: Dog-friendly

Trail contact: City of Boulder Open Space and Mountain Parks Department, Boulder; (303) 441–3408

Finding the Trailhead: From Boulder at the corner of Pearl and Twenty-eighth Streets, drive north on Twenty-eighth Street (which will lead into US 36) for roughly 2 miles to Jay Road. Continue on Twenty-eighth Street for another 1.5 miles past Jay Road before bearing right off US 36 onto the dirt, farm-access road that leads to the Foothills trailhead. Park in the lot provided at the trailhead.

The Ride

John and Maggie Williams were first to own the Boulder Valley Ranch. Since 1874, however, farmers and ranchers, as well as oil companies, owned shares in the ranch. It wasn't until 1973 that the Boulder Open Space would finally purchase the land for itself.

The route begins on the Eagle Trail as it climbs to the top of a mesa via a farm-access road. Along the way, you can see exposed sedimentary rock along the sides of

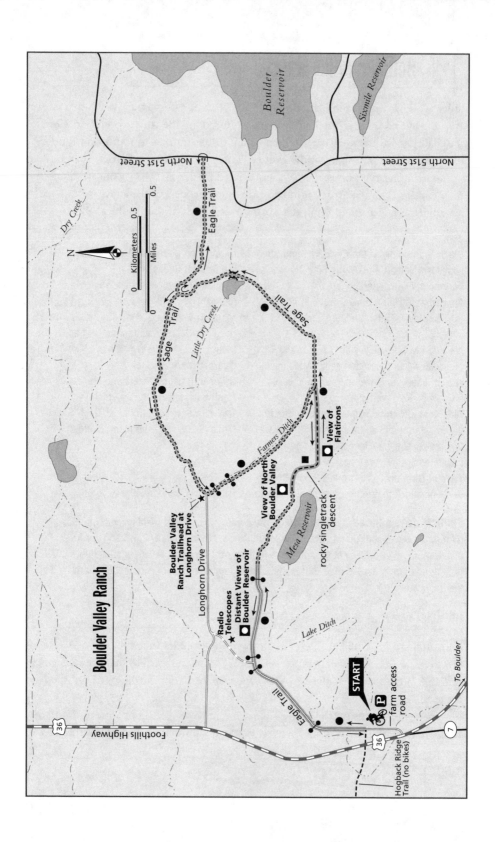

Boulder Valley Ranch

Boulder Valley Ranch Trailhead at Longhorn Drive

Longhorn Drive

Radio Telescopes

Distant Views of Boulder Reservoir

Eagle Trail

START

farm access road

P

To Boulder

Hogback Ridge Trail (no bikes)

Foothills Highway

36

7

36

Lake Ditch

Mesa Reservoir

rocky singletrack descent

View of Flatirons

View of North Boulder Valley

Farmers Ditch

Sage Trail

Little Dry Creek

Sage Trail

Eagle Trail

North 51st Street

North 51st Street

Boulder Reservoir

Sixmile Reservoir

Dry Creek

N

Kilometers
0   0.5

Miles
0   0.5

the mesas. These rocks were formed over millions of years by the ocean that covered this valley during the Cretaceous period.

From atop the mesa, riders look out onto the wondrous expanse of north Boulder Valley. This area was once prime agricultural land, but before that, the native tribes of the Arapaho and Cheyenne Indians roamed these prairies. Granted the rights to hunt and fish in the Boulder Valley in 1851 by the Fort Laramie Treaty Council, these native tribes found the area to be ripe with possibility. So much so that the Southern Arapaho Indian Tribe Chief Niwot (Arapaho for "Left Hand") once predicted that anyone who comes to live in this area will never be happy living anywhere else. The so-called Niwot's Curse is said to have been partly to blame for the Boulder Valley's expansive growth in recent years.

Returning from your own personal vision quest that being atop Boulder Valley mesa affords, the Eagle Trail eventually turns into a wide doubletrack, as it continues heading in an easterly direction toward the Boulder Reservoir. Nearing 2 miles into your ride, you descend from the mesa via a moderately rocky singletrack. Climbing this singletrack will prove a formidable challenge on your return trip. Upon reaching the bottom, the trail continues as a wide doubletrack; however, there is a singletrack carved alongside the doubletrack. Bear right at the bottom of this section, as you continue on the Eagle Trail heading in a northeasterly direction.

Once you pass the pond at 2.5 miles, the trail climbs moderately before reaching the Boulder Reservoir. The Boulder Reservoir is site to one of Boulder's most beloved traditions. Marking the passage of Spring into Summer, the KBCO/Budweiser Kinetic Sculpture Challenge is held each year at the Boulder Reservoir. Based on a race held in California since the 1960s, participants race each other in self-made, human-powered crafts on land and sea. Aside from winning the race, points are awarded for the most creative, and oftentimes bizarre, craft. The challenge also includes a Kinetic 5K run, as well as local music.

On the return trip from the reservoir, you're offered beautiful views of the entire Front Range, along with the tips of the Indian Peaks. The Sage Trail meanders quietly past farms and fields on its way to its intersection with the Eagle Trail. Once you

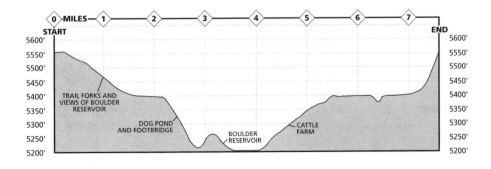

Climbing toward the top of the mesa on the Eagle Trail, with the Flatirons and a canine watering hole in the background.

arrive at this intersection, what remains is a quiet ride back to your vehicle and the challenge of, having feasted your eyes on the Boulder Valley Ranch, trying to live happily elsewhere.

Miles and Directions

0.0 Start riding in a northeasterly direction on the dirt road of the Eagle Trail.

0.5 Pass through a gate, as the trail climbs moderately in an easterly direction.

0.8 Pass through another gate where you are offered views of the distant Boulder Reservoir. From here the trail starts descending moderately.

1.0 The trail forks. Bear right at the fork and pass through another gate, as the left fork heads toward a radio tower.

1.3 The trail will turn into a wide doubletrack by a shaded canopy area. Veer left, passing through another gate, continuing on the Eagle Trail.

1.8 After a moderately rocky singletrack descent, the Eagle Trail will intersect with the Sage Trail. Bear right here, continuing on the Eagle Trail. You will be looping back around to this point via the Sage Trail on your return.

2.5 Pass a pond via a footbridge. Here is one of the better places to bring your dog.

2.8 Eagle Trail intersects with the Sage Trail again on the left. Continue straight on the Eagle Trail, heading in an easterly direction toward the Boulder Reservoir.

3.3 Reach the Boulder Reservoir and backtrack to the Eagle and Sage Trails intersection.

3.8 The Eagle Trail intersects with the Sage Trail. Bear right onto the Sage Trail, heading in a northwesterly direction.

4.6 Pass a working cattle farm off to your left.

5.0 Reach the Boulder Valley Ranch trailhead at Longhorn Drive. Ride across the road in a southerly direction. Pass through two gates and continue riding on the Sage Trail.

5.7 The Sage Trail intersects with the Eagle Trail at the bottom of the singletrack. Veer right and climb up the singletrack to the top of the mesa then retrace your path.

7.6 Arrive at your vehicle.

Ride Information

Trail Information

City of Boulder Open Space and Mountain Parks Department, (303) 441-3440 or (303) 441-4142; www.ci.boulder.co.us/openspace

Local Information

Boulder Convention and Visitors Bureau, 1850 Table Mesa Drive, Boulder 80305; (303) 442-2911

Local Events and Attractions

KBCO/Budweiser Kinetic Sculpture Challenge, May, Boulder; (303) 444-5600 or www.kbco.com

15 East Boulder Trail/White Rocks

The East Boulder Trail of the Teller Farm and White Rocks area provides an easy ride through the pastoral heartland of the Boulder Valley. Hay fields and croplands evidence the rich agricultural heritage here. Streamside areas lush with vegetation and ponds teeming with wildlife make way for the towering sandstone cliffs of the White Rocks Nature Preserve. A great ride for the family, this trail avoids any hill climbs or narrow routes and is a mild day's spin in the saddle. The route offers views of the Boulder Flatirons, Indian Peaks, and Longs Peak.

Start: The East Boulder Trail–South trailhead
Distance: 9.7-mile out-and-back
Approximate riding time: Advanced riders, 45 minutes; intermediate riders, 1–2 hours
Aerobic level: Physically easy due to the level surface area of the entire route
Technical difficulty: Technically easy due to the improved gravel surface area and width of the trail
Terrain: Improved gravel farm road, double-track, and wide singletrack
Schedule: Open year-round, 5 A.M. to midnight

Maps: DeLorme *Colorado Atlas & Gazetteer,* page 30; USGS: Niwot, CO; ZIA Maps: *Boulder County Mountain Bike Map*
Nearest town: Boulder
Other trail users: Hikers, bird-watchers, and anglers
Canine compatibility: Dog-friendly, although dogs are prohibited along much of this route, particularly in the White Rocks area
Trail contact: City of Boulder Open Space and Mountain Parks Department, Boulder; (303) 441–3408

Finding the Trailhead: From Boulder, drive east on Arapahoe Road for roughly 6 miles past Seventy-fifth Street. After driving another 0.5 mile, turn left (north) onto the dirt road of the Teller Farm trailhead entrance. Drive for roughly 1 mile on this dirt road to the East Boulder Trail–South trailhead.

The Ride

The East Boulder Trail and the White Rocks area offer hope in the face of ever-burgeoning development. As an example of responsible land use, this area was once site to numerous gravel pits used in the construction of Boulder area roads and housing. Nowadays, much of the destruction left by the gravel pits has been reclaimed and remains as preserved wildlife and wetland habitats. The great horned owls that nest in the cottonwood trees at the East Boulder Trail–South trailhead, perhaps then, serve as a fitting welcome to this area. These raptors have nested here for the last four years and always draw a curious eye.

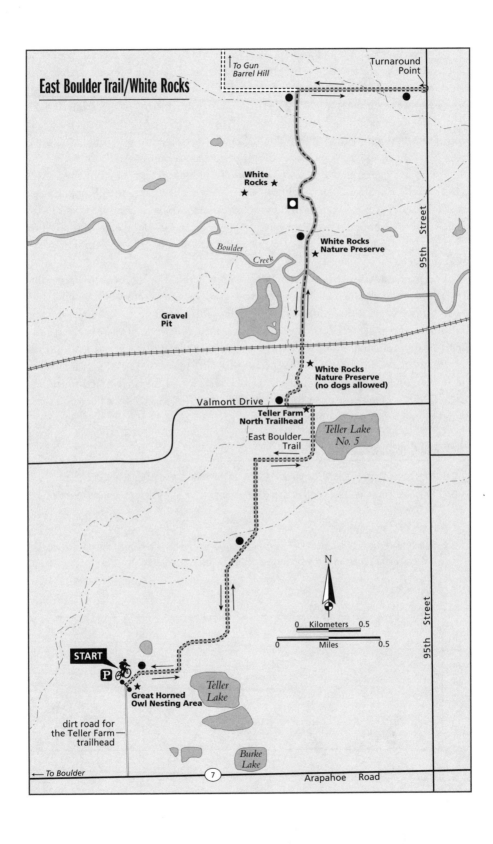

East Boulder Trail/White Rocks

To Gun
Barrel Hill

Turnaround
Point

White
Rocks ★

★

White Rocks
Nature Preserve

Boulder

Creek

Gravel
Pit

95th Street

★ White Rocks
Nature Preserve
(no dogs allowed)

Valmont Drive

★
Teller Farm
North Trailhead

*Teller Lake
No. 5*

East Boulder
Trail

N

0 Kilometers 0.5

0 Miles 0.5

95th Street

START

P

★
Great Horned
Owl Nesting Area

*Teller
Lake*

dirt road for
the Teller Farm
trailhead

*Burke
Lake*

← To Boulder

7

Arapahoe Road

As the trail meanders alongside numerous irrigation canals and by vast spreads of cropland, you'll pass through a number of gates. After crossing Valmont Drive, you enter into the White Rocks Nature Preserve.

The gravel road gives way to wide singletrack through parts of the White Rocks area, as the route passes through a variety of riparian habitats. After 3 miles, you reach one of several ponds named after Walden "Wally" Toevs. Toevs was a Boulder County commissioner in the early 1970s who supported land reclamation.

Just after crossing the Boulder Creek, you're offered distant views of the White Rocks to the northwest. You might consider bringing a good pair of binoculars, as the trail doesn't come too close to these rocks. Arapaho Indians considered this location as a prime hunting ground for pronghorn sheep and used the cliffs of the White Rocks as a bison jump. The rocks are the geological remains of a 135-million-year-old river delta.

The singletrack that passes through the White Cliffs Nature Preserve eventually turns into wide doubletrack, as it makes its way to the White Cliffs trailhead at Ninety-fifth Street. Oftentimes overlooked by riders wanting to venture into the mountains, this trail offers a look into the agricultural lifestyle of the eastern plains. With nearly 100 million acres of this country's farmland lost since the 1900s, it's important that we respect and understand this vital resource. Luckily, areas such as those surrounding the East Boulder Trail are often leased for agricultural purposes. In fact, half of Boulder's Open Space—15,000 acres—is leased for agricultural uses, thereby preserving our country's heritage.

Miles and Directions

0.0 After going through a gate, begin riding east on the wide gravel doubletrack.

0.2 The route continues in a northerly direction. Riding with a fence now to your left, cross a footbridge.

1.7 Cross over an irrigation ditch.

2.2 Reach the East Boulder Trail Teller Farm-North trailhead. Bear left through the parking lot. The trail picks up again in the northwest corner of the parking area.

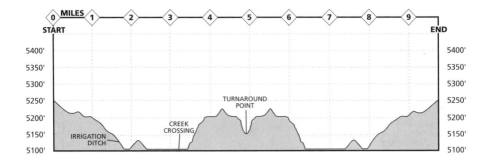

Irrigation ditches run alongside the trail and lend testimony to the area's agricultural history.

2.3 Bear right and cross Valmont Drive (watch for traffic), continuing your ride on the other side and heading in a northerly direction.

2.5 Enter into the White Rocks Nature Preserve. No dogs allowed. Here the trail follows wide singletrack before turning into gravel road again.

3.2 Cross Boulder Creek via a bridge. Shortly hereafter, the route gives way to singletrack again, as it passes a White Rocks information sign.

4.3 Exit the White Rocks Preserve. Cross a private driveway and arrive at the intersection of the East Boulder/White Rocks Trail and the East Boulder/Gunbarrel Farm Trail. Bear right at this intersection, continuing on the East Boulder/White Rocks Trail.

4.9 Reach the White Rocks trailhead at Ninety-fifth Street, and return the way you came.

9.7 Arrive at your vehicle.

Ride Information

Local Information
Boulder Convention and Visitors Bureau, 1850 Table Mesa Drive, Boulder 80305; (303) 442-2911

Local Events and Attractions
Fishing
Rocky Mountain Raptor Program, (970) 491-0398

16 Sourdough Trail

The Sourdough Trail skirts the fringes of the beautiful Indian Peaks Wilderness Area. The drive alone from Boulder to the trailhead is reason enough to head for this trail. While traveling along the Boulder Canyon, multisport adventurers can stop to enjoy great climbing and hiking opportunities before continuing on Colorado's famed Peak-to-Peak Highway. Once on the trail, however, the fun really starts. The Sourdough Trail is almost entirely covered by a thick forest canopy, providing cool, shaded relief the whole ride through. Although the climb to Brainard Lake is challenging (but enjoyable), the descent is why you ride it. A fast and smooth descent through a thick emerald forest will have you screaming, "There's no place like here and now."

Start: Sourdough trailhead off County Road 116, the road to the University of Colorado Research Station.

Distance: 12.2-mile out-and-back, with an option for a 13.2-mile loop

Approximate riding time: Advanced riders, 2–2.5 hours; intermediate riders, 3–3.5 hours for the out-and-back

Aerobic level: Physically moderate to challenging due to the extended climbing to Brainard Lake Road

Technical difficulty: Technically moderate due to a relatively smooth trail with little in the way of rocks. There are, however, a few switchbacks that make the riding moderately technical.

Terrain: Singletrack, plus some paved and dirt road if optional loop is taken

Schedule: May–October

Maps: DeLorme *Colorado Atlas & Gazetteer*, page 29; USGS: Ward, CO; Trails Illustrated: #102, Boulder; ZIA Maps: *Boulder County Mountain Bike Map*

Nearest town: Ward

Other trail users: Hikers, campers, snowshoers, and skiers

Canine compatibility: Dog-friendly

Trail contact: Roosevelt and Arapaho National Forests, Boulder Ranger District, Boulder; (303) 444-6600

Finding the Trailhead: From Boulder, drive west on Canyon Boulevard to the town of Nederland. Canyon Boulevard will become a single-lane highway (CO 119), winding its way through the steep-walled Boulder Canyon. Before reaching Nederland, you'll drive alongside Barker Reservoir and enjoy stunning views of Eldora Ski Resort. From Nederland, take CO 72 east (a.k.a. the Peak-to-Peak Highway) toward Ward for 7.5 miles until seeing the sign for the University of Colorado Research Station on the right side of the road. Turn left immediately after the sign onto County Road 116 and drive another 0.5 mile. The trailhead will be on the right.

The Ride

The Sourdough Trail is one of Boulder County's most popular singletrack routes. It's located just half a mile west of the majestic Peak-to-Peak Highway, between the historic tungsten- and gold-mining towns of Nederland and Ward. The trail brings

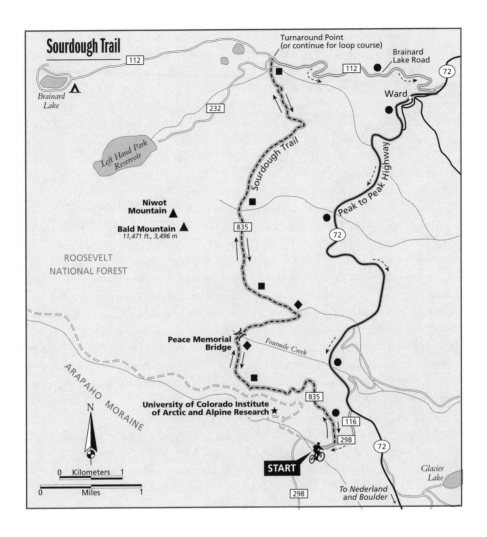

together rolling climbs with a number of narrowly negotiable switchbacks through densely mixed forests of lodgepole pine, Douglas fir, and aspen. The forest opens occasionally to reveal outstanding views of the Continental Divide above, the foothills of the Front Range below, and the Great Plains to the east. As you near the Peace Memorial Bridge, the canopy of the forest flatters its northwestern cousins by mimicking the lush woodland of Oregon and Washington. When many of the other trails in the foothills area turn sandy as the summer nears its end, the Sourdough Trail, owing to its superb tree coverage and high altitude, remains ideal with smooth-running, hard-packed singletrack.

The Sourdough Trail begins at 9,220 feet and stretches to a dizzying 10,280 feet. The trail provides some of the highest alpine mountain biking you'll find near Boulder and Denver. With elevations such as these, it's hard to believe that Sourdough's sinewy path skirts only the base of the Indian Peaks—a congeries of jagged mountain summits, ragged arêtes, windswept tundra uplands, and cirque glaciers. The range stretches southward for 27 miles and constitutes the crest of the Continental Divide in this part of Colorado.

For years Ellsworth Bethel (1863–1925), a Denver high school botany teacher, enjoyed a view of the peaks from his classroom. Moved by them, Bethel and his students went about naming each of them after various Native American tribes from Colorado's history. Though Bethel didn't succeed with all of his suggestions, he did secure approval from the U.S. Board on Geographic Names for seven tribe names on seven Front Range peaks—which constitute the Indian Peaks.

The snowfields and glaciers of the Indian Peaks are some of the most studied alpine environments in the world. Just north of the Sourdough trailhead lies the University of Colorado's Institute of Arctic and Alpine Research. Modest and cramped huts—some of them secured to the mountainside with cables as thick as a man's wrists—form the offensive line of this world-renowned field station. Rustic buildings resembling early trapper homesteads are tucked among trees just below timberline, camouflaging modern laboratories that house state-of-the-art meteorological equipment. Studies and classes are conducted on topics such as acid precipitation, climatic patterns, and alpine flora.

Just a few miles from the Sourdough Trail, amid the cutting-edge technology of the University of Colorado's Institute of Arctic and Alpine Research, are the small, onetime mining communities of Nederland and Ward. Just 12 miles from Boulder, Nederland was originally named Brownsville after its founder. Because of its proximity to Boulder, Brownsville was also called Middle Boulder. When a homesick Dutch company bought the tungsten mill, the town was renamed Nederland—an archaic spelling for Netherlands. From 1900 to 1918, Nederland produced $23 million worth of tungsten, making Boulder County the largest tungsten producer in the

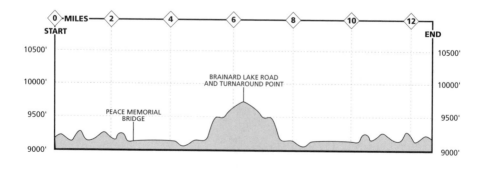

The tiny gold-mining town of Ward.

United States. The town of Ward also boasts a prosperous mining heritage. During Ward's heyday (1860 to 1900), the mining district's population peaked at 5,000 and was the largest mining camp in northern Colorado. With five hotels, eight lodges, and seven saloons—not to mention the $5 million in gold reserves—Ward achieved a certain Vegas status among Colorado mining towns of the late 1800s and early 1900s.

From state-of-the-art weather tracking devices to tungsten mines, the Sourdough Trail hangs in the balance between the new and the old. As such, it is a pleasure to ride and an education to experience.

Miles and Directions

- **0.0** Start at the Sourdough trailhead.
- **0.3** Crossing the footbridge begins a short climb through a thick pine forest.
- **1.4** After negotiating a challenging climb with a number of switchbacks, the forest opens and the trail continues under a stretch of power lines, offering views of the Peak-to-Peak Highway to the east—a good resting spot before attempting a short, technical section of trail.
- **1.9** You'll arrive at a sign that reads SOURDOUGH TRAIL and RED ROCK TRAILHEAD. Follow the Sourdough Trail.

2.7 Cross the Peace Memorial Bridge.

5.7 Sourdough Trail arrives at a trail intersection. Bearing left will take you to the Little Raven Ski Trail and Brainard Lake. Continuing straight will deliver you to Brainard Lake Road via Sourdough Trail.

6.1 Arrive at Brainard Lake Road. At the time of this writing, workers were clearcutting the forest to create a cross-country ski trail. At this point, you can either bear right onto Brainard Lake Road and do the loop or simply backtrack to your vehicle, going the way you came. I suggest backtracking and enjoying the Sourdough's fast singletrack descent.

To do the loop: Turn east onto Brainard Lake Road and follow it to the Peak-to-Peak Highway where you'll ride south along the paved highway for 6.5 miles until once again arriving at County Road 116. Turn right onto County Road 116, and ride for another 0.5 miles to your parked vehicle.

Ride Information

Local Information

Boulder Convention and Visitors Bureau,
1850 Table Mesa Drive, Boulder 80305;
(303) 442-2911

Local Events and Attractions

Eldora Mountain Resort, Nederland;
(303) 440-8700 or (888) 2-ELDORA

Nederland Old Timer Miner Days, July;
(303) 258-3580

Peak-to-Peak Highway, Colorado Highways 7, 62, and 119, connecting Estes Park and the Black Hawk/Central City gambling district

Lodging

Sundance Lodge & Stables, Nederland;
(303) 258-3797 or (800) 817-3797

Restaurants

Black Forest Restaurant, Nederland;
(303) 258-8089

Cool Beans Espresso, Nederland;
(303) 258-3435

Sundance Lodge & Cafe, Nederland;
(303) 258-0804

Organizations

Boulder Area Trails Coalition (BATCO), Boulder;
(303) 485-2162

Boulder Off-Road Alliance (BOA), Boulder;
(303) 667-2467

Front Range Mountain Bike Association,
Boulder; (303) 674-4862

17 Switzerland Trail

The Switzerland Trail is a very popular route for mountain bikes, as well as four-by-four vehicles. The former rail route offers moderate grades and is a good introduction for beginner riders. The trail descends—a bittersweet treat, as you return this way—initially into the small town of Sunset in Fourmile Canyon before climbing to terrific views of the Continental Divide and the Indian Peaks atop the Mount Alto Picnic Area. From there, the trail continues across Gold Hill Road and to an eventual scree field before connecting with Sawmill Road. Along the route, you'll find traces of bygone mining activity: old railroad tracks, abandoned mines, and rusted buckets. One of the attractions of this trail is that it passes through a number of cutouts in the hillside through which the terrain gets considerably rockier. These cutouts are a testament to the determination and heartiness of those involved in the area's earlier railroading history.

Start: Trailhead at the base of Sugarloaf Mountain

Distance: 23.1-mile lariat

Approximate riding time: Advanced riders, 2 hours; intermediate riders, 3–3.5 hours

Aerobic level: Physically moderate to challenging due to the extended climbs in exposed areas

Technical difficulty: Technically easy, due to the trail's width

Terrain: Four-by-four road, doubletrack, and singletrack that run over rocky and sandy terrain. With a 4 percent grade in spots, the trail travels through forests of aspen, ponderosa pine, lodgepole pine, and Douglas fir. At one point, riders must portage their bikes up a steep talus slope.

Schedule: May–October

Maps: DeLorme *Colorado Atlas & Gazetteer,* page 29; USGS maps: Gold Hill, CO and Ward, CO; Arapaho and Roosevelt National Forests Map; Trails Illustrated: #102, Boulder; ZIA Maps: *Boulder County Mountain Bike Map*

Nearest town: Gold Hill

Other trail users: Motor bikes, four-by-four vehicles, hikers

Canine compatibility: Dog-unfriendly, due to the length and motorized vehicular traffic of the trail

Trail contact: Roosevelt and Arapaho National Forests, Boulder Ranger District, Boulder; (303) 444-6600

Finding the Trailhead: From Boulder at the corner of Twenty-eighth Street and Canyon Boulevard, drive west on Canyon Boulevard (which will turn into CO 119) for 6.4 miles before turning right onto Sugarloaf Road. At 11.2 miles, turn right again onto the dirt Sugarloaf Mountain Road, and drive on this dirt road for another 0.8 mile before reaching its end and the trailhead to Switzerland Trail.

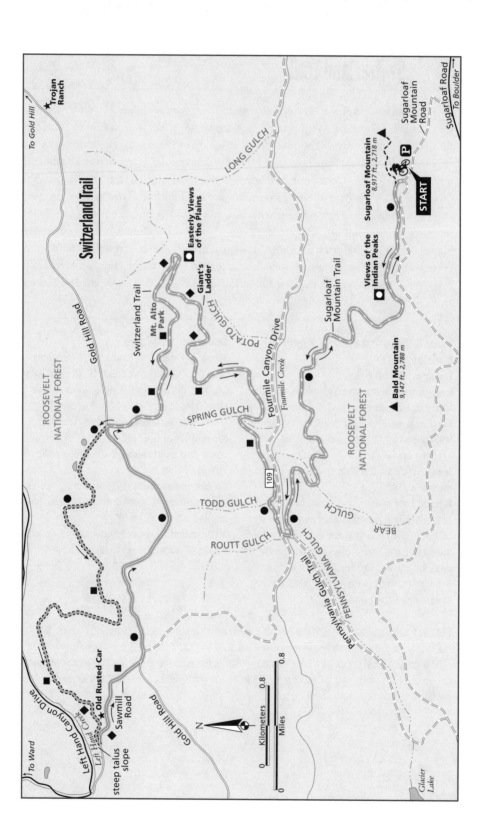

Switzerland Trail

To Ward

To Gold Hill

★ Trojan Ranch

Left Hand Canyon Drive

Left Hand Creek

◆ **Old Rusted Car**
◆ steep talus slope

Sawmill Road

Gold Hill Road

N

Kilometers
0   0.8

Miles
0   0.8

ROOSEVELT NATIONAL FOREST

Gold Hill Road

Switzerland Trail

Mt. Alto Park

Giant's Ladder

○ **Easterly Views of the Plains**

POTATO GULCH

SPRING GULCH

109

TODD GULCH

ROUTT GULCH

Fourmile Canyon Drive

Fourmile Creek

LONG GULCH

Sugarloaf Mountain Trail

▲ Sugarloaf Mountain
8,917 ft., 2,718 m

○ **Views of the Indian Peaks**

P

START

Sugarloaf Mountain Road

Sugarloaf Road

To Boulder

▲ **Bald Mountain**
9,147 ft., 2,788 m

ROOSEVELT NATIONAL FOREST

BEAR GULCH

Pennsylvania Gulch Trail

PENNSYLVANIA GULCH

Glacier Lake

The Ride

The Switzerland Trail begins with a speedy descent to the small town of Sunset. The route follows the old mining rail line of the Greeley, Salt Lake, and Pacific narrow gauge railroad, nicknamed Switzerland Trail. The line's inaugural running occurred on April 6, 1883, as it left Boulder for Penn Gulch (later named Sunset) in Fourmile Canyon. This narrow gauge railroad helped in developing the towns of Sunset, Ward, Gold Hill, Salina, and Wallstreet by running gold and silver ore during the mining boom of the late 1800s.

Having reached Sunset after a rocky and speedy descent, you begin climbing along a section of the Switzerland Trail that railroad engineers used to call "Giant's Ladder." One such engineer was James P. Maxwell, who later became Boulder's second mayor. A onetime passenger of this rail line, surveyor Ernest Greenman came to Boulder in 1896. To his credit, not only did Greenman help to form the Rocky Mountain Climbers Club, he also planted those few remaining apple trees found in Boulder Mountain Parks. Far from the serenity of any apple orchard, your climb up Giant's Ladder can be a grunt on your way to Mount Alto but one that is rewarded with wonderful easterly views of the Great Plains.

Upon reaching the Mount Alto Picnic Area, the trail begins to level off. This area was once site to the Mont Alto Lodge. Once the railway gave in to dwindling stores of gold and silver, and having suffered from the flood of 1894, the Greeley, Salt Lake, and Pacific narrow gauge railroad was reborn as a tourist line. With advertisements reading things like "One need not go to Switzerland for sublime mountain scenery," a new flood began to pour along the Switzerland Trail.

Through 1919, a flood of tourism, sometimes totaling more than 10,000 visitors in a single summer, began to ride the rails. Oftentimes, these tourist-toting trains would carry beer packed in snow for outings like moonlight walks, wildflower hikes, and aspen viewing. Mount Alto became one of the featured stops on these outings, where tourists would engage in baseball games, while the Mont Alto Lodge served as a fitting venue for concerts, lectures, and dances. A flash flood in 1919 through Fourmile Canyon would end the rail line forever. Today all that is left of the lodge

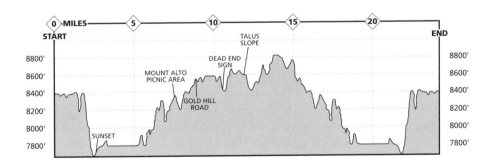

Passing through one of several cutouts through the mountain side on the old Narrow Gauge Railroad bed. PHOTO: AMANDA HLAWATY

and rail destination is an old stone chimney. But the Switzerland Trail railroad line now rests in Boulder's Central Park.

From the Mount Alto Picnic Area you continue on the Switzerland Trail as it descends to its intersection with Gold Hill Road. Bearing right onto Gold Hill Road will deliver you to the small town by the same name. Gold Hill was one of the first permanent mining camps in Colorado. The discovery of gold in 1859 led to an influx of more than 1,500 miners less than a year later. Built in 1872, the year that tellurium was also discovered in Gold Hill, the Miner's Hotel still stands today with many of its original furnishings. Unfortunately, a fire reduced much of the town to ashes in 1894.

Once across Gold Hill Road, the trail whips along level doubletrack through beautiful aspen glens. Along this stretch of the trail you can expect to find sunflowers, wild geraniums, yarrow, milkweed, Indian paintbrush, and currant bushes. By mile 11, you have to negotiate over some moderately technical and rocky terrain before reaching the talus field. Take care in portaging your bike atop the talus field, as its steep grade delivers loose rock and sand. As you bear left onto Sawmill Road, it's a bit of a grunt to the road's high point at 12.3 miles.

After reconnecting to the Switzerland Trail from Gold Hill Road, it's a fast and rocky descent to the town of Sunset. Be warned, however, from Sunset you'll still have to climb nearly 4 miles out of Fourmile Canyon to your vehicle at the base of Sugarloaf Mountain.

Miles and Directions

0.0 Start from the northwest corner of the parking lot and begin a descent over sandy and rocky terrain.

0.5 Pass views of Sugarloaf Mountain and the Indian Peaks off to your right. Stay on the main route at all times.

3.6 Arrive at the intersection of the Switzerland Trail and the Pennsylvania Gulch Trail. Bear right, passing a sign for the small town of Sunset. Cross Fourmile Creek and ride through Sunset on County Road 118 (Fourmile Canyon Drive).

3.8 County Road 118 intersects with FR 109 (Switzerland Trail). Bear left onto FR 109, climbing in an easterly direction up "Giant's Ladder."

7.3 Reach the Mount Alto Picnic Area where you'll find rest rooms and picnic tables. Continue in a westerly direction as you begin to descend moderately.

8.5 The Switzerland Trail will intersect with Gold Hill Road. Cross Gold Hill Road and continue straight on the Switzerland Trail, heading in a northwesterly direction.

10.6 You reach a sign that reads DEAD END. Pass beyond the sign and continue your riding on a wide doubletrack through a mixed conifer forest.

11.6 You pass an old, rusted, abandoned car to your left.

11.9 You reach a steep talus slope with Lefthand Canyon Drive off to your right. Portage your bike up the talus slope on your left to Sawmill Road. Bear left onto Sawmill Road.

12.6 Sawmill Road intersects with Gold Hill Road. Bear left onto Gold Hill Road.

14.4 Gold Hill Road intersects with the Switzerland Trail. Bear right onto the Switzerland Trail and return the way you came.

23.1 Arrive at the parking lot.

Ride Information

Local Information
Boulder Convention and Visitors Bureau, 1850 Table Mesa Drive, Boulder 80305; (303) 442-2911

Local Events and Attractions
Eldora Mountain Resort, Nederland; (303) 440-8700 or (888) 2-ELDORA

Gold Lake Mountain Resort & Spa, near Ward; (303) 459-3544

Peak-to-Peak Highway, Colorado Highways 7, 62, and 119, connecting Estes Park and the Black Hawk/Central City gambling district

Lodging
Gold Hill Inn, Boulder; (303) 443-6461

Organizations
Boulder Area Trails Coalition (BATCO), Boulder; (303) 485-2162

Boulder Off-Road Alliance (BOA), Boulder; (303) 667-2467

Front Range Mountain Bike Association, Boulder; (303) 674-4862

18 Betasso Preserve

Betasso Preserve delivers a short, but sweet ride and offers much to riders of any ability. The wide and smooth singletrack of the Canyon Loop Trail is ideal for beginners wanting to test their singletrack mettle. The loop also invites riders with more experience to run laps past open meadows awash with wildflowers and through cooler ponderosa pine forests. Being so close to Boulder, Betasso Preserve offers an immediate getaway from the hectic pace of Boulder during rush hour. The preserve has been the subject of much public scrutiny and environmental impact studies in the last few years, reminding us to respect our parks, open spaces, and forests.

Start: The Canyon Loop trailhead
Distance: 3.4-mile loop
Approximate riding time: Advanced riders, 20 minutes; intermediate riders, 25–45 minutes
Aerobic level: Physically easy to moderate due to the lack of significant elevation gain. There are a few short hill climbs.
Technical difficulty: Technically easy due to the wide and smooth singletrack
Terrain: Singletrack and doubletrack that roll over open meadows and hard-packed forest terrain

Schedule: April–November; open sunrise to sunset. Closed Saturdays and Wednesdays to mountain bikes.
Maps: DeLorme *Colorado Atlas & Gazetteer,* page 29; USGS: Boulder, CO; Boulder County Parks and Open Space Betasso Preserve map; ZIA Maps: *Boulder County Mountain Bike Map*
Nearest town: Boulder
Other trail users: Hikers and picnickers
Canine compatibility: Dog-friendly
Trail contact: Boulder County Parks and Open Space, Boulder; (303) 441-3950

Finding the Trailhead: From Boulder, drive west on Boulder Canyon Road (CO 119) for 5 miles and turn right onto Sugarloaf Road. Drive for roughly 1 mile to Betasso Road. Bear right onto Betasso Road, by the Betasso Preserve sign, and drive for another 0.5 mile before turning left into Betasso Preserve.

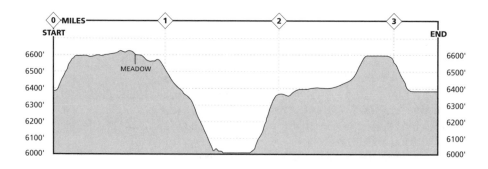

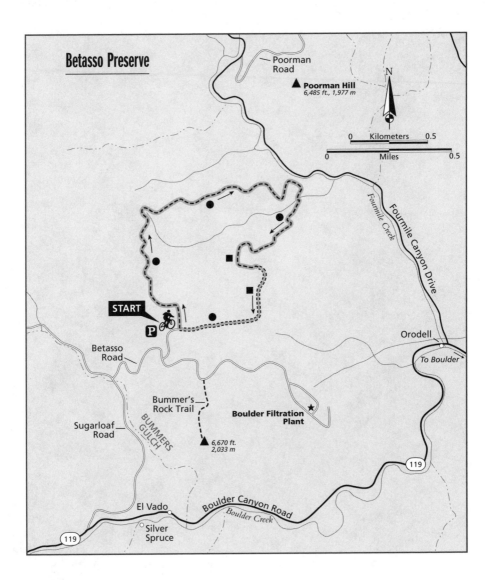

The Ride

The area surrounding Betasso Preserve was once site to the town of Orodell, which served as a stop for stagecoaches traveling from Boulder to Nederland. Situated at the junction of Boulder and Fourmile Canyons, the town serviced those working in the nearby sawmills and mines of Colorado's northeast mineral belt. Tragically, Orodell would be lost to fire in 1883, while the sawmill and gold mine were destroyed by flood.

Betasso Preserve, a Boulder County gem, is set atop an underlay of 1.7-billion-year-old Boulder Creek granodiorite (granite to you and me), one of the oldest types of rock in Boulder County. This rock formed after the slow cooling of its molten material deep underneath Earth's surface. The slow cooling process allows for the rock's crystals to be visible to the human eye, identifiable by the pink and dark feldspar and mica minerals, as well as by the clear quartz. The Bummer's Rock Trail leads to an excellent example of this granite. But Betasso Preserve offers more than just ancient archaeological jewels. Its beautiful landscapes, among which include 3.4 miles of ideal singletrack, speak to the prevailing land preservation attitudes of public opinion.

Our story begins just west of the Canyon Loop trailhead, when, in 1912, the Blanchard family homesteaded 160 acres. The Blanchards would sell their small cattle ranch, equipped with log buildings, to Steve Betasso in 1915. Steve was a hard-rock miner living in Fourmile Canyon. With earnings saved from his gold and tungsten mining, Steve continued to purchase land and built more permanent structures, maintaining a prosperous cattle business on the ranch and preparing the land for inheritance by his sons Dick and Ernie. But what Steve left his sons was more than just a ranch; he left them a legacy steeped in land stewardship.

So ingrained was their mutual respect for the land that Ernie, hoping to preserve the land so others could enjoy what he had loved for more than sixty years, sold 718 acres to Boulder County in 1976. It's reported that Ernie never once considered moving to town, arguing that "you can't leave the mountains because when you live up there one leg gets shorter than the other," and lived in the mountains until his death in 1983. Since 1976 Boulder County has added on to its original purchase and now preserves 773 acres of the original Betasso family ranch. There are even some of the ranch's original buildings still standing.

Near the Canyon Loop trailhead, there is a log cabin that was built between 1902 and 1912. Nick Fanti built the brick house for Steve Betasso in 1918, and Ernie Betasso left his mark in the clapboard house, which he built in 1948.

From the trailhead, riders begin by ascending a moderate climb over painfully manicured singletrack. After passing through a sage-filled meadow, the trail snakes its way down over an assortment of rocks, roots, and ruts.

After 2 miles, the trail again begins to climb moderately through a mixed conifer forest of ponderosa pine and Douglas fir. After a period of steady climbing through forest and field, riders return to their vehicles, where they can opt to make another lap or call it an easy, but fine day in the saddle.

The preserve offers a large group area for picnics (fifty people maximum) that can be reserved. There are also rest rooms and grills at the preserve.

◀ *Sharing the trail at Betasso Preserve.* PHOTO: AMANDA HLAWATY

Miles and Directions

0.0 Start at the Canyon Loop trailhead and begin riding in a northwesterly (clockwise) direction.

0.7 After a short climb, the Canyon Loop Trail tops out onto a meadow.

2.0-2.3 Two stream crossings.

3.0 The singletrack of the Canyon Loop trail becomes a wide doubletrack. Continue riding in a westerly direction.

3.4 Arrive at your vehicle.

Ride Information

Local Information

Boulder Convention and Visitors Bureau, 1850 Table Mesa Drive, Boulder 80305; (303) 442-2911

THE PIPELINE TRAIL
Some trail descriptions of this ride suggest accessing Betasso Preserve via the Pipeline Trail and Canyon Road. From the corner of Broadway and Canyon Road in Boulder, the Pipeline Trail lies roughly 4 miles up the Boulder Canyon on the right side of the road, just before a tunnel. Over the years, this trail has been preserved as a historic trail; however, there hasn't been too much attention given to its maintenance. At the time of this writing, the Boulder County Parks and Open Space Department, along with the Youth Corps and the Boulder Off-road Alliance (BOA), has taken on the responsibility of maintaining the Pipeline Trail. Various routes have been cut through the Pipeline Trail to Betasso Preserve. So now riders can forgo having to ride on Canyon Road and will have access to Betasso Preserve directly from the Pipeline Trail.

Unfortunately, as a result of the new and improved Pipeline Trail, we may see mountain bike restrictions for Betasso Preserve in the future. In an effort to reduce environmental impact, some restriction considerations include banning mountain bikes on Wednesdays and Saturdays, as well as alternating the direction in which bikes can travel the loop. Check with the Boulder County Parks and Open Space Department and the Boulder Off-road Alliance (BOA) for the latest information regarding this and other trails.

19 Meyers Homestead Trail

The Meyers Homestead Trail is a great beginner's ride. It offers riders a wide, doubletrack trail that doesn't deliver too many rocks, roots, or loose sand. The trail gets a bit tougher as it climbs to its terminus. As one arrives at the turnaround point, views of the Indian Peaks, Continental Divide, Boulder Canyon, and Sugarloaf Mountain (at the base of which began the Switzerland Trail, Ride 17) can be seen to the north. The end of the trail also borders private property, so do not venture off of it. Offering rest rooms and picnic tables, the Meyer's Gulch Homestead Trail is a great destination for a family of riders.

Start: The Meyers Homestead trailhead by the Group Picnic Area
Distance: 5.3-mile out-and-back
Approximate riding time: Advanced riders, 30 minutes; intermediate riders, 45–60 minutes
Aerobic level: Physically easy due to the relative lack of elevation gain as well as the trail's short distance. The hill toward the turnaround point offers riders a moderate test of their aerobic levels.
Technical difficulty: Technically easy due to the wider doubletrack that the trail runs over. There is a moderate hill climb over rockier terrain that arrives near the trail's turnaround point.

Terrain: Doubletrack over sand and rock. The trail travels through open meadows and mixed forests to its terminus.
Schedule: May–October
Maps: DeLorme *Colorado Atlas & Gazetteer,* page 39; USGS: Eldorado Springs, CO; Walker Ranch: Boulder County Parks and Open Space map; ZIA Maps: *Boulder County Mountain Bike Map*
Nearest town: Boulder
Other trail users: Hikers and picnickers
Canine compatibility: Dog-friendly
Trail contact: Boulder County Parks and Open Space, Boulder; (303) 441-3950

Finding the Trailhead: From Boulder, drive west on Baseline Road up and over Flagstaff Mountain. Baseline Road turns into Flagstaff Mountain Road after passing Chautauqua Auditorium on your left. This road is crisscrossed heavily by hiking trails, so keep an eye out for pedestrians and cyclists. After roughly 4 miles, you'll pass the sign for the Flagstaff Mountain Amphitheater and Green Mountain Lodge. Continue on Flagstaff Mountain Road for roughly another 3.5 miles before bearing right into the Meyers Homestead Picnic Area and trailhead.

The Ride

The ambling Meyers Homestead Trail that wanders past hay barn ruins is part of Walker Ranch. As such, Meyers Homestead is included among the 3,778 acres of cultural landscape, the largest parcel in Colorado to receive this designation.

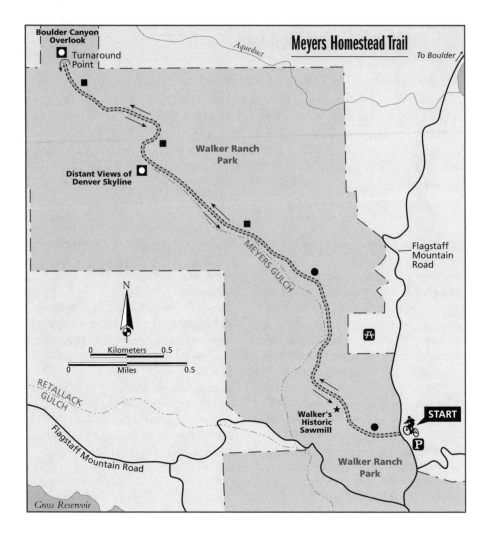

Not much is known of Andrew R. Meyers who settled the gulch north of Walker Ranch in 1890. Although Meyers would later sell his land to Walker, this trail still bears his name. A neighbor of James Walker, Meyers obtained his land during America's campaign to populate its western interior. This expansion west took shape in the Homestead Act of 1862, which called for the opening of what were then public lands to agricultural settlement.

Used primarily for logging and livestock pasture by the Walker family, the Meyers Homestead area became part of the largest cattle ranch in this part of Colorado. To his credit, James Walker built his highly successful ranch by using portable sawmills and bringing in hardy Scottish cattle that could survive in the Rocky Mountain foothills.

The trail begins by descending on a wide doubletrack as it heads in a northwesterly direction to the historic sawmill built by James Walker. After passing the sawmill, riders cruise through a couple of other meadows as the trail begins to climb more moderately. During the autumn months, these meadows are crowded with chokecherry and raspberry bushes. In preparation for their dormant season, black bears can feed for nearly twenty hours a day on these berries. In Colorado, female bears enter their dens in late October, while male bears retreat to their dens in early November. Encounters with bears are rare, but the possibility still exists. Should you encounter a bear, stay calm and speak softly to make the bear aware of your presence. If on a trail, step off the trail on the downhill slope and back away from the bear slowly.

From the dilapidated sawmill, the trail alternates from level to steeper terrain. Nearing 2 miles, riders will begin to climb more steeply as they head in and out of mixed conifer forests. In addition, riders are offered distant glimpses of the Denver skyline through a fissure in the foothills. The final approach to the trail's turnaround point arrives at nearly 2.4 miles into the ride. Here, you make your final climb through a meadow to the trail's high point and the Boulder Canyon Overlook, offering views of the Continental Divide, Indian Peaks, and Sugarloaf Mountain.

You can't help but notice the charred trees and barren ground of Sugarloaf Mountain. In 1989 a garage fire caused this devastation, destroying 44 structures along the mountain's hillsides. Now, more than ten years later, the mountainside still struggles to recover.

From the overlook, riders return to their vehicles the way they came. The descent from this turnaround point is fast. Take care when descending, as this is a popular trail for hikers and bikers alike. The route also offers a great many erosion ditches that cross the trail. These can cause a rider to flip if his or her weight isn't properly adjusted on the bicycle. For more advanced riders, these ditches make for great bunny-hop potential.

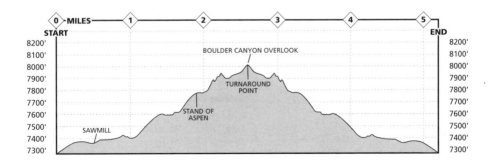

Riding past the dilapidated remains of the historic sawmill built by James Walker.

Miles and Directions

0.0 Begin riding on a wide doubletrack in a westerly direction that shortly turns toward the northwest.

0.5 Pass the historic sawmill to your left.

1.9 Ride through a beautiful stand of aspen.

2.6 Reach the trail's turnaround point and the Boulder Canyon Overlook. Return the way you came to the start.

5.3 Arrive at your vehicle.

Ride Information

Trail Information
Colorado Division of Wildlife, (303) 291–7227 or (303) 297–1192
USDA Forest Service, Boulder District, Boulder; (303) 444–6600

Local Information
Boulder Convention and Visitors Bureau, 1850 Table Mesa Drive, Boulder 80305; (303) 442–2911

Local Events and Attractions
Meyers Homestead Trail Group Shelter, accommodates up to 75 people. For reservations contact Boulder County Parks and Open Space at (303) 441–3950
Walker Ranch Tours. Contact Boulder County Parks and Open Space at (303) 441–3950

Organizations
Boulder Bicycle Commuters, Boulder; (303) 499–7466
Boulder Off-Road Alliance, Boulder; (303) 667–2467
International Mountain Biking Association (IMBA), Boulder; (303) 545–9011

20 Walker Ranch Loop

The Walker Ranch Loop is a popular ride among Boulder mountain bikers. Its initial singletrack descent to South Boulder Creek is awesome. During the spring thaw, South Boulder Creek is an impressive torrent of white water, an exhilarating sound to hear while riding along its banks. This ride weaves in and out of mixed conifer forests and offers a number of rockier singletrack sections. There is one section of the trail that requires you to portage down a steep cliff, a section that some area riders consider the Walker Ranch Loop's best and worst feature. Mountain lions have been spotted in the area, so pay attention to the mountain lion warning signs.

Start: Parking lot of Walker Ranch Open Space, at the South Boulder Creek trailhead

Distance: 8-mile loop, with other options available in Walker Ranch

Approximate riding time: Advanced riders, 1 hour; intermediate riders, 2 hours

Aerobic level: Physically challenging due to the variety of climbing involved.

Technical difficulty: Technically moderate to challenging due to smooth, fast singletrack coupled with tough rocky sections. Note: There is a section of trail called "Cliff Conditions," requiring you to portage your bicycle down steep steps and over rock faces. Take care.

Terrain: Singletrack with patches of rocks and sand; improved dirt road

Schedule: May–October

Maps: DeLorme *Colorado Atlas & Gazetteer*, pages 39 and 40; USGS: Eldorado Springs, CO; Walker Ranch: Boulder County Parks and Open Space map; ZIA Maps: *Boulder County Mountain Bike Map*

Nearest City/Town: Boulder

Other trail users: Hikers, anglers, picnickers, horseback riders, and climbers

Canine compatibility: Dog-friendly, but dogs must be on a leash at all times

Trail contact: Boulder County Parks and Open Space, Boulder; (303) 441-3950

Finding the Trailhead: From Boulder, drive west on Baseline Road to Flagstaff Mountain Road. Baseline turns into Flagstaff after Chautauqua Auditorium to your left. Stay on Flagstaff Mountain Road for about 8 miles, as it winds its way up and over Flagstaff Mountain. The road is crisscrossed heavily by hiking trails, so keep an eye out for pedestrians and cyclists. Following the sign for Walker Ranch, you'll drive past the sign for the Flagstaff Mountain Amphitheater and Green Mountain Lodge after roughly 4 miles. Flagstaff Mountain Road will eventually top out before descending down the other side of Flagstaff Mountain. Pass the Meyers Homestead Picnic Area and trailhead on the right. From there, Walker Ranch is roughly 0.5 mile farther on the left. Pull into the dirt road and drive up the short distance to the South Boulder Creek trailhead and parking lot. Riders can also park and start from the Ethel Harrold Picnic Area and trailhead, where more parking and rest rooms are available.

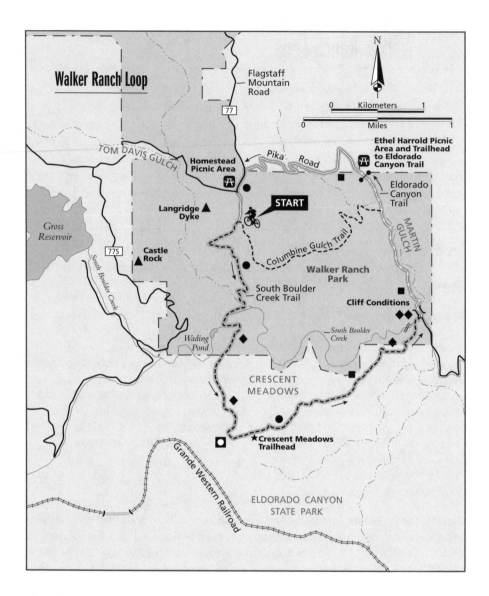

The Ride

Near Flagstaff Mountain and just west of Boulder is an area that evokes a love/hate relationship among many mountain bikers. Walker Ranch's clifflike descent from the South Boulder Creek Trail to South Boulder Creek has the reputation of being one of the more hazardous portages in Colorado. This section of trail—loved for its uniqueness, hated for its vertigo-inducing incline—has summoned many a masochist. The portage notwithstanding, Walker Ranch offers some exciting singletrack mountain biking and beautiful scenery, set amid a rich local history.

In 1869 James Walker, with only $12 in his pocket and suffering from a life-threatening illness, traveled from Missouri to Boulder on the advice of his physician. Colorado's high, dry climate would prove to be Walker's salvation. His health dramatically improved. Having reclaimed his health, Walker, along with his wife Phoebe, would reclaim their lives together by filing a homestead claim to 160 acres in 1882.

By 1883 Walker Ranch—consisting of a ranch house, barn, blacksmith shop, root cellar, granary, smokehouse, springhouse, chicken and turkey houses, corn storage house, and pig barn—afforded James and Phoebe the self-sufficient lifestyle with which they both would eventually fall in love. With various corrals, fenced pastures, and 160 acres, Walker Ranch was one of the largest cattle ranches in this region and is listed on the National Register of Historic Places.

Today, posted signs of MOUNTAIN LION TERRITORY greet the would-be mountain biker at the South Boulder Creek trailhead. If you decide to park and begin your ride at the Ethel Harrold Picnic Area and trailhead, you will begin by riding up Pika Road to the South Boulder Creek Trail. Otherwise, the route begins on the South Boulder Creek Trail, contouring to the south of Langridge Dyke and descending to Tom Davis Gulch and South Boulder Creek at mile 1.0. There are a number of great fly-fishing holes along this patch of the creek. The route to this point is fast on rock-riddled singletrack with varying patches of sand. A number of switchbacks and dips prevent the rider from going too fast. Once it reaches South Boulder Creek, the trail smooths to soft forest singletrack blanketed with pine needles. Ride upstream to a footbridge that crosses the creek at mile 1.5, whereupon the trail divides. Bear left here and continue your ride. For those requiring a bit of a dip, riding straight ahead will deliver you to a cool wading pond about 50 yards up.

After bearing left, the trail climbs out of the drainage to the Crescent Meadows trailhead at mile 2.7, offering views of the Grande Western Railroad. The climb to Crescent Meadows is a grunt but one well worth undertaking. It climbs to 7,300 feet and offers a beautiful view of Gross Dam and snowcapped peaks to the west. Ride east on the Crescent Meadows Trail, as it parallels Eldorado Canyon State Park

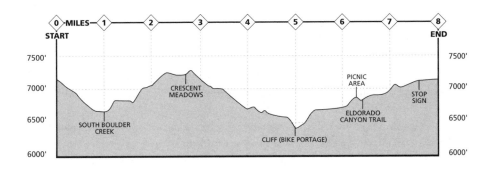

Descending the Cliff Conditions to the South Boulder Creek.

to the right. Mountain bikes are prohibited beyond the county boundary in Eldorado Canyon State Park.

This section of the route begins as a moderate descent through meadows awash with wildflowers and then becomes considerably steeper as it drops to South Boulder Creek. This may be the best section of the entire route. After dropping some big rocky hits, arrive at a sign at mile 4.8 that reads DANGER: CLIFF CONDITIONS. Dismount and carefully climb down the very technical terrain to South Boulder Creek. Once at its shores, scramble over the boulder field directly downstream, and head to the bridge that crosses the creek.

After crossing the bridge, the Crescent Meadows Trail connects with the Eldorado Canyon Trail. (Mountain bikers are prohibited from entering Eldorado Canyon State Park via the Eldorado Canyon Trail from lower Walker Ranch.) Climbing through Martin Gulch, the Eldorado Canyon Trail intersects with the Columbine Gulch Trail at mile 6.1. Here you have the option of veering left onto the Columbine Gulch Trail and shortcutting over the 1.5-mile trail back to the South Boulder Creek trailhead and to your vehicle. Or, you can continue straight ahead to Pika Road, past Ethel Harrold Picnic Area.

The Columbine Gulch Trail climbs for 400 feet via a number of steep switchbacks—testimony to this trail's designation as one "not recommended for mountain bikes." For those seeking the challenge of tough singletrack climbing, this part of the route, which ascends under thick forest cover, delivers all you'll ever want. For the spinners who prefer constant pedaling over intermittent singletrack, ride straight past the Columbine Gulch Trail to the Ethel Harrold Picnic Area. Pass the gate, ride out of the parking lot, and intercept Pika Road to the left. Pika Road offers 1.3 miles of gradual cool-down climbing before intersecting with Flagstaff Mountain Road. Turn left onto Flagstaff Mountain Road, and ride to your vehicle atop the dirt road at the South Boulder Creek trailhead.

Miles and Directions

0.0 Start at the South Boulder Creek trailhead. As the trail contours south of Langridge Dyke, descend the switchbacks into Tom Davis Gulch to South Boulder Creek.

1.0 Descend to South Boulder Creek. Follow the creek upstream.

2.7 Reach Crescent Meadows (7,300 feet). From here you can see Gross Dam due west.

5.0 Reach the Cliff Conditions Area. Dismount and carefully portage your bike down to South Boulder Creek.

6.1 Meet the junction of Columbine Gulch Trail and Crescent Meadows Trail. The Columbine Gulch Trail will return you to your vehicle, but the trail is not recommended for bicycles. Continue straight to the Ethel Harrold Picnic Area and trailhead for the Eldorado Canyon Trail.

6.3 Reach the Ethel Harrold Picnic Area and trailhead for the Eldorado Canyon Trail. Ride straight out of the parking lot and turn left onto Pika Road.

7.6 Reach a stop sign at the intersection of Pika Road and Flagstaff Mountain Road. Bear left onto Flagstaff Mountain Road toward the ride's start.

8.0 Reach the South Boulder Creek trailhead and Walker Ranch parking lot. You're at your vehicle.

Ride Information

Trail Information

City of Boulder Open Space and Mountain Parks Department, Boulder; (303) 441-3408
USDA Forest Service, Boulder District, Boulder; (303) 444-6600

Local Information

Boulder Convention and Visitors Bureau, 1850 Table Mesa Drive, Boulder 80305; (303) 442-2911

Local Events and Attractions

Walker Ranch Tours. Contact Boulder County Parks and Open Space at (303) 441-3950

Organizations

Boulder Bicycle Commuters, Boulder; (303) 499-7466
Boulder Off-Road Alliance, Boulder; (303) 667-2467
International Mountain Biking Association (IMBA), Boulder; (303) 545-9011

In Addition

Mountain Lions

Residing in areas of piñon pine, juniper, mountain mahogany, ponderosa pine, and oak brush, the mountain lion—cougar, panther, or puma—is one of North America's biggest cats and inhabits much of Colorado, including the Front Range. For this reason, it is not uncommon to see mountain lion warning signs at many mountain bike trailheads. Although mountain lion/human encounters are rare because of the big cat's calm, quiet, and elusive nature, such meetings are on the rise as a consequence, in part, of increased mountain biking in lion habitat. In fact, a standoff involving a mountain lion and a mountain biker occurred on October 22, 1997, at one of Boulder County's most popular mountain biking areas, Walker Ranch.

Varying in size from 7 to 8 feet in length and 90 to 150 pounds in weight, the mountain lion is much larger than other wild cat species in Colorado. According to Division of Wildlife experts, a mountain biker may run a higher-than-normal risk of being attacked. A mountain biker's lowered head posture may spark a lion's curiosity. Also, mountain bikers riding through the forest may be interpreted by the lion as fleeing prey, stimulating its predatory attack response. While bicycling in mountain lion habitat, keep the following information in mind; although, please be aware that every situation is different in regard to the lion, the terrain, and the people involved.

- Ride in groups
- Make noise during times of prime mountain lion activity—dawn and dusk.

If you should encounter a mountain lion:

- Never approach a lion, but keep your bicycle between yourself and the lion.
- Stay calm. Speak calmly but firmly to it.
- Back away from the lion slowly, facing the lion and standing upright; do not turn and run and chance stimulating the lion's predatory instincts.
- Make yourself larger in appearance: raise your arms, open your jacket if wearing one.
- If the lion becomes aggressive, throw stones or branches without crouching down or turning your back.
- If the lion attacks, fight back and avoid falling to the ground.

Should you have an encounter with a mountain lion, immediately contact the Colorado Division of Wildlife, Monday–Friday, 8:00 A.M.–5:00 P.M.

Northeast Region and Denver Service Center
6060 Broadway
Denver, CO 80216
(303) 291–7230

West Region and Grand Junction Service Center
711 Independent Avenue
Grand Junction, CO 81505
(970) 248–7175

Southeast Region and Colorado Springs Service Center
2126 North Weber Street
Colorado Springs, CO 80907
(719) 473–2945

21 Marshall Mesa/Community Ditch Trail

The Marshall Mesa and Community Ditch Trail is one of the most popular trails in all of Boulder County. In *Under the Devil's Thumb,* David Gessner describes another nearby trail as "a sort of StairMaster-with-view." The same description may apply to this one. The trail follows an easy route atop Marshall Mesa before descending to and crossing Colorado Highway 93 on its way toward Eldorado Springs Canyon. The views here of the Flatirons are among Boulder's best. Trail users regularly bring their dogs, as the trail runs alongside a water-filled "community ditch," as well as Marshall Lake. This trail can become quite crowded during the weekends.

Start: The Marshall Mesa trailhead on Marshall Drive

Distance: 8.0-mile out-and-back

Approximate riding time: Advanced riders, 30 minutes; intermediate riders, 45–60 minutes

Aerobic level: Physically easy with only a moderate hill climb at the outset from the Marshall Mesa trailhead

Technical difficulty: Technically easy due to the wide singletrack over smooth terrain

Terrain: Wide singletrack, doubletrack, and gravel road that rolls atop mesas, through sprawling grasslands, and past sandstone cliffs

Schedule: March–November

Maps: DeLorme *Colorado Atlas & Gazetteer,* page 40; USGS: Louisville and Eldorado Springs, CO; ZIA Maps: *Boulder County Mountain Bike Map*

Nearest town: Boulder

Other trail users: Hikers, picnickers, and horseback riders

Canine compatibility: Dog-friendly

Trail contact: City of Boulder Open Space and Mountain Parks Department, Boulder; (303) 441-3408

Finding the Trailhead: From Boulder, drive south on CO 93 for roughly 5 miles before bearing left (east) onto Colorado Highway 170 (Marshall Drive). Make a right at the stop sign, continuing on CO 170. Drive for just under 1 mile before bearing right into the Marshall Mesa trailhead. Park in the spaces provided along Marshall Drive.

The Ride

Marshall Mesa stands dominant over the site of what once was the mining town of Marshall. In 1859 William A. Kitchens discovered coal in the area and named his mine the Washington Lode, though his customers were more familiar with the term "Kitchens' Bank." With coal having been discovered at Marshall nearly twenty years before Colorado was made a state, the mesa is the site of some of the oldest coal mines in Colorado.

Coal mining flourished in Marshall from 1859 to 1946. The town grew so large that its population outnumbered Boulder's. While by today's standards this area may

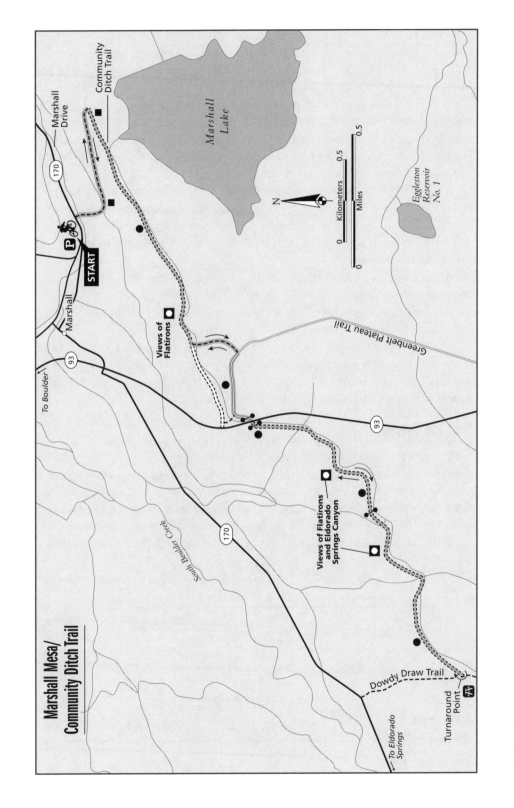

Marshall Mesa/
Community Ditch Trail

Marshall Drive

Community Ditch Trail

170

P

START

Marshall

93

To Boulder

Views of Flatirons

Marshall Lake

N

Kilometers
0   0.5

Miles
0   0.5

Eggleston Reservoir No. 1

Greenbelt Plateau Trail

93

170

South Boulder Creek

Views of Flatirons and Eldorado Springs Canyon

Dowdy Draw Trail

Turnaround Point

To Eldorado Springs

seem quiet enough, the underground coal fires that continue to burn, now for more than 130 years, remain a metaphor for Marshall's more turbulent times.

Perhaps fueled by the fires that burn beneath you, or perhaps driven by the passion of these earlier coal miners, riders now begin riding along the Community Ditch Trail as it travels to the top of Marshall Mesa. Along the way, a variety of informational tablets tell of Marshall's mining history. As you pass Marshall Lake on your left, you'll notice the water-filled ditch to your left. This community ditch once channeled water from the South Boulder Creek drainage, near the mouth of Eldorado Springs Canyon, to agricultural lands in the east.

As you connect with the Greenbelt Plateau Trail, the trail will become considerably rockier, as it climbs from the community ditch over steep and waterbarred terrain. Take caution when descending the gravel road of the Greenbelt Plateau Trail to CO 93. Near its intersection with CO 93, the trail cuts sharply to the left and delivers much loose gravel.

After crossing CO 93, riders rejoin the Community Ditch Trail. The trail delivers a fast descent along a smooth doubletrack. The doubletrack will eventually level off as it weaves through a meadow with spectacular views of the Flatirons directly in front of you.

The intersection of the Community Ditch Trail and the Dowdy Draw Trail offers riders and their dogs relief from the hot sun by providing shade from huge cottonwood trees and the cool running water of the South Boulder Creek. From here it's a short ride to the rest rooms and the turnaround point.

Miles and Directions

0.0 Begin riding by climbing Marshall Mesa in a southerly direction.

0.1 Cross a drainage and arrive at an intersection with stairs that climb to the top of Marshall Lake. Bear left here, avoiding the stairs, and continue climbing to the top of the mesa.

0.5 Bear right onto a doubletrack, as the trail levels out and heads in a westerly direction, passing Marshall Lake on your left. (No bikes are allowed in the Marshall Lake area.)

1.4 The Community Ditch Trail intersects with the Marshall Mesa Trail. Continue riding west on the Community Ditch Trail.

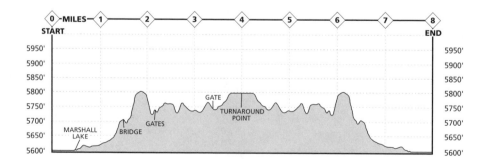

Returning from Eldorado Springs Canyon via the Community Ditch Trail, with the Flatirons in the background.

1.5 The Community Ditch Trail intersects with the Greenbelt Plateau Trail. Veer left, crossing a bridge, and continue on the Greenbelt Plateau Trail.

1.7 The Greenbelt Plateau Trail comes to a T intersection with a gravel road. Bear right at the T intersection, heading in a westerly direction, and continuing on the Community Ditch Trail. (Bearing left here will take you to the Greenbelt Plateau Trail's southern terminus at CO 128.)

2.1 After going through an iron gate, the Greenbelt Plateau Trail ends at its intersection with CO 93. Cross CO 93 carefully and continue riding on the Community Ditch Trail on the other side.

2.2 Pass through another iron gate.

3.4 Pass through another iron gate, heading toward Eldorado Springs Canyon.

3.8 The Community Ditch Trail intersects with the Dowdy Draw Trail, where no bikes are allowed. Veer right, continuing on the Community Ditch Trail to the picnic area.

4.0 Reach the western terminus of the Community Ditch Trail. Here you'll find rest rooms, as well as picnic tables. Retrace your path back to the trailhead.

8.0 Arrive at your vehicle.

Ride Information

Local Information

Boulder Convention and Visitors Bureau, 1850 Table Mesa Drive, Boulder 80305; (303) 442-2911

Local Events and Attractions

KBCO/Budweiser Kinetic Sculpture Challenge, May, Boulder; (303) 444-5600 or www.kbco.com

Organizations

Boulder Area Trails Coalition (BATCO), Boulder; (303) 485-2162

Boulder Off-Road Alliance (BOA), Boulder; (303) 667-2467

Front Range Mountain Bike Association, Boulder; (303) 674-4862

22 Fourth of July Road

The Fourth of July Road is a widely used access route for campers, hikers, riders, and four-by-four vehicles. Thus, it tends to get crowded during the weekend. Don't let the crowds turn you away, however, from enjoying the cool, refreshing runoff of Hellums Waterfall and the high-mountain scenery of Klondike and Bald Mountains. The trail delivers riders to the Fourth of July Campground and the boundary of the Indian Peaks Wilderness Area, a popular entrance point for backpackers. Located near the quirky old mining town of Eldora, the Fourth of July Road offers riders, with a yearn-to-burn attitude, a moderate to challenging ascent past the Eldora Ski Area and onto the base of the 11,340-foot Bald Mountain.

Start: The intersection of Hessie and Fourth of July Roads

Distance: 12.0-mile out-and-back

Approximate riding time: Advanced riders, 1 hour; intermediate riders, 1.5–2 hours

Aerobic level: Physically moderate to challenging. Although most of the climbing is gradual, the ride reaches elevations in excess of 10,000 feet.

Technical difficulty: Technically easy to moderate due to the route following along a dirt, albeit sometimes rutted, road

Terrain: Dirt road that can get considerably rutted as it climbs through mixed aspen and conifer forests

Schedule: July–October

Maps: DeLorme *Colorado Atlas & Gazetteer,* page 39; USGS: East Portal and Nederland, CO; Trails Illustrated: #102, Boulder; ZIA Maps: *Boulder County Mountain Bike Map*

Nearest town: Nederland

Other trail users: Hikers, backpackers, picnickers, four-by-four vehicles

Canine compatibility: Dog-unfriendly due to the vehicular traffic that is on the road

Trail contact: Roosevelt and Arapaho National Forests, Boulder Ranger District, Boulder; (303) 444-6600

Finding the Trailhead: From Boulder, drive west on Canyon Boulevard (CO 119) for 15.1 miles through the town of Nederland. At a roundabout in Nederland, bear left and continue driving south on CO 119 for another 0.6 mile. After passing a brown Eldora Ski Area sign, bear right onto Boulder County Road 130. After 1.4 miles, BC 130 will intersect with 140 Road; 140 Road bears left and continues to the ski area. Bear right here, continuing on BC 130 (which soon turns into Eldorado Avenue) toward the town of Eldora. Drive on Eldorado Avenue for 1.7 miles before entering Eldora. Drive through Eldora for 0.8 mile before Eldorado Avenue turns to dirt road. Stay on the dirt road for 0.7 mile before parking along the side of the road, next to the South Fork of Upper Boulder Creek.

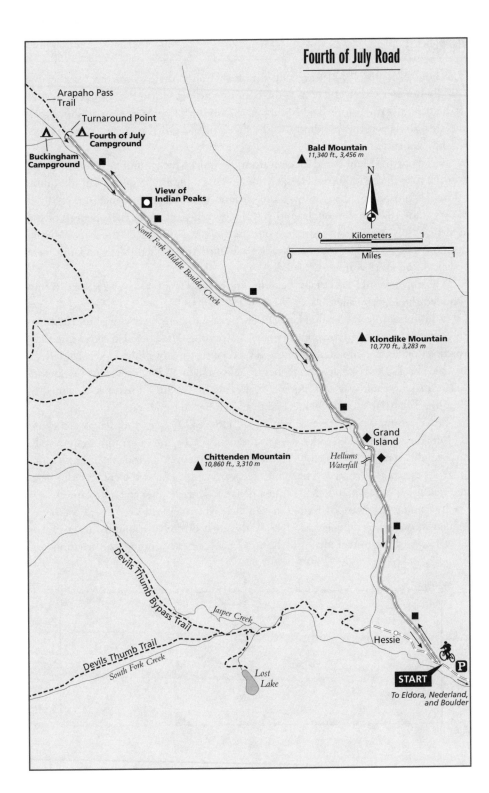

Fourth of July Road

Arapaho Pass
Trail

Turnaround Point

Fourth of July
Campground

Buckingham
Campground

View of
Indian Peaks

North Fork Middle Boulder Creek

Bald Mountain
11,340 ft., 3,456 m

N

0   Kilometers   1

0   Miles   1

Klondike Mountain
10,770 ft., 3,283 m

Grand
Island

*Hellums
Waterfall*

Chittenden Mountain
10,860 ft., 3,310 m

Devils Thumb Bypass Trail

Jasper Creek

Devils Thumb Trail

South Fork Creek

Hessie

*Lost
Lake*

START

P

*To Eldora, Nederland,
and Boulder*

The Ride

The Fourth of July Road travels up the steep-walled drainage of the North Fork Middle Boulder Creek and ends at the boundary to the Indian Peak Wilderness Area at the base of 11,340-foot Bald Mountain. As a result of periodic thundershowers in the area, along with its proximity to the creek in spots, the road can become quite muddy and rutted.

The Fourth of July Road extends from the quirky little mining town of Eldora, past the road that leads to the Hessie Mine, and onto the Buckingham Campground. Although prospectors had been poking around the Eldora area since the 1850s, it wasn't until 1875 that enough gold was discovered to warrant the opening of the Fourth of July Mine. Naturally, the Fourth of July Road serviced the mine. Mining would continue in the area at a modest pace until 1892 when thirteen claims were struck in the same year.

The town would eventually become known as Happy Valley, after John Kemp founded the Happy Valley Placer Mine in 1897.

Within no time, the name Happy Valley proved to be too provincial for the town folk, who by now had grown more than 1,500 strong. They decided to rename their town Eldorado, which lasted until the discovery that many of their personal letters, payroll checks, and the like were being delivered to Eldorado, California, before finally making their way to Eldorado, Colorado. In 1898 the townspeople voted to drop the last syllable of the name, and the town became Eldora.

Upon setting out on the trail, you'll see Eldora Ski Area to your left as you climb in a northerly direction. To the west of the drainage lie the enormous granite walls that stand before the 10,860-foot Chittenden Mountain. After roughly 1.5 miles into the ride, the trail narrows and becomes steeper, falling to meet the creek. From here, the trail levels off a bit and enters into a dense, lodgepole pine and aspen forest.

Beginning just west of Eldora, near where you now ride, a massive forest fire ripped through this drainage in 1899. With much of the surrounding area's timber now lost to fire, lumber that had been so necessary to mining construction was

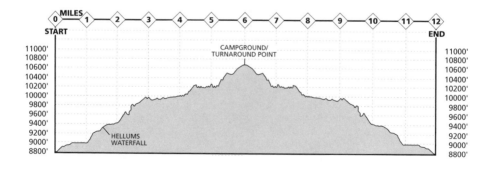

Hellums Waterfall.

nowhere to be found. The fire, coupled with the preponderance of low-grade ore, finally ended Eldora's short-lived bid to become El Dorado.

In recent years there has been renewed interest in mining Eldora. This interest is expressed most notably by the resident mining community who hope to reopen the Mogul Tunnel Mine, a gold and silver mining operation established in 1897. The fact that the mine's entrance sits only 150 yards from the center of town worries many people.

Upon reaching the trail's terminus, riders are surrounded by the towering peaks of Klondike, Pomeroy, and Bald Mountains. From here, the Indian Peaks Wilderness Area begins. No bikes are allowed in the wilderness area. Picnic areas and rest rooms are available at the Buckingham Campground.

This campground takes its name from C. G. Buckingham. The Buckingham family donated much of its mining claims around Boulder Falls (you passed it in Boulder Canyon) and offered thirty acres near Eldora to create the campground.

Before turning around and immediately speeding back to your vehicle, take time to relax, have a snack, maybe go on a hike, and then speed down to your vehicle. Take care though, as the road does support vehicular traffic.

Miles and Directions

0.0 From the intersection of the Hessie and Fourth of July Roads, begin riding in a northwesterly direction on the Fourth of July Road.

1.5 Pass the Hellums Waterfall to your left.

3.0 Pass Chittenden Mountain to your left.

5.0 The Indian Peaks come into view.

6.0 Reach the Buckingham Campground and the Indian Peaks Wilderness Area boundary. Turn around to return the way you came.

12.0 Arrive at your vehicle.

Ride Information

Local Information

Boulder Convention and Visitors Bureau, 1850 Table Mesa Drive, Boulder 80305; (303) 442-2911

Lodging

Goldminer Hotel & Rocky Ledge Cabin, Eldora: (303) 258-7770 or (800) 422-4629

Sundance Lodge & Stables, Nederland; (303) 258-3797 or (800) 817-3797

Restaurants

Black Forest Restaurant, Nederland; (303) 258-8089

Cool Beans Espresso, Nederland; (303) 258-3435

Sundance Lodge & Cafe, Nederland; (303) 258-0804

Local Events and Attractions

Eldora Mountain Resort, Nederland; (303) 440-8700 or (888) 2-ELDORA

Nederland Old Timer Miner Days, July; (303) 258-3580

Peak-to-Peak Highway, Colorado Highways 7, 62, and 119, connecting Estes Park and the Black Hawk/Central City gambling district

Organizations

Boulder Area Trails Coalition (BATCO), Boulder; (303) 485-2162

Boulder Off-Road Alliance (BOA), Boulder; (303) 667-2467

Front Range Mountain Bike Association, Boulder; (303) 674-4862

23 Eldorado Canyon State Park

Eldorado Canyon State Park offers riders a multitudinous array of recreational opportunities. The park itself is perhaps best known for its rock climbing. Climbers from around the world, and Boulder too, find a wide array of routes along the soaring red sandstone walls of Eldorado Canyon, making for an interesting sight along your ride. Standing at 7,240 feet high, Shirt Tail Peak is the highest within the canyon. The Rattlesnake Gulch Trail follows the narrow and rocky singletrack through Rattlesnake Gulch. Its sand- and rock-filled trail offers an exceptional ride to bikers with moderate to advanced technical ability. The climb through the gulch is also a bit of a grunt as it leads to the historic Crags Hotel ruin and views of the Continental Divide at the trail's westernmost portion.

Start: Along the road through Eldorado State Park

Distance: 4.9-mile lariat

Approximate riding time: Advanced riders, 1 hour; intermediate riders, 1.5–2 hours

Aerobic level: Physically challenging due to the narrow climb through Rattlesnake Gulch

Technical difficulty: Technically challenging with some steeper, rockier sections

Terrain: Singletrack and dirt road that travel through Eldorado Canyon and up the steep Rattlesnake Gulch. The trail doles out much rock and sand, as it carries riders out of Eldorado Canyon.

Fees and permits: $2.00 per cyclist/walk-in; $4.00 per vehicle (fees subject to change)

Schedule: March–October

Maps: DeLorme *Colorado Atlas & Gazetteer*, page 40; Colorado State Parks Eldorado Canyon map; USGS: Eldorado Springs, CO; ZIA Maps: *Boulder County Mountain Bike Map*

Nearest town: Eldorado Springs

Other trail users: Hikers, anglers, picnickers, and climbers

Canine compatibility: Dog-friendly

Trail contact: Eldorado Canyon State Park, (303) 494-3943

Finding the Trailhead: From Boulder, drive south on Colorado Highway 93 for roughly 5 miles before bearing right (west), after passing a brown Eldorado Canyon Park sign, onto Colorado Highway 170. Drive west on Eldorado Canyon, through Eldorado Springs, for 2.4 miles before entering the Eldorado Canyon State Park. Parking is available near the entrance to the park.

The Ride

Riders begin by traveling west on the dirt road through the park. The road follows the South Boulder Creek upstream and passes a variety of climbing walls. These sandstone walls tower 800 feet above the canyon. Routes such as the Bastille, Rotwand Wall, Wind Tower, Hawk-Eagle Ridge, Whale's Tail, Redgarden Wall, and Lower Peanuts Wall greet the rider at the outset.

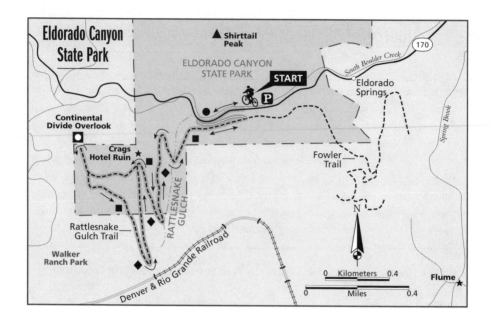

As you make your way through the canyon, keep an eye out for a small blue butterfly. The Hops Azure, one of the world's rarest butterflies, makes its home in Eldorado Canyon. The insect feeds on the hops plant found in the canyon. Found in no other known place in the world, the Hops Azure can best be seen during the summer.

Once riders connect with the Rattlesnake Gulch/Fowler Trails, the route passes over wide and smooth singletrack that travels in an easterly direction. To the left lie the massive sandstone climbing walls of Eldorado Canyon. Glimpses of the eastern plains also come into view through the mouth of the canyon. Watch out for the resident rattlesnake on the trailside boulder.

Where the Rattlesnake Gulch Trail breaks from the Fowler Trail, riders are soon delivered a tight and rocky grunt of a climb through the gulch. After roughly 1 mile, riders have to negotiate past a tight and sandy left-handed switchback, after which the trail starts veering in a southerly direction. Below you lay the tracks, if not the train, of the Denver & Rio Grande Railroad. After 1.5 miles, the trail switches back to head in a northerly direction. As riders head north, the views of the eastern plains and the thermal pools of Eldorado Springs greet them.

The thermal hot springs found in Eldorado Canyon were once the wintering grounds for resident Ute and Arapaho Indians. After white settlers arrived in 1860, their main interest was logging. As word spread of the healing hot waters of the springs, the town of Eldorado Springs started receiving visitors of a more curious type, and by 1902, the town had become a spiritualist camp for those in need of

Rattlesnake Gulch Trail in the mouth of Eldorado Canyon, with the eastern plains in the background.

healing. Soon thereafter, the town would flourish as a tourist resort with the development of the first spring-fed swimming pool in 1904. Dubbed the "Coney Island of the West," the summer would attract as many as 60,000 guests who arrived by train from Denver. Aside from the hot springs, guests would also come for Resort Days.

Resort Days included the high-wire act of Ivy Baldwin, one of America's first hot air balloonists. Baldwin would walk across a wire suspended 582 feet above the canyon floor 86 times before he retired at the age of 82 in 1948.

Once you arrive at the Crags Hotel ruin, a schematic map at the site details where the hotel once stood. Today not much remains except for the fireplace and the circular foundation where the fountain was located.

From the Crags, riders head west through dense mixed conifer forests and hillside meadows toward the overlook. This section of the route provides a welcome relief from the more exposed areas of Rattlesnake Gulch. Once arriving at the Continental Divide Overlook, riders climb moderately again on the old railroad bed before making their descent.

The descent is fast and delivers tight and rocky singletrack. Just prior to coming to the worn social path that leads to the Denver & Rio Grande Railroad and tunnels, which are on private property, the trail descends steeply over narrow and precipitously sloping singletrack. From here it's a technically challenging descent over steep and loose rock before again intersecting with the Crags Hotel ruin. What's left is a final descent of tight and sandy singletrack through big boulders back to the vehicle.

Miles and Directions

0.0 Begin riding west on the road through the park, passing the hikers-only Streamside Trail on your right.

0.5 The road intersects with the Rattlesnake Gulch Trail and Fowler Trail on the left. Bear left here, continuing on the shared route of the Rattlesnake Gulch/Fowler Trails.

0.6 The Rattlesnake Gulch Trail and the Fowler Trail split from each other. Bear right here, continuing on the Rattlesnake Gulch Trail and continue climbing in a westerly direction. The Fowler Trail continues heading east. No bikes are allowed on the Fowler Trail after this point.

1.8 The Rattlesnake Gulch Trail intersects with the Crags Hotel ruin, the Continental Divide Overlook, and the beginning of the loop. Bear right here, continuing in a westerly direction toward the Continental Divide Overlook.

2.0 Arrive at the intersection for the trail that leads to the Continental Divide Overlook. Bear right onto the trail and head north to the overlook.

2.1 Arrive at the Continental Divide Overlook. Return to the loop intersection of the Rattlesnake Gulch Trail and bear right onto it, continuing your loop in a counterclockwise direction.

2.7 The Rattlesnake Gulch Trail descends sharply and cuts left before a rail fence. Veer left here and continue a northerly descent along the Rattlesnake Gulch Trail. A worn social path travels beyond the gate to the railroad tracks and tunnels of the Denver & Rio Grande Railroad, which are on private property.

3.2 The Rattlesnake Gulch Trail intersects the Crags Hotel ruin. Bear right here and descend to the start.

4.9 Arrive at your vehicle.

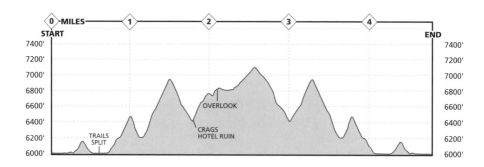

Ride Information

Local Information

Boulder Convention and Visitors Bureau, 1850 Table Mesa Drive, Boulder 80305; (303) 442-2911

Local Events and Attractions

Eldorado Springs Pool, (303) 499-9640

Organizations

Boulder Area Trails Coalition (BATCO), Boulder; (303) 485-2162

Boulder Off-Road Alliance (BOA), Boulder; (303) 667-2467

Front Range Mountain Bike Association, Boulder; (303) 674-4862

24 Rollins Pass

For years Rollins Pass has been a staple in the lexicon of high mountain riding near Boulder and Denver. Beginning on the Continental Divide's eastern slope, the ride to the top of Rollins Pass provides a long, but relatively moderate hill climb to the summit and the Continental Divide at 11,671 feet. Along the way, riders are treated to dynamic views of the Indian Peaks and the Boulder Park Valley before arriving at the top. Following the bed of an old wagon train route, the trail passes through mixed conifer forests and around high-altitude lakes before arriving at the caved-in Needle Eye Tunnel and Rollins Pass. Since much of this route travels above timberline, riders should start early in the day to lessen the chances of being caught above timberline during a midafternoon thunderstorm, a common occurrence for this area.

Start: The east portal of the Moffat Tunnel
Distance: 30.2-mile out-and-back
Approximate riding time: Advanced riders, 3 hours; intermediate riders, 3.5–4.5 hours
Aerobic level: Physically moderate due to the trail's length and high elevations. The trail leading from the Needle Eye Tunnel to Rollins Pass is physically challenging with steep terrain at high elevations.
Technical difficulty: Technically easy, although the trail leading from the Needle Eye Tunnel to Rollins Pass is technically challenging with steep and rocky terrain
Terrain: Two-wheel-drive road, doubletrack, and singletrack that travel through mixed conifer forests and across hillside meadows to above timberline and the Continental Divide.

Schedule: June–September
Maps: DeLorme *Colorado Atlas & Gazetteer,* page 39; USGS: Nederland and East Portal, CO; Trails Illustrated: #103, Winter Park, Central City, Rollins Pass; ZIA Maps: *Boulder County Mountain Bike Map*
Nearest town: Nederland
Other trail users: Hikers, anglers, campers, two- and four-wheel-drive vehicles
Canine compatibility: Dog-unfriendly due to the vehicular traffic and the trail's long distance
Trail contact: Roosevelt and Arapaho National Forests, Boulder Ranger District, Boulder; (303) 444-6600

Finding the Trailhead: From Boulder, drive west on Canyon Boulevard for 16 miles to Nederland and a roundabout. Bear left at the roundabout and continue driving west on Colorado Highway 119 for 5 miles to Rollinsville before turning right onto the dirt Rollins Pass Road (RD 16). Continue on Rollins Pass Road for 7.4 miles to the intersection of the road leading to the east portal of the Moffat Tunnel and Forest Road 149 (Moffat Road "Hill Route").

The Ride

Originally a mule trail linking Denver and Winter Park, the route across Rollins Pass served as a major thoroughfare for Native Americans, fur trappers, and miners alike.

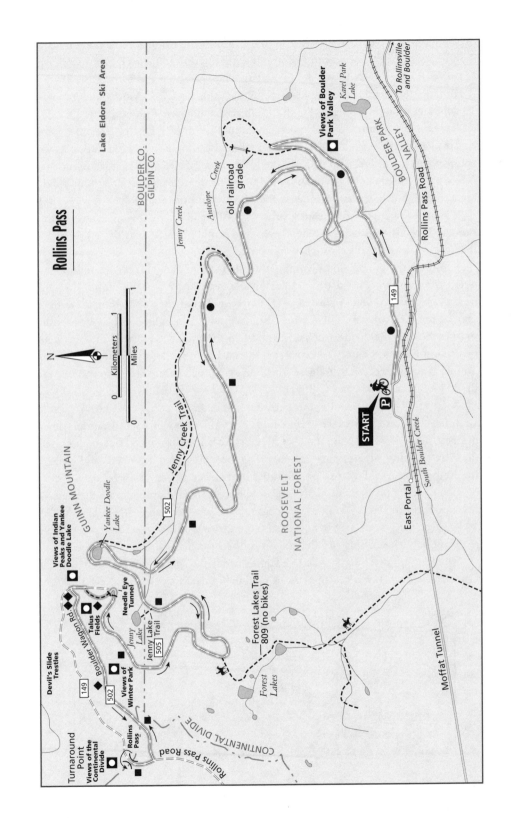

Rollins Pass

Lake Eldora Ski Area

BOULDER CO.
GILPIN CO.

**Views of Indian
Peaks and Yankee
Doodle Lake**

GUINN MOUNTAIN

Yankee Doodle
Lake

Jenny Creek

Antelope Creek

old railroad grade

**Views of Boulder
Park Valley**

Karel Park
Lake

BOULDER PARK
VALLEY

To Rollinsville
and Boulder

Rollins Pass Road

149

Jenny Creek Trail

502

ROOSEVELT
NATIONAL FOREST

START

P

East Portal

South Boulder Creek

N

Kilometers

Miles

0   1

0   1

Turnaround
Point
**Views of the
Continental Divide**

**Devil's Slide
Trestles**

Rollins Pass

149

Views of Winter Park

502

Boulder Wagon Rd.

**Talus
Fields**

**Needle Eye
Tunnel**

Jenny
Lake

Jenny Lake
505 Trail

Forest Lakes Trail
809 (no bikes)

Forest
Lakes

CONTINENTAL DIVIDE

Rollins Pass Road

Moffat Tunnel

In 1865 John A. Rollins built a wagon toll road over the original mule trail and laid the foundation for what was to become the rail line of the Denver, Northwestern, & Pacific Railway (DN&PR), the highest rail line ever built in North America.

Built in 1903 by Denver banker and railroad pioneer David Moffat, the line was actually a compromise, opting for the Rollins Pass line when funding for a tunnel underneath the Continental Divide fell through. The line ran for 23 miles over Rollins Pass and descended into Winter Park and operated until 1913 when it was bought by William Freeman and renamed the Denver Salt Lake Railroad. Unfortunately, having died in 1911, Moffat would never come to realize his dreams of building a tunnel, but Freeman considered the idea worth pursuing.

The first few miles of the route climb gradually and offer expansive views of the Boulder Park Valley. Behind you lies the eastern portal of the Moffat Tunnel, an engineering marvel that cuts through James Peak.

Although the brainchild of Moffat, it would be Freeman who eventually orchestrated the tunnel's construction, requiring the removal of 750,000 cubic yards of rock by way of 2.5 million pounds of dynamite. The tunnel cost the lives of twenty-nine of the men who routinely worked ninety-hour weeks for forty-eight months to bore through the divide. But on February 26, 1928, it secured its first safe passage of a train to Grand County's west portal. Measuring 6.2 miles in length, the Moffat Tunnel is the world's sixth longest and highest railroad tunnel, passing underneath the Continental Divide at 9,239 feet.

After roughly 8 miles into your ride, the trail becomes considerably rockier, as it continues to climb in a westerly direction. Here riders are afforded beautiful views of Bryan and Woodland Mountains to the northeast. Inviting riders to stop and smell the flowers, blue lupine, pink mountain globemallow, red fireweed, and yellow meadow goldenrod all blaze along hillsides like islands of fragrant wildfires.

Once the trail reconnects with the Jenny Creek Trail, riders continue their gradual ascent northwest, making a 180-degree turn around Yankee Doodle Lake. At 10,711 feet, the lake sits in a basin before Guinn Mountain. A cascading waterfall can regularly be seen flowing into the lake from the snowfields above.

The long approach to Needle Eye Tunnel suddenly appears from around a curve. Once at the tunnel, you must portage your bikes up and over it and along a narrow

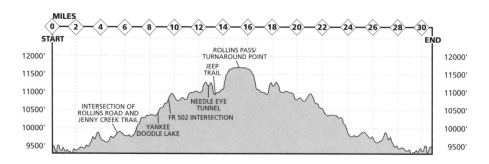

Climbing up and over the Needle Eye Tunnel.

and rocky path through talus fields. This portage is all the more troublesome when you consider that there is only about 20 feet of earth between you and the top of the tunnel. During spring thaw, boulders from the tunnel's ceiling have been known to pry loose, dropping into the tunnel without warning.

Having safely made it to the top of the tunnel, two stone foundations welcome you and serve as fitting lookouts to views of the Indian Peaks, as well as Yankee Doodle Lake, nearly 1,000 feet below. The tailless, mouselike creatures that you'll see ducking in and out of surrounding talus fields are called "pika." Now above timberline, riders descend along rocky singletrack to the Boulder Wagon Road.

Below this road lie the Devil's Slide Trestles, also known as Twin Trestles. While an interesting sight to see, the Devil's Slide Trestles are unsafe and should be avoided. The doubletrack of the Boulder Wagon Road is burdened by steep grades and football-size rocks, making it a physically and technically challenging section of trail.

Upon reaching Rollins Pass, take some time, if not hurried by thunder and lightning, to absorb miles of unobstructed views from the Continental Divide. Here lies the site of the small railroad town of Corona.

With little to no food available atop Rollins Pass, riders make their speedy, if not hungry, return. After crossing back over Needle Eye tunnel, it's a top-ringing descent to your vehicle.

Miles and Directions

0.0 Begin riding east on Rollins Pass Road 117 (FS 149).

5.6 Rollins Pass Road intersects with the Jenny Creek Trail (FS 502) on the right. Continue straight, gradually climbing on the Rollins Pass Road. **Option:** More advanced riders can choose to branch off here and continue on the Jenny Creek Trail, as it descends on a physically and technically challenging narrow four-by-four road to Jenny Creek before making its eventual climb to reconnect with Rollins Pass Road at Yankee Doodle Lake.

9.6 Rollins Pass Road reconnects with the Jenny Creek Trail and arrives at Yankee Doodle Lake. You'll be able to spot Needle Eye Tunnel high above the lake on the ridgeline.

10.4 Rollins Pass Road intersects with the Jenny Lake Trail (FS 505) on the right. Continue straight on Rollins Pass Road, climbing in a westerly direction.

11.4 Rollins Pass Road intersects with the foot and horse Trail 809 on the left. Continue climbing on Rollins Pass Road as you approach Needle Eye Tunnel.

13.0 Arrive at Needle Eye Tunnel. Skirt the tunnel to your right and portage your bicycles over the narrow talus-field trail to the other side.

13.1 Arrive at the top of the Needle Eye Tunnel. Here, cairns along a rocky singletrack mark the proper route. Follow the cairns and the singletrack to the intersection with the Boulder Wagon Road.

13.4 The singletrack intersects with the Boulder Wagon Road. Bear left onto the physically and technically challenging Boulder Wagon Road and continue climbing steeply to the north. The road that leads to the Devil's Slide Trestles will be below you on the right, blocked off by logs, and is marked by a DEVIL'S TRESTLES sign. **Option:** riders can either ride or hike this road to view the trestles before returning and reconnecting with the Boulder Wagon road.

13.5 The Boulder Wagon Road crumbles into a wider jeep trail as it veers toward the west and Rollins Pass. Continue riding along a moderate grade to the pass, passing a KEEP VEHICLES ON ROAD sign to your left.

14.9 The Boulder Wagon Road intersects with Rollins Pass Road 149 at a T intersection. Bear right here onto Rollins Pass 149 and head to the old townsite of Corona and Rollins Pass. FS 149 continues left and descends to Winter Park.

15.1 Arrive at the top of Rollins Pass and the Continental Divide. Return the way you came, back to your vehicle.

30.2 Arrive at your vehicle.

Ride Information

Local Information
Boulder Convention and Visitors Bureau, 1850 Table Mesa Drive, Boulder 80305; (303) 442-2911

Local Events and Attractions
Eldora Mountain Resort, Nederland; (303) 440-8700 or (888) 2-ELDORA
Nederland Old Timer Miner Days, July; (303) 258-3580
Self-guided auto tours with a mile-by-mile account of the "Hill Route." Brochures are available at various businesses at Winter Park and Rollinsville.
Winter Park, Mountain Bike Capital, USA

Lodging
Sundance Lodge & Stables, Nederland; (303) 258-3797 or (800) 817-3797

Restaurants
Black Forest Restaurant, Nederland; (303) 258-8089
Sundance Lodge & Cafe, Nederland; (303) 258-0804

Organizations
Boulder Area Trails Coalition (BATCO), Boulder; (303) 485-2162
Boulder Off-Road Alliance (BOA), Boulder; (303) 667-2467

DENVER'S SKI TRAIN

For more than sixty years, the Denver Ski Train has been transporting skiers from Denver's Union Station to the Winter Park Ski Resort. But once the snows melt, the town of Winter Park transforms itself from ski resort to Mountain Bike Capital, USA.

It would seem natural, then, for the Ski Train to want to open its doors to mountain bikers. And it has.

In the summer of 2000, the train began transporting mountain bikers and their bikes to Mountain Bike Capital, USA. Fresh off the success of its 2000 summer run, the Ski Train continued its mountain biking services through the summer of 2001.

The Ski Train usually departs from downtown Denver's Union Station in the morning and returns by late afternoon. A specifically designed car fits all of the bicycles on board, leaving passengers to simply enjoy the ride through the Rockies. As the train parallels South Boulder Creek, it passes the towns of Pinecliffe and Rollinsville. After going through a barrage of tunnels, the Ski Train arrives at the 6.2-mile-long Moffat Tunnel, the highest railroad tunnel in the United States, before coming to a stop fewer than 100 yards from the ski lifts. The trip to Winter Park only takes two hours, as much as it would if driven by car.

Passengers may choose to pay a $45 round-trip coach price, where they can purchase snacks at the Cafe Lounge cars, or they may pay a $70 round-trip club price, where they can enjoy a complimentary continental breakfast buffet to Winter Park and snacks on the way back. Moreover, the club car affords more seating room, with smaller crowds.

If you want to board the Ski Train for some summer mountain biking at Winter Park, it's best to book your reservations three to four weeks in advance.

For more information, contact the Ski Train at (303) 296–4754 or visit the Web site at www.skitrain.com.

25 Mountain Lion Trail

Golden Gate Canyon State Park offers riders a network of prime singletrack. Prior to the summer of 2000, Golden Gate Canyon State Park only allowed bikes on its trails located in Jefferson County. In the summer of 2000, however, portions of the park in Gilpin County were opened to bikes. Now the park offers riders more trail miles than it ever had before. Voted the "Best Bike Ride" in *Westword's* "Best of Denver 2001" issue, the Mountain Lion Trail stands as a legacy of when riders were only allowed to ride the portion of Golden Gate Canyon that extended into Jefferson County. However, this trail stands the test of time and continues to invite more advanced riders to challenge themselves on its rocky and narrow singletrack. Weaving across meadows, through forests, up hillside climbs, and down creek sides, the Mountain Lion Trail offers a lot of incredible terrain.

Start: The Burro trailhead at Bridge Creek

Distance: 8.2-mile loop

Approximate riding time: Advanced riders, 1.5 hour; intermediate riders, 1.5–2 hours

Aerobic level: Physically moderate to challenging due to the sustained climbing along wide doubletrack and singletrack

Technical difficulty: Technically moderate to challenging due to rockier sections along the creeks

Terrain: Singletrack and doubletrack that passes through open meadows, along rocky creeks, and through mixed conifer forests

Fees and permits: $4.00 daily pass park fee (fees subject to change)

Schedule: June–October

Maps: DeLorme *Colorado Atlas & Gazetteer,* page 39; Colorado State Parks Golden Gate Canyon map; USGS: Ralston Buttes, CO; USGS: Black Hawk, CO illustrates the Gilpin County side of Golden Gate Canyon State Park; Trails Illustrated: #102, Boulder

Nearest town: Nederland

Other trail users: Hikers, horseback riders, picnickers, anglers, campers, and hunters

Canine compatibility: Dog-friendly

Trail contact: Golden Gate Canyon State Park, (303) 582–3707

Finding the Trailhead: From Boulder, drive south on Colorado Highway 93 for roughly 17 miles before bearing right onto Golden Gate Canyon Road. Drive on Golden Gate Canyon Road for roughly 13 miles before pulling off to the right to pay the daily use fee. After paying, bear right on 57 Road (Ralston Creek Road or Drew Hill Road) by the Visitors Center, and drive for roughly 3 miles to the Burro trailhead at Bridge Creek.

The Ride

Golden Gate Canyon State Park includes 14,000 acres of sweeping meadows, mixed conifer and aspen forests, and high mountain peaks. Elevations within the park range from 7,600 feet to 10,400 feet.

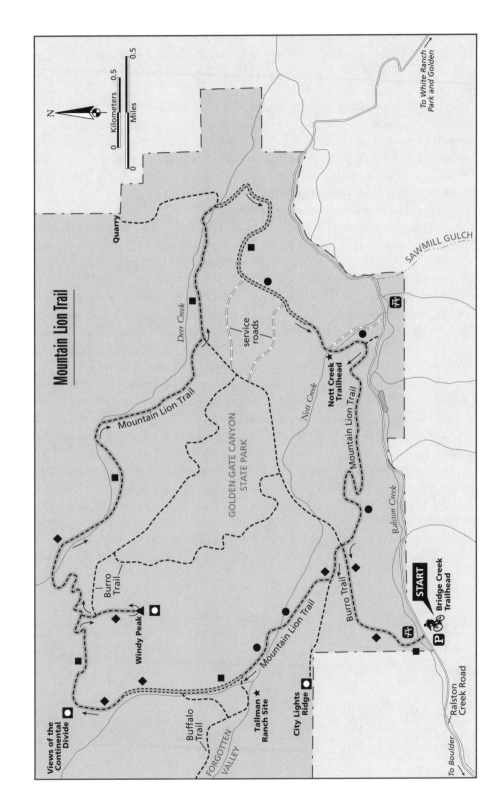

The trail begins by climbing steadily on the Burro Trail, heading in a north-northwest direction across south-facing meadows. Within the first mile of riding, a right-handed switchback delivers steep, sandy, and rocky terrain, before leveling off atop a ridge.

Soon after connecting with the Mountain Lion Trail, the route travels through a tall stand of ponderosa pine. Here the trail is much smoother than the rockier and sandier sections of the Burro Trail. After passing the turnoff for the City Lights Ridge, riders descend on wide singletrack through stands of aspen and over occasionally rocky terrain before beginning their climb again at roughly 1.6 miles. Soon thereafter, riders reach the site of the old Tallman Ranch.

The area surrounding the ranch has been occupied by four generations of Swedish descent. Anders Tallman and his family homesteaded the land in 1876. Here the Tallman family raised milk cows, beef cattle, and chickens. To supplement their income, the Tallmans also cut timber and kept a garden whose produce they would sell to residents of the nearby town of Black Hawk.

Originally, Anders homesteaded this site because it reminded him of his homeland in Sweden. When they came of age, Anders's son Nells and daughter Anna homesteaded neighboring land to a combined Tallman ranch holding of 400 acres. It would appear as though riders were climbing through all 400 of these acres as they make their way up the meadow toward a cool stand of aspen trees.

At about 2.7 miles, the trail narrows to singletrack and climbs more steeply as it switches back toward Windy Peak over physically and technically challenging terrain. Riders are rewarded with views of the Continental Divide along the way, however, before entering into a thick ponderosa pine forest at nearly 3 miles into the ride.

From where the Mountain Lion forks and heads to Windy Peak, it's a short burst to the top at roughly 9,000 feet.

The descent from Windy Peak is fast and takes the form of tight and rocky switchbacks, as well as big root ledges. Riders blaze through a meadow and cross Deer Creek a few times, following it downstream. During the summer, the Tallman family diverted water from nearby Nott Creek and channeled its cooling waters

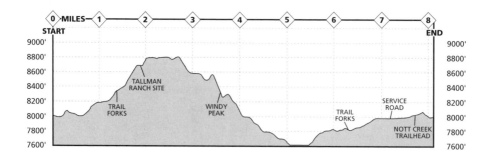

Arriving at the site of the old Tallman Ranch.

across the milk house floor. This was the family's only refrigeration system for the milk, eggs, butter, and meat stored there.

Descendants from the Tallman family continued to work this land until 1955, when it was sold to a developer. It wasn't long before the first section of park was purchased in 1960. In 1970 the Colorado State Parks bought the remaining land, which today totals more than 14,000 acres, preserving it for future generations, Swedish or otherwise. Due to its historical significance, the Tallman Ranch was added to the State Registry of Historic Properties in 1995.

Once crossing Deer Creek at the Mountain Lion Trail's intersection to the Quarry, riders climb on doubletrack and pass two service roads before descending to their vehicles.

Miles and Directions

0.0 Begin by climbing along the Burro Trail singletrack, heading in a north-northwest direction.

0.1 The Burro Trail comes to a fork. Bear left here, continuing your climb and heading in an easterly direction.

1.2 The Burro Trail intersects with the Mountain Lion Trail. Turn left onto the Mountain Lion Trail, heading toward Forgotten Valley.

1.4 The Mountain Lion Trail forks. Continue straight here on the Mountain Lion Trail as it heads in a more northerly direction. The left fork heads toward the City Lights Ridge. No horses or bikes are allowed on the City Lights Ridge route of the Mountain Lion Trail.

1.9 Arrive at the Tallman Ranch site. Continue climbing north on the Mountain Lion Trail's doubletrack.

2.2 The Mountain Lion Trail intersects with the Buffalo Trail to the left. Bear right here, continuing on the Mountain Lion Trail and heading toward Windy Peak.

3.3 The Mountain Lion Trail forks at a rock wall. Bear right (straight) here and continue along the out-and-back trail to Windy Peak.

3.6 Arrive at Windy Peak. Turn around and backtrack to where the Mountain Lion Trail forked.

4.0 Arrive at the Mountain Lion fork for Windy Peak and the trail's continuation to Nott Creek. Bear right here, heading in a northerly direction. Careful inspection of the area will reveal a yellow trail sign that reads MOUNTAIN LION TRAIL TO KNOTT CREEK and points in the correct direction.

5.6 The Mountain Lion Trail intersects with the Burro Trail. Continue descending on the Mountain Lion Trail.

6.3 The Mountain Lion Trail forks. Bear right, crossing Deer Creek, and begin climbing in a southerly direction. The left fork is an out-and-back to the Quarry.

7.1 Pass a service road.

7.3 The Mountain Lion Trail intersects with a service road. Bear left here continuing on the Mountain Lion Trail, descending in a southerly direction and following the Nott Creek parking sign.

7.7 Arrive at the Nott Creek trailhead. Ride through the parking area and continue on the singletrack on the other side, located near the rest room.

8.2 Arrive at your vehicle.

Ride Information

Trail Information

Colorado State Parks, (303) 866–3437

Local Information

Boulder Convention and Visitors Bureau, 1850 Table Mesa Drive, Boulder 80305; (303) 442-2911

Local Events and Attractions

Panorama Point Scenic Overlook group events, (303) 582-3707

Mining towns of Black Hawk and Central City, 6 miles south of the park on CO 119

Organizations

Boulder Area Trails Coalition (BATCO), Boulder; (303) 485-2162

Boulder Off-Road Alliance (BOA), Boulder; (303) 667-2467

Front Range Mountain Bike Association, Boulder; (303) 674-4862

26 White Ranch

White Ranch offers grueling climbs; steep, narrow descents; and tight switchbacks. The route described here includes all of these aspects but is still only a small sampling of what White Ranch has to offer. With steep grades, loose rock, and plastic erosion bars strewn across the trail, the initial climb from the parking lot is one of the toughest on the Front Range. From there, riders are offered fast descents along precipitously sloping terrain and through mixed conifer and piñon forests. Although within a short distance of Golden, Boulder, and Denver, White Ranch, because it's viewed as a more advanced area to mountain bike, is seldom crowded.

Start: From parking lot off Pine Ridge Road

Distance: 8.4-mile lariat (with many options to add and/or subtract from this distance)

Approximate riding time: Advanced riders, 1.5 hours; intermediate riders, 2-2.5 hours

Aerobic level: Physically challenging due to the climbing involved in exposed and hot terrain

Technical difficulty: Technically moderate to challenging due to its steep and rocky climbs and descents with many tight switchbacks

Terrain: Singletrack and doubletrack run over very rocky terrain as well as very smooth, forested terrain

Schedule: April–November

Maps: DeLorme *Colorado Atlas & Gazetteer,* page 40; USGS: Golden, CO; Ralston Buttes, CO; Trails Illustrated: #102; White Ranch Park Map, Jefferson County Open Space

Nearest town: Golden

Other trail users: Hikers, horseback riders, campers, and picnickers

Canine compatibility: Dog-friendly, but bring plenty of water for the pooch. Dogs must be on a leash at all times.

Trail contact: Jefferson County Open Space, Golden; (303) 271-5902

Finding the Trailhead: From Canyon Boulevard and Broadway Road in Boulder, drive south on Colorado Highway 93 (Broadway) for 17.4 miles until you see the WHITE RANCH OPEN SPACE sign to your left. Turn right before the sign onto Fifty-sixth Avenue. Drive for approximately 1 mile on Fifty-sixth Avenue before turning right again onto Pine Ridge Road, which will lead you to the White Ranch parking lot.

The Ride

Once a cattle operation, today White Ranch is a 3,040-acre Open Space Park. Taking its name from a local homesteader, Paul R. White, the park includes roughly 18 miles of multiuse trails. Only a half-mile northwest of Golden, White Ranch offers mountain bikers living in the Denver metro area a great escape from the city grind.

The majority of the park is exposed, particularly the east side, which traverses a steep slope, so White Ranch receives ample amounts of sunlight making it one of

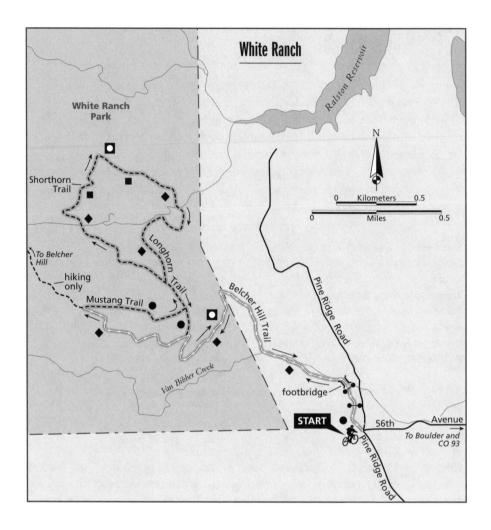

the first mountain bike areas of Colorado's higher foothills region to open for the mountain biking season. Because of the jump on the season, White Ranch tends to get sandy toward the end of summer. Because of the exposure, you'd be well advised to bring plenty of water and sunscreen with you while riding the ranch.

From advanced riding to novice riding, White Ranch offers it all. Rugged and rocky steep climbs challenge even the best of riders, while smooth and gentle meadow shots tempt weary neophytes to release the death grip on the brakes. From the many vantage points in the park, mountain bikers are offered sweeping views of the Great Plains and the Denver skyline.

The first part of the route ascends a steep, sandy, and rocky doubletrack. Even the best riders will feel the burn after 2.4 miles of this kind of climbing. Luckily, the singletrack descent of Mustang Trail to Longhorn Trail offers a brief respite. After passing the continuation of the Longhorn Trail and continuing to climb up the Shorthorn Trail, the route winds its way through a dense pine forest. The terrain of the singletrack here is narrow and smooth. The trail eventually exits the forest and winds its way north along an east-facing slope.

Along the slope you'll find patches of what is more commonly referred to as Indian T.P. (toilet paper). Botanists would probably rather you call the plant by its proper name, mullein (also spelled "mullen"). The plant's wide leaves account for the nickname. Tea made from brewing mullein leaves is said to relieve respiratory problems—useful info when riding at higher altitudes.

At mile 4.3, the northern junction of Shorthorn and Longhorn trails marks the beginning of your return. The most challenging part of this entire route begins once you turn onto the Longhorn Trail. At mile 5.0, the route hits a steep and rocky descent, followed by tight switchbacks and big drop-offs, eventually delivering you to the bottom of a steep-walled drainage. What follows is a steep and rocky ascent up the other side, with tight switchbacks. From here, it's a fast race back to the Belcher Hill Trail and an even faster race back to the parking lot.

With elevations raging from 6,150 feet to 8,000 feet (atop Belcher Hill), White Ranch offers some tough climbing but rewards you with bombing singletrack. One note of caution: Because of the many narrow trails leading around blind curves, it's likely that you may run into someone. Control your speed while descending. Mountain bikers are responsible for yielding to all other trail users, and downhill riders yield to uphill riders.

Miles and Directions

0.0 Start from the parking lot at the trailhead of Belcher Hill Trail. You'll pass through two gates and cross Van Bibber Creek via a footbridge within the first half-mile. Please close both gates behind you and begin climbing up Belcher Hill Trail after crossing the creek.

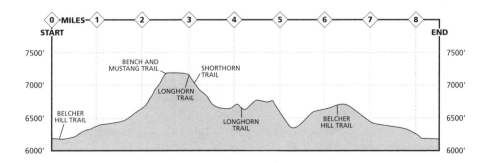

The steep and rocky intial climb of Belcher Hill Trail.

1.8 Arrive at the junction of Longhorn (to your right) and Belcher Hill trails. You will eventually return via Longhorn Trail, but for now, forgo turning right onto Longhorn Trail and continue pedaling west up Belcher Hill Trail. To the east, views of the Denver skyline and its surrounding towns sprawl out before you.

2.4 Belcher Hill Trail intersects with Mustang Trail. Here is a good place to rest, as your initial climb has ended—not to mention there's a bench seat to sit on. Hang a right, now descending on the singletrack of the Mustang Trail.

3.0 Arrive at the junction of Mustang and Longhorn trails. Veer left onto the Longhorn Trail, which within 0.25 mile will quickly Y: Longhorn to your right, Shorthorn to your left. Continue left and begin climbing, now on the Shorthorn Trail.

4.3 Arrive at the northern junction of Shorthorn and Longhorn trails. Bear right onto the Longhorn Trail.

6.0 Arrive at the southern junction of Shorthorn and Longhorn trails. Bear left, continuing your ride on Longhorn. Within 0.3 mile you will once again arrive at the junction of Mustang and Longhorn. Continue on Longhorn for another 0.1 mile.

6.4 Arrive at the junction of Longhorn and Belcher Hill Trails. Veer left onto Belcher Hill Trail and descend, what previously you had climbed, back to the parking lot.

8.4 Arrive at the parking lot.

Ride Information

Trail Information

Jefferson County Open Space Trails Hotline,
Evergreen; (303) 271-5975

Local Information

Boulder Convention and Visitors Bureau, 1850
Table Mesa Drive, Boulder 80305; (303)
442-2911

Local Events and Attractions

Coors Brewing Company Tours, Monday–Friday,
10:00 A.M.–4:00 P.M., Golden; (303)
279-6565

Hakushika Sake Tours, Monday–Friday, 10:00
A.M.–3:00 P.M., Golden; (303) 278-0161

Books

Under the Devil's Thumb by David Gessner
(Tucson: The University of Arizona Press, 1999)

Honorable Mentions

Boulder Region

Six more rides in the Boulder area deserve mention, even though they didn't make the "A" list. They may be a bit out of the way or more heavily traveled, but they still deserve your consideration when choosing a destination.

F Buchanan Pass Trail

Most riders who attempt the Buchanan Pass Trail come away from it either loving or hating the experience. For rock hounds who enjoy putting their body and bike through battle with boulders, Buchanan Pass lies close to their hearts. For riders who prefer more of a spinner's route, this trail leaves little in the way of smooth sailing.

As part of the 16-mile trail that eventually leads into the Indian Peaks Wilderness Area, the Buchanan Pass Trail begins near the Camp Dick campground and incorporates sections of the South St. Vrain Trail and the Sourdough Trail. The South St. Vrain Trail and the Buchanan Pass Trail follow a shared route parallel to the St. Vrain Creek over relatively smooth singletrack and past the Sourdough Trail. This smooth singletrack is short-lived, however, delivering the blows of rocks and roots soon thereafter.

The first eastern 4.5 miles of the Buchanan Pass Trail are open to mountain bikes, after which, however, the trail leads into the Indian Peaks Wilderness Area. Here riders will connect with Coney Flats Road (FS 507) and then with the Beaver Reservoir Cut-off Trail #835. From this cut-off trail, riders will intersect and negotiate the rocky Sourdough Trail before reconnecting with the smoother singletrack trail of the Middle St. Vrain.

This trail can be quite confusing for riders unfamiliar with the area. Riders would benefit from checking with the *Boulder County Mountain Bike Map* by ZIA Maps.

For more information, contact the Arapaho and Roosevelt National Forests, Boulder Ranger District, Boulder, CO at (303) 444–6600.

To reach the Buchanan Pass Trail, drive west on Canyon Boulevard (Colorado Highway 119) to Nederland. In Nederland, bear right onto Colorado Highway 72 and drive north for roughly 15 miles to the turnoff for Camp Dick on the left. Drive for another mile, and park at the trailhead on the left.

G Bald Mountain Trail

Next time you think there's no time to go mountain biking, think again. In a word, Bald Mountain is short, 1.1 miles short, but one worth riding nevertheless. For beginners who haven't yet conditioned their bodies to Colorado standards, this is a great ride whose singletrack delivers baby-bottom's smoothness in as small a package. For the more advanced riders, Bald Mountain offers mountain bikers the opportunity to run laps, a unique outside reinterpretation of the velodrome.

From Boulder, drive west on Mapelton Avenue, which will turn into Sunshine Canyon Drive (CR 52), for 4.6 miles to the Bald Mountain Scenic Area trailhead on the left. Park in the spaces provided by the Bald Mountain Scenic Area trailhead.

For more information, contact the Boulder County Parks and Open Space Department, (303) 441–3950.

⊢ Boulder Creek Path

The Boulder Creek Path is one of the most recognizable bicycle thoroughfares in all of Boulder. The paved path parallels the Boulder Creek for roughly 7.5 miles and continues through the Boulder Canyon, where it eventually becomes a wide, natural surface trail.

Riders typically access the Boulder Creek Path at the Boulder Public Library on Tenth and Arapaho Streets. From there, the path passes the Children's Fishing Pond, an ideal resting spot for littler anglers; the Red Rocks/Settler's Park, where vertical red rock formations jut dramatically skyward; and the Boulder Creek Kayak Course, where 'yakers brave the rapids during the runoff season of late spring and early summer. Later in the season, you will often find tubers running the same, if not somewhat mellowed, rapids.

Parts of the path are located just a few blocks from the outdoor pedestrian Pearl Street Mall, which offers such diversions as shopping, street performers, food, and cool beverages.

From these creekside attractions, the trail continues through Boulder Canyon. The sheer cliff walls of the Boulder Canyon are a popular climbing place for would-be Spidermen and -women.

For more information on the Boulder Creek Path or the Pearl Street Mall, contact the Boulder Parks Department at (303) 413–7200 or the Boulder Chamber of Commerce at (303) 442–1044.

| Eaton Park

Located behind the Shelby Museum at Sixty-third and Spine in East Boulder, Eaton Park has been converted from an old dumpsite to a city park. Although Eaton Park does not offer any trail system per se, it does cut another facet in the ever-burgeoning gemstone of mountain biking.

Also know as Red Fox Hills or the GunBarrel Jumps, Eaton Park has been described by Judd De Vall, international coordinator for the International Mountain Bicycling Association, as a "bicycle challenge area." The area is roughly one-half acre in size and delivers tabletops and single and double jumps. Unique to this dirt jump park is the fact that riders are encouraged to bring their own shovels to dig their own jumps. Moreover, the park supplies water to make the ground more malleable for shoveling and shaping. Also offering a gazebo for hikers and other park-goers, Eaton Park marks a new trend in the area of mountain biking.

As the sport evolved to include downhilling and cyclecross, freestyle jumping can now be included among mountain biking's offshoots. Perhaps even more important, Eaton Park offers resident mountain bikers and BMX riders a safe and legal alternative to back-alley jumping. This bicycle challenge area affords neighborhood kids, as well as adults, the opportunity to express themselves physically, as individuals, much like players in a sandlot baseball game do as team members.

For more information about the area, contact the city of Boulder at (303) 413–7228.

J Winniger Ridge Dot Trail System

Located in Nederland, the Dot Trail System begins behind the Nederland High School. While there is presently a network of trails in the area, the Forest Service, the Boulder Off-road Alliance (BOA), and the International Mountain Bicycling Association (IMBA) are in the planning stages of creating a mapped and well-constructed trail system that would extend from Nederland to Boulder.

The current network of trails can be ridden; however, due to its circuitous arrangement and spotty trail markings, it's recommended that riders ride with someone who knows the area. Riders have been known to get lost here.

K West Magnolia Trail

The West Magnolia Trail has been a long-standing favorite for area mountain bikers of Boulder and Nederland. With no real physically or technically challenging terrain, the West Magnolia Trail is a great beginner's ride. At several vantage points, you're offered beautiful views of the Indian Peaks. The trail offers numerous routes to Rollinsville and links to the numerous singletrack trails and access roads found in the surrounding Roosevelt National Forest. The West Magnolia Trail offers mountain bikers, hikers, and horseback riders an easy to difficult route through the densely wooded areas of the Magnolia area.

To reach the West Magnolia trailhead, drive south on CO 119 from Nederland toward Rollinsville. After passing the Sundance Cafe Lodge, bear right onto West Magnolia, County Road 132W. Park in the pullout provided and begin riding through the densely wooded mixed conifer forest. Roughly a mile farther down 132W is another Forest Service Road on the left that links with a variety of other roads and singletrack trails.

For more information, contact the Preserve Unique Magnolia Association (PUMA) at P.O. Box 536, Nederland, CO 80466.

Denver Region

D enver is one of the few cities in history that was not founded on a road, railroad, lake, navigable river, or body of water. The discovery of gold in 1858 along the banks of Cherry Creek first brought settlers to the site that would later become Colorado's capital. Prior to the "Pikes Peak or Bust Gold Rush" of the late 1850s and early 1860s, however, the site had already enjoyed a reputation as a meeting place for trappers, traders, and the Native tribes of the Sioux, Cheyenne, Arapaho, Ute, and Crow. But it would be by rail that Denver would secure its dominance as a western city.

Not put off by the Trans-Continental Railroad bypassing its city, Denver residents opted, instead, to start their own railroad company and connect it with the Union Pacific in Cheyenne, Wyoming. Awarded capital status of the Colorado Territory in 1867, Denver would later remain the capital after Colorado was admitted to the union in 1876.

Located nearly 300 miles west of the United States' geographic center and covering more than 154 square miles of land, Denver is the largest city within a 600-mile radius of itself. Nestled between the eastern plains and the central Rocky Mountains, Denver serves as gateway to more than 8.8 million visitors a year, not the least of whom come to enjoy the area's fine cycling opportunities.

While there are 20,000 acres of parks in nearby mountains, Denver itself boasts 205 parks, most linked by bike paths within the city limits—the largest city parks system in the country. In particular, the incredible Open Space Parks of Jefferson County, Denver's most populated county, have been rated the best in the nation by the American Hiking Society. Nearly three-fourths of Jefferson County lie in the surrounding Rocky Mountains. While the hills surrounding Denver offer riders more than 85 miles of off-road trails, the city itself includes more than 450 miles of bike paths and lanes, all of which are frequently used by the Denver-based bicycle touring company, Two Wheel Tours, (303) 798–4601. The backbone of Denver's urban bicycling network includes the Platte River and Cherry Creek Trails. From these trails, riders can link to all of Denver's bike paths and lanes, enabling riders to get anywhere in the city without having to compete with vehicular traffic. Receiving over 300 days of sunshine a year and warm Chinook winds periodically throughout the winter, Denver offers mountain bikers year-round riding. Not surprising then that *Bicycling* ranked Denver number one in the magazine's November

2001 issue among its Best Cycling Cities for those with a population ranging from 200,000 to 500,000. And if that wasn't enough, Denver is one of the largest cities ever to have been honored by the League of American Bicyclists as a Cycling Friendly Community.

But bikers beware. Denver also boasts one of the highest per-capita motor vehicle ownership rates in the country, which amounts to one licensed vehicle for every person in the city. Luckily, Denver provides bike transport on all of its buses.

Currently, the Denver metro area counts its population at 2.3 million, three-fourths of whom live in the suburban counties of Adams, Arapaho, Boulder, Denver, Douglas, and Jefferson. As the largest city between the Great Plains and the Pacific Coast, Denver offers all the amenities of a large city, while providing all the recreational activities normally found only in smaller mountain towns.

For more information on Denver, contact the Denver Visitor Information Center at (303) 892–1112 or (303) 892–1505 or (800) 645–3446; the Colorado Tourism Board at (303) 592–5410; the Colorado Travel and Tourism Authority, (800) COLORADO; or the Denver Metro Chamber of Commerce, (303) 534–8500.

27 Chimney Gulch Trail

The area surrounding Lookout Mountain, aside from being great for mountain biking, is also a well-known hang gliders' stomping ground. But for those of us who prefer the terra firma to the terrifying, the Chimney Gulch Trail is all we mountain bikers need to know about the Lookout Mountain area. The first part of this route takes riders over red dirt singletrack and through patches of scrub oak. The exposed terrain and many switchbacks make this initial approach a tough one. The next part of the trail climbs steadily as it snakes its way up Chimney Gulch to Windy Saddle. The last section of this route follows through dense stands of pine and aspen on its way to the top of Lookout Mountain. In short, Chimney Gulch offers a lot of bang for your buck. The initial descent from Lookout Mountain runs over a smooth bed of pine-needle singletrack before continuing over rocky and exposed terrain. A great option is to combine this ride with Apex Park (Ride 28).

Start: The Chimney Gulch trailhead at base of Lookout Mountain
Distance: 9.4-mile out-and-back
Approximate riding time: Advanced riders, 1-1.5 hours; intermediate riders, 1.5-2 hours
Aerobic level: Physically moderate due to the climbing through exposed terrain, with a good deal of tight and steep switchbacks
Technical difficulty: Technically moderate due to some steeper, short sections. There are also a number of waterbars with which to contend.
Terrain: Singletrack that runs over exposed hillsides, around tight switchbacks, and through deep forests. Riders will also have to ride on a dirt drive and paved road for a short while.

Schedule: March–November; open daily from 8:00 A.M. to dusk. The Nature Center hours are Tuesday–Sunday, 10:00 A.M.–4:00 P.M.
Maps: DeLorme *Colorado Atlas & Gazetteer*, page 40; USGS: Morrison, CO; Lookout Mountain Nature Center and Preserve Map
Nearest town: Golden
Other trail users: Hikers and horseback riders
Canine compatibility: Dog-friendly, although no dogs, bikes or horses are allowed on the Forest Loop and Meadow Loop
Trail contact: Jefferson County Open Space, Golden; (303) 271-5925

Finding the Trailhead: From Denver, drive west on Interstate 70 for 8 miles before taking exit 265 to Colorado Highway 58, following signs for Golden and Central City. Drive west on CO 58 for 5 miles to its intersection with U.S. Highway 6 at a stoplight in Golden. Bear left at the stoplight and drive south on US 6 for roughly a quarter of a mile before turning right into the dirt pullout of the Chimney Gulch trailhead. Park in the pullout by the trailhead.

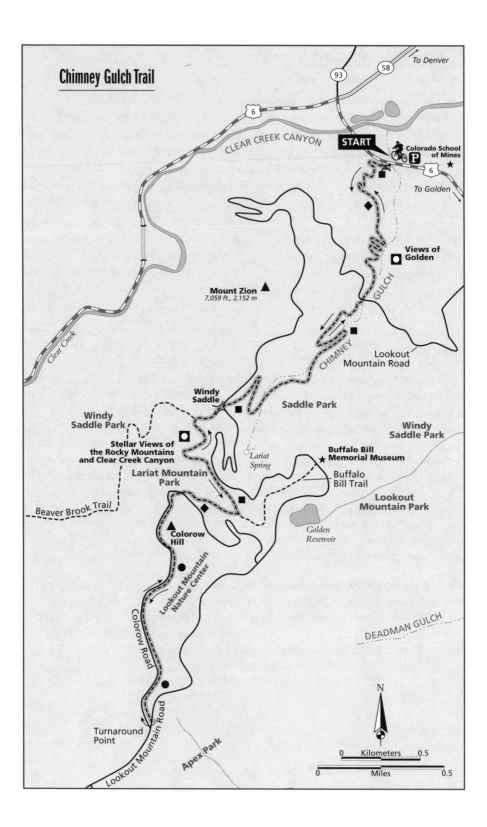

Chimney Gulch Trail

93
58
To Denver
6
CLEAR CREEK CANYON
START
Colorado School
of Mines
P
6
To Golden

Views of
Golden

GULCH

Mount Zion
7,059 ft., 2,152 m

CHIMNEY

Lookout
Mountain Road

Clear Creek

Windy
Saddle

Saddle Park

Windy
Saddle Park

Windy
Saddle Park

Stellar Views of
the Rocky Mountains
and Clear Creek Canyon

Lariat
Spring

Buffalo Bill
Memorial Museum

Lariat Mountain
Park

Buffalo
Bill Trail

Lookout
Mountain Park

Beaver Brook Trail

Colorow
Hill

Golden
Reservoir

Lookout Mountain
Nature Center

DEADMAN GULCH

Colorow Road

Turnaround
Point

Lookout Mountain Road

Apex Park

N

0   Kilometers   0.5

0   Miles   0.5

The Ride

To the observant and ambitious rider, the Chimney Gulch Trail affords lessons in recycling and sustainable resources. At the end of the trail, riders are introduced to the sustainable design of the Lookout Mountain Nature Center. From there, riders can also easily access a second area ride in Apex Park before "re-cycling" back to the start. But these lessons begin even before you reach the top.

As you make your way up the initial switchbacks of the trail, you may notice a slight hint of roasting barley and malt wafting through the air. That's not your mind playing tricks on you; it's the Coors Brewing Company just over your left shoulder. The Coors Brewing Company has operated in Golden since 1873 and boasts being the world's largest brewery. So where's the lesson in recycling and economy, you might ask?

After World War II had ended in 1945, Coors began looking into alternatives for packaging its product. Having relied exclusively on kegs and bottles up to this time, the Coors company introduced the country's first all-aluminum beverage can on January 22, 1959. Moreover, following the can's successful introduction, the company offered a penny for every can returned to the brewery. And thus, a recycling revolution was born. Today, Coors owns and is an operating partner in the nation's largest aluminum-can manufacturing plant in Golden. Who says recycling can't be profitable?

After a mile of steady climbing, the trail begins to level out a bit, offering a few rockier and more technical sections. After crossing the footbridge at 1.7 miles, you begin riding up the Lookout Mountain drainage of Chimney Gulch. Sections of Chimney Gulch offer some shaded relief from the otherwise exposed terrain of the lower reaches of the trail.

Arriving at the Windy Saddle, you're offered stellar views of the Rocky Mountains and Clear Creek Canyon. It is from the cool springs of Clear Creek that water is drawn for the brewing of Coors beer, thus lending credence to the slogan "Brewed with Pure Rocky Mountain Spring Water."

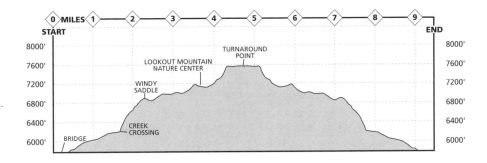

Heading southwest from Windy Saddle toward the Lookout Mountain Nature Center.

This section of trail that leads from Windy Saddle is one of the most beautiful of the entire route. As it climbs steadily through thick stands of mixed conifers, the trail's singletrack is laden with pine needles and an occasional rocky section. After nearly 3 miles of riding, you pass a scree field where you're offered beautiful views of Golden to the east.

As you near the top of Lookout Mountain, you're thrown a technical rock- and root-filled section as a last little test of your strength. Once atop Lookout Mountain, take time to explore the Lookout Mountain Nature Center.

Riders can continue from the nature center via the Lookout Mountain Trail to Apex Park. Should your stamina be sustainable, you might consider combining this ride with one through Apex Park. This combination is truly a Front Range epic.

If you choose to save this epic for another day, you'll undoubtedly enjoy the fast descent from the top of Lookout Mountain to your vehicle.

Miles and Directions

0.0 Begin riding west, staying to the left of US 6, following a trail along the steel guardrail. Cross a small bridge that will deliver you to the start of the Chimney Gulch Trail.

0.2 After crossing the bridge, the trail climbs as it switches back a number of times in a southwesterly direction.

0.7 The singletrack of the Chimney Gulch Trail will intersect with a dirt drive that leads to a private home. Bear left onto this dirt road and ride for roughly 50 feet before bearing right, following a trail marker sign, and continuing on the singletrack.

0.9 The Chimney Gulch Trail will intersect with the paved Lookout Mountain Road. Cross the road and continue riding on the Chimney Gulch Trail, heading in a westerly direction. Use caution when crossing the road, as Lookout Mountain Road sees a good deal of vehicular traffic. It is also a popular road biking route.

1.7 Cross a creek via a footbridge.

2.0 Cross over another bridge, as the trail continues through mixed conifer and aspen forests.

2.3 Arrive at the Windy Saddle. Here, the Chimney Gulch Trail will again intersect with the paved Lookout Mountain Road. Bear left onto the paved road and ride for roughly 50 yards before bearing right, following a sign for the hikers-only Beaver Brook Trail. At this point, the Chimney Gulch Trail and the Beaver Brook Trail follow the same route.

2.6 Arrive at the point where the Chimney Gulch Trail breaks from the Beaver Brook Trail. The hikers-only Beaver Brook Trail bears right and continues heading in a southwesterly direction. Bear left here, following a sign for the Jefferson County Conference and Nature Center. This section of trail is known as the Lookout Mountain Trail.

3.3 The Lookout Mountain Trail (a.k.a. Chimney Gulch Trail) intersects with the Buffalo Bill Trail to the left. Bear right and continue riding on the Lookout Mountain Trail, heading for the Lookout Mountain Nature Center.

3.6 Reach the top of Lookout Mountain and the Lookout Mountain Nature Center and Boettcher Mansion. Cross the paved Lookout Mountain Road and continue riding on the Lookout Mountain Trail toward Apex Park.

4.2 Pass Ellsworth Park to your right.

4.7 Lookout Mountain Trail will intersect with the Lookout Mountain Road trailhead to Apex Park. At this point, turn back and retrace your path. **Option:** You may wish to descend into Apex Park via the Apex Trail and Enchanted Forest Trail. See Apex Park, Ride 28.

9.4 Reach your parked vehicle.

Ride Information

Local Information

Greater Golden Chamber of Commerce, 1010 Washington Avenue, P.O. Box 1035, Golden 80402; (303) 279-3113

Local Events and Attractions

Buffalo Bill Memorial Museum and Grave, Lookout Mountain; (303) 526-0747

Historic Boettcher Mansion, Lookout Mountain; (303) 526-0855

Lookout Mountain Nature Center Group Programs, Golden; (303) 526-0212

Restaurants

Cody Inn, Golden; (303) 526-0232

28 Apex Park

Apex Park offers a network of trails within a short drive of Boulder, Denver, and Golden. Hence, it can get crowded on weekends. But don't let its proximity fool you into believing that Apex Park doesn't have some of the toughest trails surrounding the metropolitan area. Delivering rocky singletrack, steep climbs, and exposed hillsides, Apex Park is sure to deliver quintessential Front Range riding. Be sure to wear sunscreen and drink plenty of water while on the trail. The route described below covers the northeasterly sections of Apex Park. To add roughly 3 more miles of singletrack to your ride, continue heading west through the park on the Apex Trail to its terminus at Lookout Mountain Road. From its terminus, I highly recommend returning via the Enchanted Forest Trail.

Start: Apex Park trailhead by the Heritage Square Shopping Center

Distance: 5.5-mile lariat, with options to extend

Approximate riding time: Advanced riders, 30–45 minutes; intermediate riders, 1–2 hours

Aerobic level: Physically moderate to challenging due to some extended climbs over varied terrain in exposed areas

Technical difficulty: Technically moderate to challenging due to the rocky terrain, tight singletrack, and big drop-offs

Terrain: Singletrack with a good deal of large, loose rocks and sand

Schedule: April–November

Maps: DeLorme *Colorado Atlas & Gazetteer*, page 40; USGS: Morrison, CO; Jefferson County Open Space Apex Park Map

Nearest town: Golden

Other trail users: Hikers and horseback riders

Canine compatibility: Dog-friendly

Trail contact: Jefferson County Open Space, Golden; (303) 271-5925

Finding the Trailhead: From Denver, drive west on Interstate 70 and exit at 265 onto Colorado Highway 58. Drive west on CO 58 for 5 miles to its intersection with U.S. Highway 6 at a stoplight in Golden. Bear left at the stoplight and drive south on US 6 for roughly 2.3 miles before turning right onto Heritage Road (the Jefferson County Complex will be on your left). Drive on Heritage Road for 1 mile and turn right into Apex Park, marked by a brown park sign. Park in the northeast corner of the Heritage Square Parking Lot.

The Ride

Apex Park offers outstanding views of the unique geological formations of the Hogback (see Dakota Ridge and Red Rocks Trail, Ride 31), Green Mountain (see Hayden/Green Mountain Park, Ride 30), and the Table Mountains. With nearly 7 miles of prime singletrack over 530 acres, Apex Park is sure to offer mountain bikers the good life. Or will it?

Before setting out on the Apex Trail, take notice of the looming old cottonwood tree overhead. Word in the West has it that some misguided horse rustler once

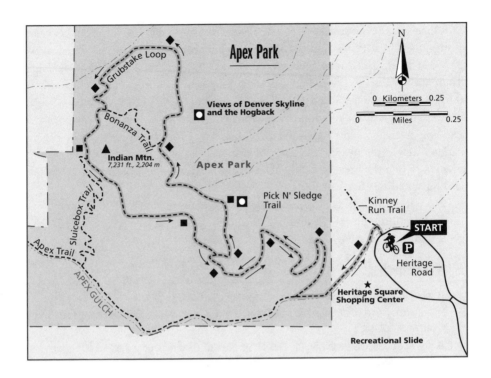

Apex Park

Views of Denver Skyline and the Hogback

Pick N' Sledge Trail

Indian Mtn.
7,231 ft., 2,204 m

Grubstake Loop

Bonanza Trail

Sluicebox Trail

Apex Trail

APEX GULCH

Kinney Run Trail

START

Heritage Road

Heritage Square Shopping Center

Recreational Slide

N

0 Kilometers 0.25

0 Miles 0.25

swung—and I don't mean on a swing—from one of its branches after he was caught stealing horses. In fact, the *Rocky Mountain News* of July 24, 1861, reported, "he was arrested yesterday and preparations were made to bring him to Denver to trial; but last night he was taken in charge by a body of men who preferred that his trial should cost nothing." You can almost feel the tightness of the rope as you climb up the first mile of Apex Gulp's—I mean Gulch's—tight, rocky, and sandy singletrack. But this is only a primer of what's to come.

The site of the park used to be occupied by the town of Apex. During Colorado's mining craze of the late 1800s, a toll road ran through the town that connected to the gold mining districts of Central City, or as people of the day liked to call it, "Gregory Diggins." The Apex and Gregory Wagon Road through Apex Gulch was one of the area's first thoroughfares to the gold fields of Central City. The tolls were collected from miners on their way to strike it rich near where the present Heritage Square Shopping Center stands today. I guess you had to spend money to make money even back then. The toll road remained in operation from the 1860s through the mid-1880s. While riding the trails, visitors to Apex Park may still catch glimpses of the old roadbed.

The Pick N' Sledge Trail is marked by steeper and more exposed sections than those the first mile of the ride has to offer. While the climb up the Pick N' Sledge Trail is a killer (no pun intended), you are rewarded with sweeping views of the Great Plains and the Denver skyline to the east.

Once on the Grubstake Loop Trail, you're again offered views of the Front Range, the Great Plains, and the Denver skyline. More important, however, you're provided with shaded relief from the more exposed sections of the Pick N' Sledge Trail. The Grubstake Loop Trail courses swiftly over smooth singletrack as it runs through mixed conifer forests and skirts the perimeter of Indian Mountain. Sitting in Apex Gulch, near the confluence with Lena Gulch, the area surrounding Apex Park was a great value to early Native Americans. From the higher reaches of the park, as well as the nearby Hogback, Native Americans could stand watch over any invaders, while they reaped the benefits of the numerous buffalo, deer, and elk that also inhabited nearby areas.

From the top of Indian Mountain, it's a speedy descent across a meadow, passing the intersection with the Grubstake Loop, to the Apex Trail. Your ride closes with a short and rocky descent along the Apex Trail to your vehicle.

Miles and Directions

0.0 Start from the Apex Park parking lot and trailhead and begin climbing in a westerly direction, crossing a small seasonal creek via footbridge. After crossing the creek, bear left by an Apex Trail sign.

0.6 The Apex Trail intersects with the Pick N' Sledge Trail. Bear right onto the Pick N' Sledge Trail, which takes a number of switchbacks as it continues to climb in a northwesterly direction.

1.6 The Pick N' Sledge Trail intersects with the Grubstake Loop. Continue on the Grubstake Loop as it descends in a northwesterly direction.

2.1 The Grubstake Trail intersects with the southern tip of the Bonanza Trail to your left. Continue straight on the Grubstake Trail as it descends in a northerly direction over smooth singletrack and through densely wooded forests.

2.6 You begin climbing again via a number of switchbacks; although, this time, you're in the shade.

3.0 The Grubstake Loop intersects with the northern tip of the Bonanza Trail to the left. Continue on the Grubstake Loop as it continues to the top of Indian Mountain.

3.1 The Grubstake Trail intersects with the Pick N' Sledge Trail and the Sluicebox Trail. Veer left onto the Pick N' Sledge Trail.

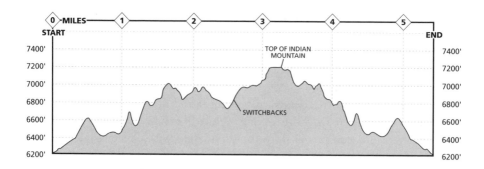

Climbing the Pick N' Sledge Trail, with views of the eastern plains and the Denver skyline.

3.4 Reach the top of Indian Mountain. From here, the trail descends in an easterly direction on smooth singletrack.

3.8 The Pick N' Sledge Trail intersects with the Grubstake Loop. Continue on the Pick N' Sledge Trail, keeping right, on your way to the Apex Trail.

4.8 The Pick N' Sledge Trail intersects with the Apex Trail. Bear left onto the Apex Trail and return to Apex Park trailhead.

5.5 Arrive at your vehicle.

Ride Information

Trail Information

Jefferson County Open Space Trails Hotline, Evergreen; (303) 271-5975

Local Information

Greater Golden Chamber of Commerce, 1010 Washington Avenue, P.O. Box 1035, Golden 80402; (303) 279-3113

Local Events and Attractions

Astor House Museum, Golden; (303) 278-3557

Hakushika Sake Tours, Monday–Friday, 10:00 A.M.–3:00 P.M., Golden; (303) 278-0161

Heritage Square Alpine Slide and Bungee Jump, Golden; (303) 279-1661

29 Barbour Forks

The Barbour Forks Trail is one of the lesser-traveled trails in the Denver/Boulder region. This may be due to the variety of trails that cross its main route. For this reason, riders should always be familiar with the trail's route and bring a map of the area. The trail supplies hillside meadows full of wildflowers, tall stands of aspen and mixed conifers, as well as—dare I say it—little in the way of other trail users. Combining four-by-four road with prime singletrack, the trail travels up the Soda Creek drainage of Idaho Springs to connect with a looped singletrack trail. While not particularly long, this trail can be enjoyed by novice and advanced riders alike. The singletrack stands out among the best in the area. Perhaps more important, after the ride is done, riders can soak their sores away in the thermal pools of the Indian Springs Resort.

Start: Head southwest, up the four-by-four Barbour Forks Road

Distance: 5-mile lariat

Approximate riding time: Advanced rider, 45 minutes; intermediate riders, 1–1.5 hours

Aerobic level: Physically moderate to challenging due to the trail's steeper climbs along the four-by-four road

Technical difficulty: Technically moderate due to the significant amount of rocky sections both when climbing on the four-by-four Barbour Forks Road and when descending on the Barbour Forks singletrack

Terrain: Four-by-four road and singletrack that pass through dense woodland and open meadows

Schedule: June–October

Maps: DeLorme *Colorado Atlas & Gazetteer,* page 39; USGS: Idaho Springs, CO; Trails Illustrated: #104, Idaho Springs–Georgetown–Loveland Pass, CO

Nearest town: Idaho Springs

Other trail users: Hikers, horseback riders, four-by-four vehicles, and ATVs

Canine compatibility: Dog-friendly

Trail contact: Roosevelt and Arapaho National Forests, Boulder Ranger District, Boulder; (303) 444-6600

Finding the Trailhead: From Denver, drive west on Interstate 70 for 30.6 miles to Idaho Springs, exiting at 241A, the first Idaho Springs exit. Drive through Idaho Springs on Colorado Boulevard for 1 mile, passing the Argo Gold Mine and Mill on your right and the Safeway on your left, before bearing left after the 7-11 store onto Miner Street. Here, Miner Street and Colorado Avenue form the V of a Y intersection. Colorado Avenue splits to the right, as Miner Street continues to the left. After bearing left here onto Miner Street, a brown sign reading steve canyon will be on the right as you pass the Idaho Springs Visitors' Center. Drive past the visitor center for roughly 0.3 mile on Miner Street before turning left onto Soda Creek Road, heading underneath the interstate. You'll drive on Soda Creek Road for 1.6 miles, passing the Indian Springs Resort on your left, before the road turns to gravel at the county dump site. From the dump site, drive for another 1.7 miles on the gravel Soda Creek Road before bearing left into the pullout parking space and the Barbour Forks trailhead. Park in the dirt pullout by the trailhead.

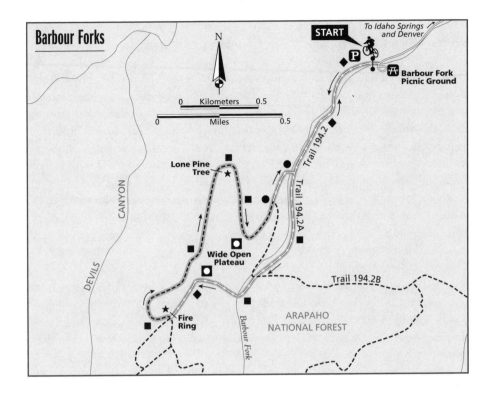

The Ride

Although relatively short in length, the Barbour Forks Trail does dole out its share of technical and physical abuse. No matter, though. Riders can rest assured knowing that the healing waters of the Great Spirit pour forth just down the road at the Indian Springs Resort.

The first recorded mention of the hot springs was made by George A. Jackson, the man who first discovered placer gold in the Rockies. In his journal of 1859, Jackson wrote that he "camped at warm springs near mouth of small creek, coming in on south side." That small creek was none other than Soda Creek. But before Jackson was bathing his wares in these hot mineral springs, the Arapaho and Ute Indian tribes used these healing waters of the Great Spirit as spiritual centers. In fact, Soda Creek divided the Ute and Arapaho Nations. Each Nation, then, came to view the hot springs as neutral ground. Needless to say, once gold was discovered here, the Ute and Arapaho were soon permanently removed from the area.

Upon beginning the trail, riders are immediately tossed a grunt of a hill climb, as the trickling waters of the Barbour Forks of Soda Creek lend a teasing voice to the sound of your heavy breathing.

Far from any healing hot waters at this point, you pass through a dense evergreen forest whose underbrush more closely resembles that of someplace far more tropical than Colorado.

After about a mile of climbing, riders are greeted with a moderately physical and technical climb, complete with sand and loose rock. Soon thereafter, however, the trail levels out as it passes under the dark canopies of mixed conifers. After crossing the fork of Soda Creek at 1.2 miles, you ride into a beautiful meadow. Shortly after bearing left in the meadow, you'll bear right at an intersection and climb up a very steep and rocky technical section. As you near the top, Barbour Forks Road will come into view below before the trail lets out onto a wide-open plateau.

Once passing through what appears to be a small aspen revegetation stand, you'll want to look for the singletrack that darts off to the right. Once on the Barbour Forks singletrack, it will curve around to the right, nearly 180 degrees, back toward the direction from where you came.

The singletrack initially follows the edge of the clearing next to where you had just ridden on the road, delivering rocks and roots that eventually give way to smooth and hard-packed trail. The trail descends in a northerly direction to deliver you behind the big boulder north of the grassy plateau. The descent becomes considerably faster from here, as the trail's smooth surface invites riders to let go of their death-grip on the brakes.

Upon entering into the meadow after 3 miles of riding, you'll again have to carefully look for the singletrack that veers off to the right. After connecting with this singletrack, the trail doubles back and drops into a pine forest below the trail on which you were just riding. This trail runs over smooth singletrack through dense evergreen forest to a logging skid road. Bearing left on the skid road and again onto trail 194.2, you return to your vehicle. Hopefully, you'll add your name alongside the likes of Walt Whitman, Frank and Jesse James, Teddy Roosevelt, and Sarah Bernhardt, who have all taken comfort in the healing waters of the Great Spirit that pour forth just down the road.

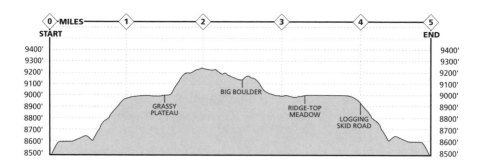

The Barbour Forks singletrack.

Miles and Directions

0.0 Ride out of the parking lot and bear left onto Soda Creek Road. Passing through a gate, begin climbing southwest up the four-by-four Barbour Forks Road.

0.7 The Barbour Forks Road comes to a trail intersection. Bear left here onto trail 194.2A (still the Barbour Forks Road) and pedal in a southwesterly direction through a hillside meadow awash with wildflowers. The trail to the right is listed as 194.2 and continues in a more immediate westerly direction as it crosses the fork of Soda Creek. You will eventually connect to 194.2, but not now.

1.2 Trail 194.2A (Barbour Forks Road) intersects with 194.2B to your left and climbs in an easterly direction. Bear right here, heading in a westerly direction and crossing the fork of Soda Creek. Once arriving in the meadow, intersect the 194.2 trail and bear left onto it, climbing in a southerly direction.

1.3 Trail 194.2 (Barbour Forks Trail) intersects with a road that cuts left through a pine forest and heads in a southerly direction. At this point, bear right, continuing on the main Barbour Forks Trail, as it climbs in a northwesterly direction along a technically challenging, steep climb.

1.5 Reach the top of an open and grassy plateau. Just beyond the big boulder to the north of the plateau lies the singletrack with which you'll eventually connect. For now, however, look to the southwest (left), where you'll continue riding along the main Barbour Forks Trail. There, in the woods, you may spy the remains of an old hunter's shelter. Bear left here, continuing on the main trail and heading in a southwesterly direction through the pine forest.

1.9 Pass through a small aspen revegetation stand. Here, the four-by-four Barbour Forks Road that you are on continues to the left, heading in a southeasterly direction, as it passes through another tall stand of pines and begins to climb significantly over loose rock. At this point, look to connect with the Barbour Forks singletrack on your right. The singletrack is identifiable by a large fire ring and an old rusted pipe. Bear right onto the singletrack and head in a southwesterly direction.

2.5 Arrive behind the big boulder located in the northernmost section of the grassy plateau. Bear left here, continuing on the singletrack, continuing your descent in a northerly direction.

3.3 Arrive at a ridge-top meadow. Ride slowly through the meadow for roughly 40 yards (at 3.4 miles), before veering right onto the inconspicuous singletrack that wraps around a lone pine tree to doubleback into the woods directly below the trail on which you were just riding. Should you miss this turnoff, and continue straight on the more obvious trail, you'll still return to your vehicle, but at the expense of a couple of miles.

4.0 Arrive at an old logging skid road. Bear left, and continue on the skid road, heading in an easterly direction.

4.1 The skid road intersects with the 194.2 trail. Bear left onto 194.2.

4.3 Trail 194.2 will cross the fork of the Soda Creek and intersect with 194.2A (Barbour Forks Road). Bear left onto Barbour Forks Road and return to the start the way you came.

5.0 Arrive at your vehicle.

Ride Information

Local Information

Clear Creek County Tourism Board, P.O. Box 100, Idaho Springs 80452; (303) 567-4660 or (800) 88-BLAST

Idaho Springs Visitors Center, 2060 Miner Street, P.O. Box 97, Idaho Springs 80452; (303) 567-4382 or (800) 685-7785

Local Events and Attractions

Argo Gold Mine and Mill, Idaho Springs; (303) 567-2421

Mount Evans Scenic and Historic Byway, (303) 567-4660 or (800) 88-BLAST

Lodging

Indian Springs Resort, Idaho Springs; (303) 989-6666

Restaurants

Jiggies Cafe, Idaho Springs; (303) 567-9942

Two Brothers Deli, Idaho Springs; (303) 567-2439

30 Hayden/Green Mountain Park

By offering smooth singletrack, beautiful views of Red Rocks Park and the Denver skyline, and a fast and sometimes rocky descent from the 6,800-foot summit, Hayden/Green Mountain Park is sure to please. It makes for a great introduction to mountain biking. Due to its proximity to Denver, the park can be crowded on weekends. During the spring and early summer riding season, Green Mountain is blanketed with wildflowers.

Start: The Florida trailhead on the north side of Alameda Parkway, just past Florida Avenue

Distance: 6.4-mile loop

Approximate riding time: Advanced riders, 30–45 minutes; intermediate riders, 1–2 hours

Aerobic level: Physically easy to moderate due to the modestly rolling nature of the terrain. There is one extended hill climb on the park's western slope that many will find challenging as they head to the summit.

Technical difficulty: Technically easy to moderate due to the smooth singletrack. There are some rockier and narrower sections of single-track that might require an intermediate level of technical expertise.

Terrain: Mostly smooth singletrack with some varying rocky sections. Dirt roads lead to the top and extend across the summit of Green Mountain.

Schedule: April–November

Maps: DeLorme *Colorado Atlas & Gazetteer,* page 40; USGS: Morrison, CO

Nearest town: Lakewood

Other trail users: Hikers and horseback riders

Canine compatibility: Dog-friendly

Trail contact: Jefferson County Open Space, Golden; (303) 271-5925

Finding the Trailhead: From Denver, drive west on U.S. Highway 6 (exit 209B from Interstate 25) toward Lakewood for roughly 7 miles. Exit at Simms Street/Union Street and bear left onto South Union. Drive south on Union for 1.7 miles before bearing right onto Alameda Parkway. Drive west on Alameda Avenue for 1.5 miles before bearing right into the Green Mountain trailhead. Park in the lot by the Florida trailhead.

The Ride

Offering 2,281 acres of lush hillsides awash with wildflowers and wildlife, Hayden/Green Mountain Park is an oasis set on the outskirts of an otherwise bustling metropolis. Aside from this, what makes Green Mountain Park special is that it represents a true Foothills ecosystem. As one of a few large parcels of Foothills ecosystem left in the Denver metro area, it is important that we respect and maintain this vital resource.

Green Mountain sits at the terminus of two distinct regions: the easternmost edge of the Rocky Mountains and the westernmost edge of the short grass prairie.

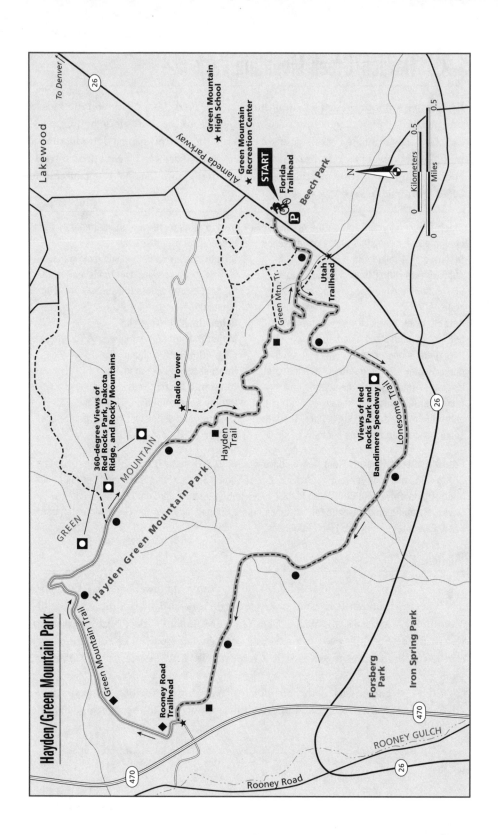

In a beautifully blended tribute to both regions, the 6,800-foot mountain is covered in a wavy plume of open grassland, highlighted, at times, with yucca and cacti.

Starting on Lonesome Trail, the first 3 miles offer relatively smooth terrain as they skirt the base of Green Mountain. Should you be riding during the spring and early summer season, you'll appreciate the green lushness of the hillsides. In full bloom, Green Mountain reminds one of Marin County, California, mountain biking's birthplace.

Spring attracts a lot of attention to Green Mountain for reasons long known to nature lovers. In March, you can expect to find the red and purple blooming colors of cranesbill and alyssum. In keeping with the season's colors, red-tail hawks return to nest at Green Mountain, as do robins. The territorial singing of the red-winged blackbird is often heard, while foxes and coyotes settle in dens with their pups. Later in the spring, the lilac-colored locoweed begins to bloom. Love for locoweed is not shared by all, however, as the weed is a problem for ranchers because it is poisonous to many kinds of livestock. In fact, deriving from the Spanish word that means "crazy," the "loco" in locoweed recalls a long-standing belief that animals, particularly horses, that eat the weed become addicted to it, made "crazy" by it, and eventually die from it.

Spring wears on to uncover a rookery of nesting Swainson's hawks, night herons, pelicans, meadowlarks, and bluebirds. Butterflies become active flitting through forests of white and yellow sand lilies; purple, bell-shaped harebells; and the reds and oranges of Indian paintbrush and mallow.

Passing through this kaleidoscope for the senses, you're treated to stunning views of the Hogback and Dakota Ridge. These pleasantries soon fade, however, as you reach the Green Mountain Trail and start climbing to the top of Green Mountain.

Once reaching the summit of Green Mountain, you're offered 360-degree views of the Red Rocks Park, Dakota Ridge, and the higher Rocky Mountains to the west; Boulder and the Flatirons to the north; the Great Plains and Denver skyline to the east; and 14,110-foot Pikes Peak to the south. As you look around, realize that this area was once predominantly prime buffalo habitat. Today, the black-tailed prairie dog communities surrounding the base of the mountain take up a good deal

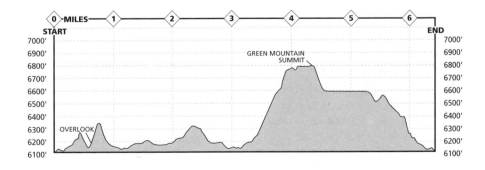

Descending on the singletrack, with views of Red Rocks Park to the west.

of that habitat. From your roost atop Green Mountain, however, you may come across seeing coyotes, hawks, and rattlesnakes. There is, of course, the very rare occasion of spotting a mountain lion.

Once connecting with the Hayden Trail from atop Green Mountain, you begin a savage descent over smooth and sometimes rocky terrain. While descending the eastern ridge of the park, the Hayden Trail continues to provide incredible views of Red Rocks Park. This speedy descent returns you to the Lonesome Trail.

After basking in the beauty that Hayden/Green Mountain Park has to offer, bear left on the Lonesome Trail and return from a day well spent.

Miles and Directions

0.0 Begin climbing moderately in a southwesterly direction on the Lonesome Trail.

0.4 The Lonesome Trail intersects with the Utah Trail. Continue heading west on the Lonesome Trail.

0.6 You're offered an overlook of Red Rocks Park and Bandimere Speedway to the west and the Denver skyline to the east.

3.3 Lonesome Trail meets the Rooney Road trailhead and the beginning of the Green Mountain Trail. Bear right onto the dirt road of the Green Mountain Trail and begin climbing in a northerly direction.

4.4 Reach the summit of Green Mountain and continue a fast cruise on the Green Mountain Trail heading in an easterly direction.

4.9 The Green Mountain Trail intersects with the Hayden Trail on the right, roughly 100 yards before the tall radio tower. Only cairns mark the singletrack of the Hayden Trail. Bear right onto the Hayden Trail singletrack. If you pass the radio tower, there are other singletrack trails that lead to your vehicle.

5.6 The Hayden Trail intersects with the Green Mountain Trail at a T intersection. Bear right at the T, continuing your descent on the Hayden Trail, as it crosses over waterbars and occasional switchbacks.

5.9 The Hayden Trail intersects with the Utah trailhead and the Lonesome Trail. Bear left onto the Lonesome Trail and return toward your vehicle.

6.4 Reach your vehicle.

Ride Information

Local Information

Bear Creek/Lake Park Information Visitor Center, 13411 West Morrison Road, Morrison 80465; (303) 697-6159

City of Lakewood, 480 South Allison Parkway, Lakewood 80226; (303) 987-7800

Local Events and Attractions

Bandimere Speedway, Morrison; (303) 697-6001

Dinosaur Ridge, Morrison; (303) 697-DINO; www.dinoridge.org

Red Rocks Park and Amphitheater, Morrison; (303) 697-6486; www.Red-Rocks.com

Restaurants

The Fort (specializes in big game entrees), Morrison; (303) 697-4771

In Addition

HandleBar & Grill

Combine the favorite pastime of riding a bicycle with food and drink, and what do you get? Denver's own HandleBar & Grill (HB&G). In a place where cookie-cutter theme restaurants vie for dominance by "über-sizing" their market share, the HandleBar & Grill remains a Colorado original and true to its tagline: "We ain't no chain."

Opened in 1997 by owner Mike Miller, the restaurant offers a relaxed and playful atmosphere. Adorned with vintage bicycles, racing jerseys, and autographed photographs of cycling's legends, the HandleBar & Grill is a veritable "velohead" museum. According to Miller, 99 percent of the people who have ever ridden a bicycle have had a good first experience. For this reason, Miller believes that the cycling memorabilia in his restaurant "make people feel good."

Menu items—like Big Chain Rings (onion rings), Singletrack Club (sandwich), and Marley's Jamaican Chicken Breast (HB&G's bow to Jamaica's own "Soul Avenger")— speak to cyclists and attest to the cuisine being "American with a heavy Caribbean twist." The fully stocked bar also serves some of Colorado's finest microbrews, among which include, not surprisingly, Fat Tire Amber Ale and Singletrack Copper Ale.

What makes the HandleBar & Grill special isn't just its food and drink offerings but its connection to the larger Colorado cycling community. Miller acknowledges that by melding a successful business with a fun concept, "the cycling community has embraced and welcomed us." And for its part, the HandleBar & Grill has reciprocated.

HB&G is actively involved with Bicycle Colorado, the American Cycling Association, the Bob Cook Mount Evans Hill Climb, the MS 150, the Courage Classic, and the Lance Armstrong Foundation. The HandleBar & Grill also sponsors the Spirit of the Rockies, the only Colorado-exclusive intrastate mountain bike race series. To all this Miller adds, "We're involved; we're not just beating the drum" and avoiding the fight; "we try . . . to give back to the cycling community."

Even the bar and grill's own racing team is required to "give back." Formed in 1998 and managed by Dean Crandall, member of the Mountain Biking Hall of Fame, HB&G's racing team can oftentimes be found repairing and maintaining mountain bike trails. The team works closely with the Boulder Off-road Alliance's (BOA) "Colorado Pay Dirt Program." Make no mistake; the team's alter ego to all this goodwill is a highly competitive beast that rears its head at every race.

This same spirit resonates even when off the trail. The HandleBar & Grill provides cable locks and keys for cyclists wishing to lock their bicycles while dining, as

This Denver restaurant, which is decorated with cycling products and memorabilia, proudly proclaims, "We ain't no chain!"

well as air pumps, tools, and tubes for any last-minute adjustments. It is this kind of energy and word-of-mouth appeal that has made the HandleBar & Grill an endearing icon for the Colorado cycling community. "The longer we were here, the more credible we'd become," admits Miller, and so, "people in the cycling community started liking to have their stuff on display here."

From signed jerseys of Rishi Grewal and Lance Armstrong, to autographed photos of Ron Kiefel and Bobby Julich, to Yeti, Morgul-Bismark, and Schwinn bicycle frames, there isn't much wall space left. Some of cycling's elite have also enjoyed dining at the HandleBar & Grill, among whom include Greg LeMond, Greg Demgen, Eddy Merckx's son Axel, and more recently, Stephen Hlawaty, author of the widely popular FalconGuides, *Mountain Biking Colorado's Front Range* and *Mountain Biking Colorado.*

HandleBar & Grill
Washington Park
305 S. Downing
Denver, CO 80209
Phone (303) 778–6761
Web site www.handlebarandgrill.com

31 Dakota Ridge and Red Rocks Trail

The Hogback is a popular mountain bike ride within easy reach of Denver or Golden. From its highest points, you can see stunning views of Red Rocks Amphitheater. The ride demands sound legs and technical skills. With some of the most technically challenging terrain in the Front Range, the Hogback is not for the faint of heart. Its rocky drop-offs and narrow singletrack, tightening atop a steep ridge of tilted strata, have left many cyclists crying "mommy." Once you descend from the hogback, the ride continues within Red Rocks Park and among its beautiful sanguine rocks.

Start: Village Walk parking lot of the Matthews/Winters Park

Distance: 6.5-mile loop

Approximate riding time: Advanced riders, 1 hour; intermediate riders, 2 hours

Aerobic level: Physically moderate to challenging due to some short, but steep climbs

Technical difficulty: Technically moderate to challenging due to steep, sandy drop-offs and climbs

Terrain: Singletrack, dirt road, and paved highway. The terrain is very rocky and sandy in spots. This is a good early-season ride, as it tends to get too sandy after long dry spells. Not recommended as an autumn ride.

Schedule: April–November

Maps: DeLorme *Colorado Atlas & Gazetteer*, page 40; USGS: Morrison, CO; Matthews/Winters Park Map: Jefferson County Open Space

Nearest town: Golden

Other trail users: Hikers, concert-goers, and picnickers

Canine compatibility: Dog-friendly (but watch out for the rattlesnakes). Dogs must be on a leash at all times.

Trail contact: Jefferson County Open Space, Golden; (303) 271-5902

Finding the Trailhead: From Denver, head west on Interstate 70 to exit 259, following signs to Morrison. Exit at 259, and turn left, driving under I-70. Now on Colorado Highway 26, turn right into Matthews/Winters Park, marked by a brown sign on the right side of the road. Park at the Village Walk parking lot in Matthews/Winters Park.

The Ride

Dakota Ridge is part of the Dakota Group, a 14-mile-long ridge of steeply sloping or tilted strata—otherwise known as a "hogback." The ridge extends from Golden to Roxborough Park and is composed of Lower Cretaceous rock units. Formed roughly 66 million years ago, the hogback is the result of the upward thrust of the Rocky Mountains' Front Range. Due to the abundance of Jurassic dinosaur fossils this area has yielded, the section of the Dakota Hogback stretching from I-70 to the town of Morrison has recently been renamed "Dinosaur Ridge," a geologically famous national landmark.

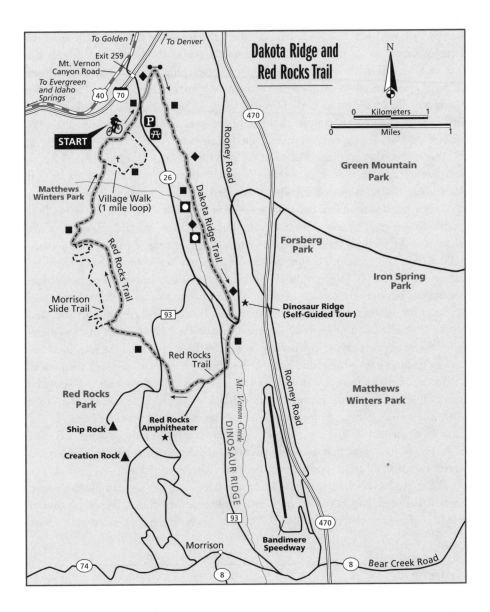

Dakota Ridge and Red Rocks Trail

To Golden
To Denver
Exit 259
Mt. Vernon Canyon Road
To Evergreen and Idaho Springs
40
70
START
P
Matthews Winters Park
Village Walk (1 mile loop)
26
Red Rocks Trail
Morrison Slide Trail
93
Red Rocks Trail
Red Rocks Park
Ship Rock ▲
Creation Rock ▲
Red Rocks Amphitheater ★
Dakota Ridge Trail
Rooney Road
470
Green Mountain Park
Forsberg Park
Iron Spring Park
Dinosaur Ridge (Self-Guided Tour)
Matthews Winters Park
Mt. Vernon Creek DINOSAUR RIDGE
Rooney Road
93
Morrison
Bandimere Speedway
470
74
8
8
Bear Creek Road

N

0   Kilometers   1
0   Miles   1

Dinosaur discoveries near Morrison date back as early as 1877 when Arthur Lakes, a part-time professor at what became the Colorado School of Mines, found a stegosaurus vertebra with a 33-inch circumference. Aside from being the first dinosaur fossils found in the western United States, many of the discoveries near Morrison were the first of their kind.

With fossilized remains of Jurassic dinosaurs, millions of years old, tucked in its geological folds, the hogback invites the mountain biker not with the terrors of a

Jurassic Park but with a subtlety that whispers the secrets of the ages. Riders begin their journey with an instant lung-buster to the top of the hogback and onto the Dakota Ridge Trail. From this knife-like ridge, sweeping views of the High Plains lie to the east, marked distinctly by Green Mountain and Denver. The Rocky Mountains lie to the west, with Mount Morrison and Red Rocks Park in plain view. The crest is marked by plentiful patches of sand and rock, remnants of a 135-million-year-old sea moving westward across Colorado.

The trail snakes atop the Hogback for roughly 2 miles. Rattlesnakes are occasionally spotted here, though they typically stick to the rock piles and tall grasses that dot Dakota Ridge. It's recommended that riders carry—and know how to use—a snake-bite kit. If you stick to the trails, it's unlikely you'll have an encounter, but better safe than sorry. The southern end of the Dakota Ridge Trail delivers some of the trickiest rocky sections found along the entire route. At mile 2.1 there's a rock face imbedded in the ground. The line to the left requires deft technical skills, particularly as it cuts sharply to the right along the edge of a big drop-off. The center line is attractive but delivers a strong blow to your front tire, not to mention your ego.

Ride for another mile before entering Red Rocks Park, en route to the Red Rocks Trail. The town of Morrison opened the park as "The Garden of the Titans" in 1906. Students studying mythology at nearby Episcopal College imagined the park to be the Titans' playground and ascribed fitting names to each rock formation.

To the north of the stage of the Red Rocks Amphitheater stands the 400-foot monolith Creation Rock. Facing Creation Rock is Shiprock, so named because it looks like a sinking ship. The formation behind the stage is the Rock of Mnemosyne, named for the Greek goddess of song and memory. Iron oxide deposits, left over from the vast inland sea that once engulfed Red Rocks Park, hardened as the ancient waters receded and are responsible for the many shades of red.

Today, Red Rocks Park is best known for its naturally formed amphitheater. Nestled between two 400-foot high red sandstone formations, the amphitheater provides near-perfect acoustics. The 9,200-seat theater provides concert-goers with

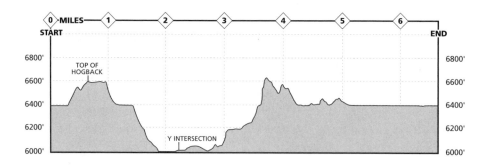

View of Red Rocks Amphitheater, with Creation Rock (left), Shiprock (right), and Rock of Mnemosyne (center).

an intimate listening experience—complete with a 30-mile panoramic view of hued plains and the stunning Denver city lights.

Once on the Red Rocks Trail, be sure to keep bearing right (north) at all trail crossings. The Red Rocks Trail offers rolling hills and mild climbs, mixed with some smooth descents. At mile 4.2 the Red Rocks Trail intersects with the Morrison Slide Trail at Cherry Gulch. Taking the Morrison Slide Trail on your left for 1.2 miles adds about a half-mile and some more climbing to your route. Continue on the Red Rocks Trail until you reach the intersection with the Village Walk. This is a 1-mile loop that will lead you back to your vehicle, whichever way you decide to turn.

Miles and Directions

0.0 Start at the Village Walk parking lot in the Matthews/Winters Park. Ride back out of the parking lot and cross CO 26. Begin ascending the rock- and sand-laden dirt road to the top of Dakota Ridge.

0.3 Bear right at the gate onto the Dakota Ridge Trail. Do not ride beyond this gate.

0.7 Top of the Hogback. To your right will be I-70, leading west into the mountains. There are some big drop-offs from here until you reach a killer, but short, climb.

1.0 Killer, but short, climb. What makes this climb difficult is its steep pitch coupled with large waterbars across the trail.

2.2 The trail comes to a Y intersection. Hang a left. By continuing straight, you'll end up having to duck under a gate to get back onto the main trail. Ride down the trail with caution. Arrive at a staircase and bear right onto the paved road (Dinosaur Ridge). Ride to where the road curves to the right and cross over the cement barricade and rejoin the trail on your left. Climb briefly and then descend sharply.

3.0 After riding down a fast singletrack, the trail once again lets out onto a paved road (Jefferson County Road 93). Be cautious here and stay in control, as the trail leads you right onto the road. Bear right here again, following signs for the Red Rocks Trail. Cross the paved road and hang an immediate left onto an access road into the Red Rocks Park. Pedal for 0.2 mile and bear right onto the singletrack Red Rocks Trail.

4.2 Junction of Morrison Slide Trail and Red Rocks Trail. Bear right here, continuing on the Red Rocks Trail.

5.8 Second intersection with Morrison Slide Trail. Stay to the right.

6.5 Arrive back at the Village Walk parking lot in the Matthews/Winters Park.

Ride Information

Trail Information

Jefferson County Open Space Trails Hotline, Evergreen; (303) 271-5975

Local Information

Denver Metro Chamber of Commerce, 1445 Market Street, Denver 80202; (303) 534-8500

Local Events and Attractions

Bandimere Speedway, Morrison; (303) 697-6001

Dinosaur Ridge, Morrison; (303) 697-DINO; www.dinoridge.org

Red Rocks Park and Amphitheater, Morrison; (303) 697-6486; www.Red-Rocks.com

Restaurants

The Fort (specializes in big game entrees), Morrison; (303) 697-4771

32 Argentine Pass

This trail leads to the top of the Continental Divide and the 13,132-foot Argentine Pass, the highest crossing of the Continental Divide in North America. From the top of the Divide, riders are rewarded with sweeping views of the Rocky Mountains, including 14,270-foot Grays and 14,267-foot Torreys Peaks to the northwest and 14,264-foot Mount Evans to the southeast. Because this trail travels above timberline, be ever mindful of rapidly changing weather conditions. By following the singletrack of the old railroad bed of the Argentine Central Grade, riders connect with FS 248 that leads to the Waldorf townsite at 11,594 feet before taking the very rocky and hazardous Argentine Pass Trail to the top. The entire route is fantastic, offering incredible singletrack, long climbs, stellar views, and a bit of Colorado mining history. This ride is best suited for well-conditioned riders.

Start: The Georgetown Loop Historic Mining and Railroad Park

Distance: 23.2-mile out-and-back

Approximate riding time: Advanced riders, 2–2.5 hours; intermediate riders, 3–3.5 hours

Aerobic level: Physically challenging due to a number of switchbacks, as well as a long, extended climb at high elevations

Technical difficulty: Technically moderate to challenging due to some rockier sections through gullies and on sections nearest the trail's higher elevations

Terrain: Four-by-four road and singletrack. The singletrack passes over an old railroad grade through dense forest, while the four-by-four road climbs to elevations of more than 13,000 feet through rocky, above-timberline terrain.

Schedule: July–September

Maps: DeLorme *Colorado Atlas & Gazetteer*, page 39; USGS: Georgetown, Gray's Peak, and Montezuma, CO; Trails Illustrated: #104, Idaho Springs-Georgetown-Loveland Pass, CO

Nearest town: Georgetown

Other trail users: Hikers and horseback riders on the Argentine Central Grade; four-by-four vehicles on FS 248

Canine compatibility: Dog-unfriendly

Trail contact: Roosevelt and Arapaho National Forests, Boulder Ranger District, Boulder; (303) 444-6600

Finding the Trailhead: From Denver, drive west on Interstate 70 for 45 miles to the town of Silver Plume. Take exit 226 from I-70 and bear left at the end of the ramp. Having driven under I-70, bear right following the historic site parking sign. You can park either in the Georgetown Loop Historic Mining and Railroad Park parking lot or along the frontage road of I-70.

The Ride

Riders begin this trail by leaving what was once the old Silver Plume depot, the first depot that served the tiny mining town. The depot began operating on September 11, 1884, and stayed in operation until 1939. Today, the depot still stands at the south edge of Silver Plume.

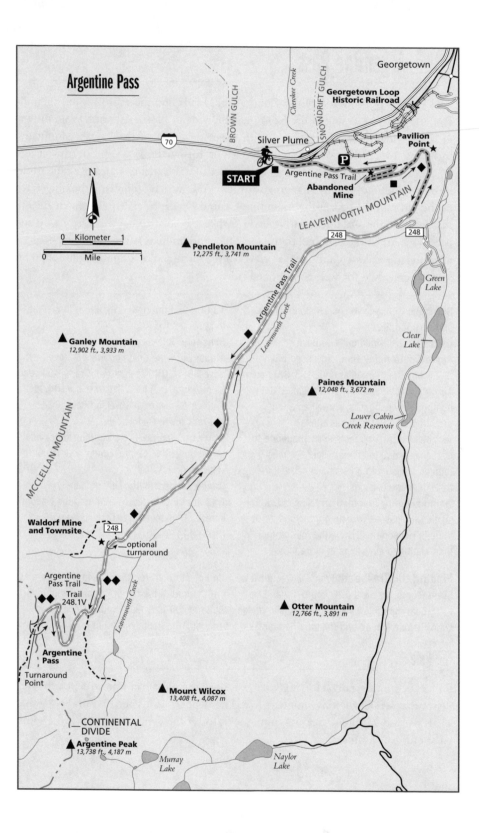

Argentine Pass

Georgetown

BROWN GULCH

Cherokee Creek

SNOWDRIFT GULCH

**Georgetown Loop
Historic Railroad**

70

Silver Plume

**Pavilion
Point**

P

START

Argentine Pass Trail

**Abandoned
Mine**

N

0   Kilometer   1

0   Mile   1

LEAVENWORTH MOUNTAIN

248

248

Green
Lake

▲ **Pendleton Mountain**
12,275 ft., 3,741 m

Argentine Pass Trail

Leavenworth Creek

Clear
Lake

▲ **Ganley Mountain**
12,902 ft., 3,933 m

▲ **Paines Mountain**
12,048 ft., 3,672 m

*Lower Cabin
Creek Reservoir*

MCCLELLAN MOUNTAIN

**Waldorf Mine
and Townsite**

248

optional
turnaround

Leavenworth Creek

**Argentine
Pass Trail**

Trail
248.1V

▲ **Otter Mountain**
12,766 ft., 3,891 m

**Argentine
Pass**

Turnaround
Point

▲ **Mount Wilcox**
13,408 ft., 4,087 m

CONTINENTAL
DIVIDE

▲ **Argentine Peak**
13,738 ft., 4,187 m

*Murray
Lake*

*Naylor
Lake*

As you leave the station, Republican Mountain lies to the right (north) across Clear Creek Canyon. A flock of bighorn sheep can often be seen on the mountain's south slope. The population of these sheep dwindled from the thousands during the early 1900s to just forty in 1950. Their decrease in numbers was due, in part, to development of local mountain towns, as well as an invasion of a parasitic lung worm causing many sheep to die of pneumonia. Aside from development and disease, some sheep were swept to their deaths in avalanches during the winter. Snow Drift Gulch is an avalanche path located on the south slope of Republican Mountain. The gulch is marked by the bright green impression that extends from the tundra of the mountain's summit to its subalpine forests. Luckily, the Colorado Division of Wildlife came to the flock's aid, restoring Colorado's state animal to its normal population.

Upon connecting with the singletrack of the Argentine Pass Trail, riders turn south underneath a canopy of aspen, as they climb across Leavenworth Mountain. Along this route, riders pass a number of relics from Colorado's bygone mining days: water tanks, abandoned mines, trestles, and mining roads. One such road appears as you near 1 mile. Here the trail becomes narrower as you pass the old mining road on your right. Continue straight, heading in an easterly direction, staying on the main trail. Generally speaking, railroad grades follow the path of least resistance and, thereby, travel along moderate inclines. Be sure to avoid any conspicuous roads that leave from the main trail.

Nearing 2 miles into the ride, the trail bears right and continues in a southwesterly direction. Oftentimes, while riding this trail, you can hear the steam-whistle blow of the Georgetown Rail making its loop through what was once one of the greatest silver-producing regions in the world.

Constructed in 1877, the Georgetown narrow gauge railroad served the mining camps between Denver and Silver Plume. Aside from hauling freight, the rail line also delivered passengers amazed at where these trains could run. Although Georgetown and Silver Plume lie only 2 miles from each other, it took 4.5 miles of track to cover the twisty 600 feet in elevation that separate the two towns. But this curious fact pales in comparison to the engineering feat accomplished at Devil's Gate.

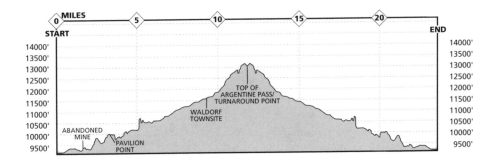

Waldorf Townsite.

Considered by some to be one of the most complex railroad loops in the world, the Devil's Gate Viaduct spans a gorge nearly 100 feet high as it crosses Clear Creek. The viaduct stretches nearly 300 feet long and forms a spiral where the track actually crosses over itself. It would take 200 men to lay the 4 miles of track of which the Devil's Gate Viaduct is a part before its completion in 1884.

After 3 miles into your ride, the contrasting views of the Continental Divide rising above and the tiny town of Silver Plume falling below are astounding when you consider what men and women had to endure during Colorado's early mining history. Perhaps, then, it comes as no surprise to discover that these hearty men and women needed some kind of relief from the hardships of the day. That relief came in the form of a dance hall atop Pavilion Point. Today, all that remains of the hall is a freestanding stone fireplace and chimney.

Once it connects with FS 248, the route passes a variety of cascading hillside waterfalls, particularly if you're riding during June and early July. As you continue on FS 248, an old telegraph line will be to your left. Upon reaching the townsite of Waldorf, it's a grueling 2.3 miles to the top of Argentine Pass along the Argentine Pass Trail.

Constructed in 1869 under the management of Stephen Decatur, Argentine Pass attempted to connect the ore smelters in Denver to the gold and silver mines near Breckenridge. When finished, the direct wagon route would cross the Continental Divide at 13,132 feet, making it the highest crossing of the divide in North America.

Once atop the pass and the Continental Divide, you're rewarded with incredible views. Looking to the northwest, the most prominent peak is 14,270-foot Grays Peak; 14,267-foot Torreys Peak lies just behind and to the right. Mount Evans, ever-popular for the road that carries drivers to its 14,264-foot summit, lies to the southeast.

The descent from Argentine Pass is fast and rocky. Be careful of vehicular traffic along FS 248. The trail offers speed freaks a top-ringing good time the whole way down.

Miles and Directions

0.0 Starting from the Georgetown Loop Historic Mining and Railroad Park, begin riding westward along the frontage road.

0.4 Bear left, heading in a southeasterly direction, following the Argentine Pass Trail.

1.6 Pass an abandoned mine. Keep your eyes open here, as you'll eventually bear right before passing any other abandoned mines.

1.9 The route cuts to the right. While a path continues straight ahead and eventually passes a second abandoned mine on the right, you should bear right at this time, continuing your ride and heading in a southwesterly direction. The trail is considerably narrower singletrack than in the first 2 miles. If you pass this second mine, you've gone too far. Turn around, and reconnect to the main route.

2.3 Arrive at a trail intersection. One trail cuts sharply to the left and heads in an easterly direction. Another trail crosses the Argentine Pass Trail and descends in a westerly direction. Be sure to continue climbing here on the main trail of the Argentine Central Grade.

3.3 Arrive at Pavilion Point.

4.2 The Argentine Pass Trail will intersect with FS 248. Do not be put off by the sign at this intersection that identifies this road as 248.1. Regional maps identify this road as FS 248. Continue riding on FS 248 toward the Waldorf townsite about 5 miles down the trail. Be advised that this road is open to vehicular traffic.

6.6–7.3 FS 248 forks two times. At each fork, continue straight on FS 248.

9.3 Reach the townsite of Waldorf. At this point, FS 248 cuts right (north) on its way to McClellan Mountain. Continue heading straight, in a southerly direction, following the very steep and rocky Argentine Pass Trail to the top of Argentine Pass. **Option:** The Waldorf townsite makes for a good turnaround point for riders less than gonzo-abusive to their bikes and bodies.

10.2 The trail forks. The left fork has a posted sign that reads 248.1U. The right fork has a posted sign that reads 248.1V. Bear right here onto Trail 248.1V, taking the higher of the two trails and switchbacking toward Argentine Pass.

11.6 Reach the top of Argentine Pass and the Continental Divide. Return the way you came.

23.2 Arrive at your vehicle.

Ride Information

Local Information

Georgetown Visitors Center, P.O. Box 834, Georgetown 80444; (800) 472-8230; www.georgetowncolorado.com

Local Events and Attractions

Georgetown Loop Historic Mining and Railroad Park, Georgetown; (303) 569-2403 or (800) 691-4-FUN; www.georgetownloop.com

Hamill House Museum, Georgetown; (303) 569-2840

Hotel de Paris Museum, Georgetown; (303) 569-2311

Lodging

Georgetown Motor Inn, Georgetown; (303) 569-3201 or (800) 884-3201

Restaurants

Alpine Inn Restaurant, Georgetown; (303) 569-2931

Crazy Horse Bar and Restaurant, Georgetown; (303) 569-3032

In Addition

Narrow Gauge Railroad

As mountain bikers, we owe a debt of gratitude to the narrow gauge railroad lines whose beds have since become some of our finest mountain bike rides. The Argentine Pass Trail, the Switzerland Trail, and the Narrow Gauge Trail paralleling the North Fork of the South Platte River in Pine Valley Ranch Park all owe their existence to the narrow gauge railroad.

In a way, the mountain bike and the narrow gauge railroad share a similar evolution. Both fed from the need for finding an easier way of transportation through the Rocky Mountains. The only difference may be that recreation, not profit, prompted the development of the mountain bike. No one can argue, however, that either of these modes of transportation doesn't share elements of both.

To circumvent the difficulties of construction along steep canyon walls and high mountain passes, the narrow gauge railroads were built on a 3-foot-wide track bed, rather than the industry standard of a 4-foot, 8.5-inch track bed. Overall, this allowed the narrow gauge railroads greater flexibility in negotiating around sharper curves and up and down steep grades than ever before.

In 1870 the Denver & Rio Grande Railroad (D&RGR) laid Colorado's first narrow gauge line, which extended north from Denver through Wyoming. Following the D&RGR's lead, and spurred by the growing mining industry, the Colorado Central Railroad was first in building a narrow gauge line that extended into the Rocky Mountain interior in 1872. The line would provide service for the booming mining industries up Clear Creek. At one-third the expense of standard rail construction, the narrow gauge railroad soon became the new standard for rail building in Colorado's Rocky Mountains.

The emergence of narrow gauge lines greatly attributed to the expansion of mines throughout the western portion of Colorado during the 1870s and 1880s. A waning gold and silver mining economy, coupled with the higher costs of converting standard rails to narrow gauge rails, caused the eventual decline of the narrow gauge railroad by the mid-1890s.

But while narrow gauge lines stopped being constructed, those that had been laid in previous years remained as a tourist attraction for passengers wishing to view the splendid mountain scenery past which these trains rode. Indeed, the D&RGR included an Around the Circle tour that began in Denver and traveled south to New Mexico before heading northwest to Durango. From Durango, passengers could board the Rio Grande Southern Railroad and experience a similar adventure throughout Colorado's southwest before returning to Denver.

Today, with our adapted version of the "iron horse," we can experience our own self-guided tours over the same narrow gauge track beds and marvel at the industry of those who built the rails in some of our country's most beautiful, and sometimes hostile, environments.

For more information, contact

Colorado State Parks
1313 Sherman Street
Room 618
Denver, CO 80203
(303) 866–3437

Trails and Rails Downhill Mountain Bike Tours
P.O. Box 217
Georgetown, CO 80444
(970) 569–2403 or (800) 691–4FUN

Rails-to-Trails Conservancy's National Headquarters
1100 Seventeenth Street NW
Tenth Floor
Washington, D.C. 20036
(202) 331–9696

33 Elk Meadows and Bergen Peak

The trails that weave through Elk Meadow Park are some of the finest in all of Jefferson County. While the climb to the top of Bergen Peak is a bit of a grunt, the views of Pikes Peak, Mount Evans, Mount Bierstadt, and the Continental Divide are not to be missed. Not only that, but the descent from the peak packs enough punch for the climbing to seem like a distant memory. The singletrack throws out smoother softer sections, but you leave remembering the screaming descent of threading tight rock outcroppings and barreling over big drop-offs. Oh yeah, there are more switchbacks here than pine cones.

Start: The Sleepy S Trail at the Lewis Ridge Road parking lot and trailhead

Distance: 11.3-mile loop

Approximate riding time: Advanced riders, 1.5 hours; intermediate riders, 2–3 hours

Aerobic level: Physically challenging due to the climb to Bergen Peak

Technical difficulty: Technically moderate to challenging due to some tighter singletrack that weaves through rock outcroppings and over big drop-offs

Terrain: Wide and narrow singletrack and doubletrack that roll over smooth terrain through meadows; also steeper ascending and descending sections that roll over rocky terrain and through mixed conifer forests

Schedule: Late May–October

Maps: DeLorme *Colorado Atlas & Gazetteer*, page 39; USGS: Squaw Pass and Evergreen, CO; Jefferson County Open Space Elk Meadow Park Map

Nearest town: Bergen Park

Other trail users: Hikers, horseback riders, and picnickers

Canine compatibility: Dog-friendly, with a dog training area located on the south side of Stagecoach Boulevard

Trail contact: Jefferson County Open Space, Golden; (303) 271-5925

Finding the Trailhead: From Denver, drive west on Interstate 70 for 22.5 miles to exit 252 and the Evergreen Parkway. Drive east (heading south to the town of Evergreen) on the Evergreen Parkway (CO 74) for 4.5 miles through the town of Bergen Park. Bear right onto Lewis Ridge Road and then right again into the Elk Meadow Park parking lot. Park in the Lewis Ridge Road lot.

The Ride

Elk Meadow Park descended from a long line of ranchers. The barn that stands in Elk Meadow speaks to its ranching history. As part of the Homestead Act of 1862, the U.S. government awarded homesteaders Robert Strain, Charles Abbott, Thomas Audrey, and Charlotte Dow 160-acre tracts. These four were the original homesteaders of Elk Meadow.

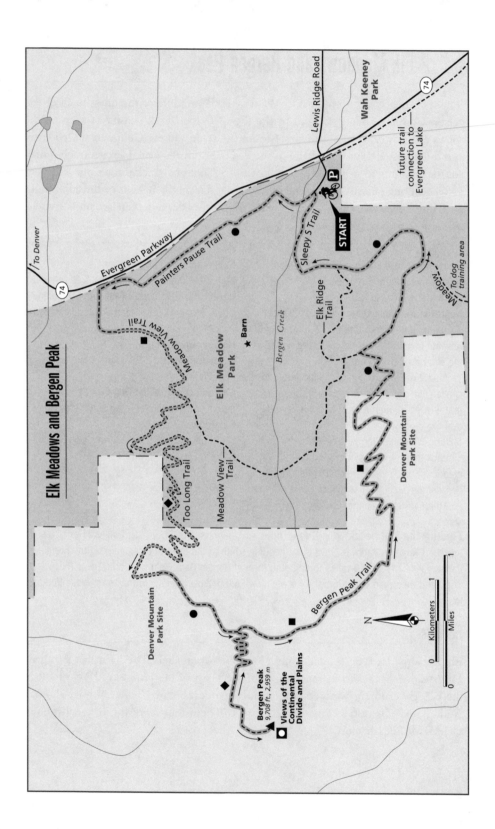

Elk Meadows and Bergen Peak

To Denver

74

Evergreen Parkway

Lewis Ridge Road

Wah Keeney Park

74

future trail connection to Evergreen Lake

P

START

Painters Pause Trail

Sleepy S Trail

Elk Ridge Trail

Meadow View Trail

Bergen Creek

Barn

Elk Meadow Park

Meadow

To dog training area

Meadow View Trail

Too Long Trail

Denver Mountain Park Site

Denver Mountain Park Site

Bergen Peak Trail

Denver Mountain Park Site

Bergen Peak
9,708 ft., 2,959 m
Views of the Continental Divide and Plains

N

Kilometers

Miles

0   1

To this, Theodore Johnson would add his own 1,140 acres of homesteaded land through various land acquisitions from 1905 to 1943. Two years after Johnson's final land acquisition, Darst Buchanan would purchase all 1,140 acres for his purebred Hereford cattle. In 1949 Cole Means bought the land from Buchanan as summer pasture for his Texas herds. In 1977 the area surrounding Elk Meadow would again be sold. This time, however, the buyer was Jefferson County, and those that roamed the meadow weren't Herefords or Longhorns but, rather, citizens of Jefferson County and the surrounding area.

Perhaps the reason Elk Meadow passed through so many hands is that it offered those who would acquire it such a variety of wildlife habitat. Indeed, Elk Meadow Park includes a wide diversity of ecosystems.

The first mile of trail rolls over smooth, wide singletrack, climbing moderately in a northern direction. The Meadow View Trail passes through meadow and grassland ecosystems over wide singletrack, turning into doubletrack at roughly 1.5 miles. The less steep and lower elevations found within the meadow and grassland ecosystems provide riders with an abundance of grasses, shrubs, wildflowers, and wavy terrain. The Richardson ground squirrel, a relative of the prairie dog, thrives in this ecosystem. In fact, there are a number of these squirrel colonies in the park itself.

As the Meadow View Trail continues to rise to meet the Too Long Trail, riders are introduced to a number of tough switchbacks. After these switchbacks, riders begin to enter the transitional zone, through which the Too Long Trail runs. The scattered forest of ponderosa pine growing at a distance from one another marks the transitional zone. This ponderosa parkland ecosystem offers shelter and food to the many deer and elk (hence the park's name) that frequent this area during the winter months.

By 2.5 miles, the trail gets a bit tougher as it continues to climb, delivering a number of rocky sections with which to contend. This section of trail leads through an aspen grove that introduces riders to the foothills zone. The foothills zone will typically offer steeper slopes and an abundance of densely populated Douglas fir, with islands of aspen groves thrown in the mix. Not to be outdone by their more numerous neighbors, aspen provide the shade required for young conifers to grow.

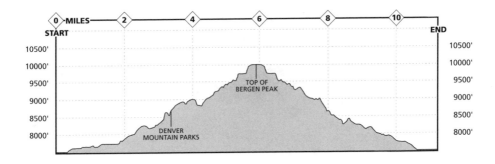

Having ridden for about a mile through the Denver Mountain Parks area, riders enter into an incredible lodgepole pine forest. The singletrack here is soft with pine needles as the trail whips through these dense stands of evergreens. Enter the montane zone. The slopes here are steeper than in the foothills zone and are generally covered with lodgepole pine.

Once connecting with the Bergen Peak Trail, riders have to contend with a pretty grueling climb to reach the top of Bergen Peak, where they are rewarded with westerly views of the Continental Divide and easterly views of the Great Plains. Bergen Peak introduces riders to the subalpine environment: little plant life, save for the green lichen that grows on exposed rock outcroppings.

The descent from Bergen Peak is a screamer. After a technical rocky section, riders reach the intersection of the Bergen Peak Trail and the Too Long Trail. Continuing south along the Bergen Peak Trail, riders have to negotiate over some huge drop-offs, as well as tighter, rockier sections. After a fun switchback section, riders connect with the Meadow View Trail and return to their vehicles. Since the descent can be very fast, be aware of other trail users.

Miles and Directions

0.0 From the parking lot, bear right and begin riding on the Sleepy S Trail, heading in an easterly direction toward the Evergreen Parkway.

0.1 The Sleepy S Trail intersects with the Painters Pause Trail. Bear left onto the Painters Pause Trail and begin riding in a northerly direction.

1.1 The Painters Pause Trail intersects with the Meadow View Trail. Bear left onto the Meadow View Trail and begin riding in a southwesterly direction.

2.1 The Meadow View Trail intersects with the Too Long Trail. Bear right onto the Too Long Trail and begin climbing up the tight switchbacks.

3.2 Enter into Denver Mountain Parks.

4.5 The Too Long Trail intersects with the Bergen Peak Trail. Continue climbing on the Bergen Peak Trail in a westerly direction as it makes its way to the top of Bergen Peak.

5.6 Reach the top of Bergen Peak. From here, backtrack to the intersection of the Bergen Peak Trail and the Too Long Trail.

6.7 Reach the intersection of the Bergen Peak Trail and the Too Long Trail. Bear right, continuing on the Bergen Peak Trail and heading in a southerly direction.

9.4 Bergen Peak Trail intersects with the Meadow View Trail. Bear right onto the Meadow View Trail.

◀ Navigating the rocky descent of the Bergen Peak Trail.

10.1 Meadow View Trail intersects with the Sleepy S Trail. Bear left onto the Sleepy S Trail and ride in a northerly direction.

10.8 The Sleepy S Trail intersects with the Elk Ridge Trail to the left. Stay on the Sleepy S Trail, continuing in a northerly direction.

11.3 Arrive at your vehicle.

Ride Information

Local Information

Evergreen Chamber of Commerce, P.O. Box 97, Evergreen 80437; (303) 674-3412

Local Events and Attractions

Evergreen Music Festival at Evergreen Lake, July; (303) 674-3412

Hiwan Homestead Museum, Evergreen; (303) 674-6262

Restaurants

The Whipple Tree, Evergreen; (303) 674-9944

34 Mount Falcon Park

With 2,130 acres and 11.1 miles of trails to its credit, Mount Falcon Park delivers some of Denver's finest singletrack. The park's multiuse trail system leads visitors to a variety of historical sites and overlooks: the Summer White House ruins, the remains of John Brisben Walker's castle in the mountains, Eagle Eye Shelter, and the panoramic views of Mount Evans and the Continental Divide, the Great Plains, and Red Rocks Park. Riders cross meadows and gullies and pass red sandstone boulders on their climb up Mount Falcon. Picnic tables and rest rooms are provided at trailheads.

Start: The eastern Mount Falcon trailhead
Distance: 9.6-mile lariat
Approximate riding time: Advanced riders, 1-1.5 hours; intermediate riders, 1.5-2 hours
Aerobic level: Physically moderate to challenging due to a few steep climbs
Technical difficulty: Technically easy to moderate due to wide singletrack and a moderate degree of rocks and roots on the trail
Terrain: Singletrack and doubletrack, mostly on smooth, hard-packed dirt; some rocks and roots with which to contend through semiarid conditions
Schedule: April–November
Maps: DeLorme Colorado Atlas & Gazetteer, page 40; USGS: Morrison, CO
Nearest town: Morrison
Other trail users: Hikers and horseback riders; Turkey Trot Trail is a hikers-only trail
Canine compatibility: Dog-friendly
Trail contact: Jefferson County Open Space, Golden; (303) 271-5925

Finding the Trailhead: From Denver, drive west on Interstate 70 for roughly 13 miles to the Golden/Morrison exit. Bear left (east) onto Colorado Highway 26 and drive for roughly 4 miles to the town of Morrison. In Morrison, bear right onto the one-way Stone Street and then right (west) again onto Main Street and drive through the town to Colorado Highway 8. Bear left (south) onto CO 8 and drive for a little over a mile to Forest Avenue. Bear right (west) onto Forest Avenue and drive for 0.2 mile before taking your first right (north) onto Vine Avenue, following the signs to the trailhead and the eastern access of Mount Falcon. Park in Mount Falcon Park's east parking area, off CO 8.

The Ride

Your ride begins immediately with a tough climb up Castle Trail. Although the singletrack is wide and smooth, the climb is particularly challenging because of the various waterbars that cross the trail. As if that wasn't enough, the first few miles also deliver some intermittent rockier sections with which to contend before retreating into the cooler confines of a mixed conifer forest.

As the Castle Trail switches back a number of times, you're offered beautiful views of the Denver skyline and Red Rocks Park. While riding up to Mount Falcon, you'll often hear the high winding engines of the race cars at nearby Bandimere Speedway.

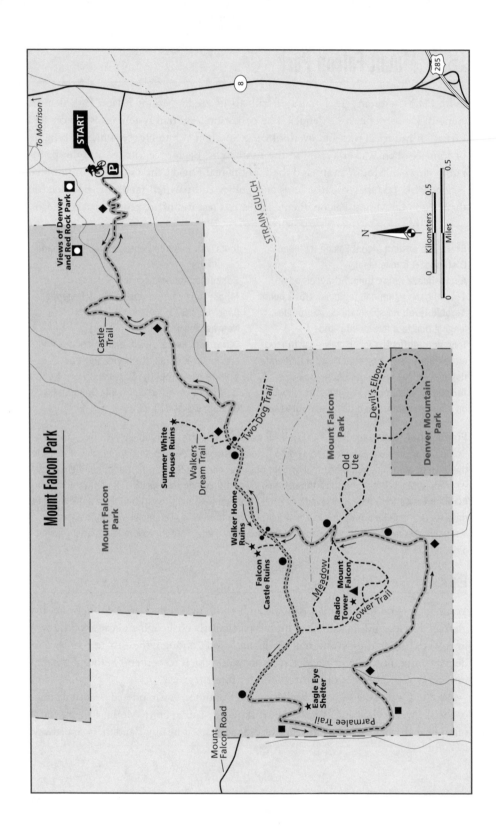

Mount Falcon Park

Mount Falcon Park

Mount Falcon Park

To Morrison

START

P

Views of Denver
and Red Rock Park

Castle
Trail

STRAIN GULCH

285

8

Summer White
House Ruins

Walkers
Dream Trail

Two-Dog Trail

Walker Home
Ruins

Falcon
Castle Ruins

Meadow

Mount Falcon
Park

Old
Ute

Devil's Elbow

Denver Mountain
Park

Radio
Tower

Mount
Falcon

Tower Trail

Mount
Falcon Road

Eagle Eye
Shelter

Parmalee Trail

N

Kilometers

Miles

0   0.5

0   0.5

Once you intersect with Walker's Dream Trail, you can hike or ride the short 0.3 mile to the Summer White House ruins. Named after John Brisben Walker, the trail leads to the site of his once-cherished dream: to have a summer home for the presidents of the United States.

With funds collected from ten-cent contributions by the children of Colorado, among other donations, Walker began the campaign for the presidents' home in 1911. Part of the campaign included displaying the marble cornerstone—mined locally from Marble, Colorado—in Denver to generate local interest. By 1914 Walker had already written a number of letters to President Woodrow Wilson, inviting him to join in the laying of the cornerstone. After commissioning Denver architect J. B. Benedict to design the Summer White House, Walker funded the foundation himself. By the fall of 1914, sans President Wilson, the cornerstone for the Summer White House had been positioned. President Wilson's absence would prove to be a fitting omen to what lie ahead for the summer retreat.

Though thousands of dollars had been collected for the Summer White House project, construction never resumed due to the onset of World War I and Walker's dwindling financial resources. Today, all that is left of this dream is the foundation and the marble cornerstone, which reads "Summer home for the presidents of the United States, the gift of the people of Colorado, 1911." Today, however, what was once a gift *of* the people has become a gift *for* the people, a gift that takes its shape in the beautiful views of the Continental Divide.

From the site of the Summer White House, our ride continues southwest along the Castle Trail. From here to its intersection with the Meadow Trail, the Castle Trail becomes a smooth doubletrack, as it runs through mixed conifer forests. The cruise is mellow and sweet along the ridgeline, offering views of the Continental Divide to the west and Eastern Plains to the east. At the intersection of the Castle and Meadow Trails, you can take a short hike to the ruins of Walker's castle home, along the ridge just west of the Summer White House site.

Begun in 1909, Walker's elaborate stone mansion included a northwest tower that encompassed a library, living room, master bedroom, and observation deck, while the north wing of the mansion included a reception room, dining room, and

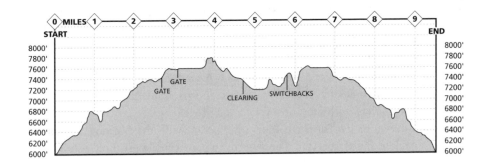

Walker home ruins.

kitchen. The south wing provided a den, a large music room, and several bedrooms. Unfortunately, lightning would, indeed, strike twice for Walker: once figuratively in the collapse of the Summer White House project and once literally when it struck the mansion in 1918. The lightning caused a fire that burned the mansion to the ground. Today, only the mansion's stone walls and its numerous fireplaces are all that remain of this onetime castle—that and a trail connecting riders to the past, the present, and the Parmalee.

The Parmalee Trail is quite sinuous as it runs through some of the most beautiful sections of Mount Falcon Park. In an ironic twist, however, riders must first pass through the scarred remains of a forest fire (not the one responsible for the loss of Walker's castle) before connecting with the Parmalee Trail. At this intersection of the Castle and Parmalee Trails, you'll find a rest area with rest rooms. Riding the tight singletrack of the Parmalee Trail, you descend through mixed conifer forests over moderately technical terrain of rock and sand. After speeding through a clearing below the Eagle Eye Shelter, you cross a stream and are immediately thrown into a steep climb, complete with erosion-resistant waterbars.

After climbing to the Parmalee Trail's intersection with the Meadow Trail, it's a short run back to the Castle Trail. The descent to your vehicle via the Castle Trail is an impressive one. While there are a number of opportunities to catch air, be aware of other trail users and check your speed.

Miles and Directions

0.0 Heading in a westerly direction, begin riding on the Castle Trail singletrack.

0.1 The Castle Trail intersects with the Turkey Trot Trail, a hikers-only trail. Bear left, continuing on the Castle Trail.

1.4 The Castle Trail again intersects with the Turkey Trot Trail. Bear left, continuing on the Castle Trail.

1.7 The Castle Trail leads up a steep and rocky climb through a mixed conifer forest.

2.6 Arrive at the high point with a gazebo and picnic table off to your right. Here, the Castle Trail intersects with Walker's Dream Trail, a short 0.3-mile trail that leads to the Summer White House ruins.

2.7 After passing through a gate, the Castle Trail intersects with the Two-Dog Trail to your left. Continue straight on the wide doubletrack of the Castle Trail.

3.1 After passing through another gate, the Castle Trail intersects with the Meadow Trail to the left and the Walker Home ruins trail. Caution: The foundation of the castle is unstable, so keep off. Continue on the Castle Trail in a southwesterly direction.

3.5 The Castle Trail again intersects with the Meadow Trail on the left. Continue on the Castle Trail, which leads to the Eagle Eye Shelter, heading in a northerly direction.

3.8 The Castle Trail intersects with the Parmalee Trail. Bear left onto the Parmalee Trail, continuing in a southerly direction. The doubletrack rejoins the singletrack on the Parmalee Trail.

4.7 The Parmalee Trail enters into a clearing where you'll see the Eagle Eye Shelter, an old fire-watch tower.

5.8 Begin a switchback ascent.

6.1 The Parmalee Trail intersects with the Meadow Trail and the Tower Trail. Veer right onto the Meadow Trail, heading in an easterly direction, toward your reconnection with the Castle Trail.

6.5 The Meadow Trail intersects the Castle Trail near the Walker Home ruins. Bear right onto the Castle Trail and retrace your path to the start.

9.6 Arrive at your vehicle.

Ride Information

Trail Information

Mount Falcon Park's trails are sometimes closed due to heavy rains. To check on closures, call (303) 271-5975

Local Information

Denver Metro Chamber of Commerce, 1445 Market Street, Denver 80202; (303) 534-8500

Local Events and Attractions

Bandimere Speedway, Morrison; (303) 697-6001

Red Rocks Park and Amphitheater, Morrison; (303) 697-6486; www.Red-Rocks.com

Restaurants

The Fort (specializes in big game entrees), Morrison; (303) 697-4771

35 Alderfer/Three Sisters Park

Alderfer/Three Sisters Park offers riders a network of great trails. From smooth to rocky singletrack along speedy descents and tough climbs, the trails offer something for everyone. The rock formations of Three Sisters and the Brother have served as area landmarks for years and are an incredible sight to see. Evergreen Mountain rewards the tireless rider with great views of the town of Evergreen. Offering a variety of picnic areas, rest rooms, and terrain, this park can be great for families, as well as loner mountain-bike types. As such, it can get pretty crowded on the weekends.

Start: The Alderfer/Three Sisters Park trail-head. Cross Buffalo Park Road and begin riding on the East Evergreen Mountain Trail on the south side of the road.
Distance: 7.7-mile loop
Approximate riding time: Advanced riders, 45 minutes; intermediate riders, 1–1.5 hours
Aerobic level: Physically moderate due to some extended climbs
Technical difficulty: Technically moderate due to the wide singletrack; more technical with rocks on the tight Three Sisters Trail

Terrain: Singletrack over sometimes smooth and wide or rocky and tight trail; rocky sections, meadows, and forests
Schedule: May–October
Maps: DeLorme *Colorado Atlas & Gazetteer*, page 39; USGS: Evergreen and Conifer, CO; Jefferson County Open Space Alderfer/Three Sisters Park Map
Nearest town: Evergreen
Other trail users: Hikers and horseback riders
Canine compatibility: Dog-friendly
Trail contact: Jefferson County Open Space, Evergreen; (303) 271-5975

Finding the Trailhead: From Denver, drive west on Interstate 70 for 22.5 miles to exit 252 and the Evergreen Parkway. Drive east (heading south to the town of Evergreen) on the Evergreen Parkway (CO 74) for 8.4 miles before turning right after Evergreen Lake onto Seventy-third Road. Drive on Seventy-third Road for 0.6 mile before turning right onto Buffalo Park Road, following the brown sign for Alderfer/Three Sisters Park. Drive on Buffalo Park Road for 1.5 miles to the east parking lot and trailhead on the right (a second parking lot is located another 0.5 mile up the road). Cross the road and begin riding.

The Ride

Alderfer/Three Sisters Park partly takes its name from the Alderfer family, who still owns and operates the nearby ranch. E. J. Alderfer and his wife, Arleta, moved into the Dollison ranch house in 1945. The Alderfers first raised silver fox (hence, the trail name) and Aberdeen Angus cattle (best-tasting roast beef sandwiches' main ingredient). In 1970 the Alderfers switched from raising silver fox to pasturing horses. From 1977 to 1986 the Alderfer family donated portions of their more than 1,000 acres to Jefferson County Open Space.

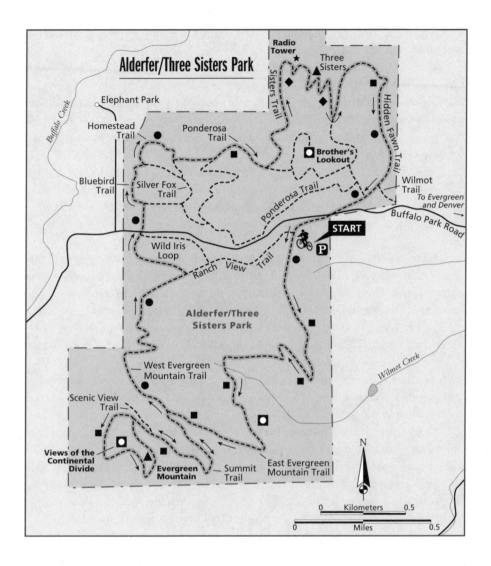

We begin riding in a clockwise direction along the East Evergreen Mountain Trail, on the south side of Buffalo Park Road. The East Evergreen Mountain Trail climbs moderately over wide, smooth singletrack as it switches back up Evergreen Mountain. All of these switchbacks are difficult but manageable to varying degrees. The waterbars strewn across the trail add to the degree of difficulty. Don't be tempted by the bench you pass on your right. The more ambitious mountain biker knows better and will press on. After crossing Wilmot Creek, riders are offered a fine overlook of the surrounding hillsides to the south. Once atop Evergreen Mountain, beautiful views of the Continental Divide are the climber's spoils.

The descent along the Summit Trail and the West Evergreen Mountain Trail is incredibly fast over smooth and wide singletrack and through mixed conifer forests. Parts of these forests have been thinned of much of their lodgepole pine in an attempt to revitalize the forest. Before thinning, there were roughly 5,000 lodgepole pine per acre. With this many trees crowding such a small space, there was little room for new trees to grow.

The Wild Iris Loop, Bluebird Trail, and Homestead Trails offer easy rides through wide-open meadows. It's not until you get to the Sisters Trail that the route becomes considerably tougher. After 6 miles, the terrain becomes very rocky as the trail climbs more steeply through large boulders on its way north to the Three Sisters rock formation.

The second half of the park's name derives from these rock outcroppings. Made of metamorphic rock of the Precambrian era, these outcrops consist largely of silver plume quartz. These dominant rock formations are a familiar landmark for Evergreen residents old and new and lie in the park's northernmost corner.

Spencer Wyant originally owned this area of the park, which included the Three Sisters Peak. Luckily, like E. J. Alderfer, Spencer Wyant also donated much of his land to Jefferson County Open Space.

Once arriving at the top of a saddle between two of the Three Sisters summits, your troubles of climbing seem to vanish as you digest the meaning of the words that are inscribed in a nearby rock, "Meetings, whether between moments or lifetimes, are certain when you are friends." Perhaps this is a sentiment that we can share not only with whom we now ride, but also with the Alderfer and Wyant families.

Wishing newfound friends well, riders descend south from the Three Sisters Peak along the Sisters Trail. The first part of this descent delivers tight, rocky sections, big drop-offs, and a number of steeps. After connecting with the Hidden Fawn Trail, the route offers a welcome contrast to the Sisters Trail in the form of a smooth and mellow cruise on wide singletrack back to your vehicle.

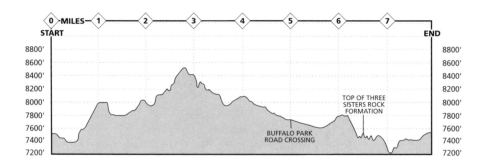

Working through the rough stuff. PHOTO: AMANDA HLAWATY

Miles and Directions

0.0 Start riding on the East Evergreen Mountain Trail, heading in a southwesterly direction.

0.2 The East Evergreen Mountain trail will intersect with the Ranch View Trail. Bear left here, continuing on the Evergreen Mountain Trail, heading in a southerly direction.

2.2 The East Evergreen Mountain Trail becomes the West Evergreen Mountain Trail and intersects with the Summit Trail on the left. Bear left onto the Summit Trail, passing the Scenic View Trail on your right. Just after passing the Scenic View Trail, bear right where the Summit Trail loops back to itself, heading up Evergreen Mountain in a counterclockwise direction. **Option:** Riders can opt to take the short 0.2-mile Scenic View Trail to an overlook of an old ranch house.

3.6 Return to the junction of the East/West Evergreen Mountain Trail and the Summit Trail. Bear left, continuing on the West Evergreen Mountain Trail.

4.7 The West Evergreen Mountain Trail intersects with the Wild Iris Loop Trail. Bear left onto the Wild Iris Loop Trail, as it heads west through a meadow.

5.0 Cross Buffalo Park Road and enter into the west parking area of Alderfer/Three Sisters Park. Bear left onto the Bluebird Trail, heading in a northerly direction. **Option:** At this point riders can also bear right onto the Buffalo Park Road and return to their vehicles.

5.3 The Bluebird Trail intersects with the Homestead Trail. Bear left onto the Homestead Trail.

5.7 The Homestead Trail intersects with the Silver Fox Trail. Bear left onto the Silver Fox Trail, heading in an easterly direction.

5.8 The Silver Fox Trail intersects with the Ponderosa Trail. Bear left onto the Ponderosa Trail, continuing in an easterly direction.

5.9 The Ponderosa Trail intersects with the Sisters Trail. Bear left onto the Sisters Trail, heading in a northerly direction.

6.5 Reach the top of the Three Sisters rock formation. Descend via the Sisters Trail.

6.9 The Sisters Trail intersects with the Hidden Fawn Trail. Bear left onto the Hidden Fawn Trail, as it continues in a northerly direction.

7.5 The Hidden Fawn Trail intersects with the Wilmot Trail on your left. Continue riding in a southerly direction on the Hidden Fawn Trail toward the trailhead.

7.7 Arrive at the trailhead and your vehicle.

Ride Information

Trail Information

Evergreen Park and Recreation District, Evergreen; (303) 674-6441

Local Information

Evergreen Chamber of Commerce, P.O. Box 97, Evergreen 80437; (303) 674-3412

Local Events and Attractions

Evergreen Music Festival at Evergreen Lake, July; (303) 674-3412

Hiwan Homestead Museum, Evergreen; (303) 674-6262

Restaurants

The Evergreen Inn, Evergreen; (303) 674-5495

36 Meyer Ranch Park

Meyer Ranch Park offers riders one of the milder singletrack rides in all of Jefferson County. As such, it makes for a great beginner's ride. However, the area network of trails accommodates riders of all abilities. The easier Owl's Perch and Lodge Pole Loop Trails are ideal for beginners, while the Sunny Aspen and Old Ski Run Trails steadily climb to an overlook. There are no sections of the route that are particularly strenuous or technical; although, riding in excess of 8,000 feet elevation does require one to be in good physical condition. The short 4.4 miles of this route takes riders through wide-open meadows and dense woodland.

Start: The Meyer Ranch Park trailhead

Distance: 4.4-mile double lariat

Approximate riding time: Advanced riders, 30 minutes; intermediate riders, 30–60 minutes

Aerobic level: Physically easy to moderate due to the short length of the trail. The going gets tougher as you climb along the Sunny Aspen and Old Ski Run Trails, near the trail's high point.

Technical difficulty: Technically easy to moderate due to smoother, hard-packed singletrack that occasionally rolls over more technical rockier sections

Terrain: Singletrack and doubletrack through meadows and mixed conifer forests over hard and smooth terrain

Schedule: May–October

Maps: DeLorme *Colorado Atlas & Gazetteer*, page 40; USGS: Conifer, CO; Jefferson County Open Space Meyer Ranch Park map

Nearest town: Aspen Park

Other trail users: Hikers, bird-watchers, and horseback riders

Canine compatibility: Dog-friendly

Trail contact: Jefferson County Open Space, Evergreen; (303) 271-5975

Finding the Trailhead: From North Denver, drive west on Interstate 70 to Colorado Highway 470. Drive south on CO 470 for roughly 5.8 miles before bearing right and heading west onto U.S. Highway 285 (Hampden Avenue). Drive on US 285 for roughly 11.6 miles before turning right onto South Turkey Creek Road. Pull into the Meyer Ranch Park parking lot.

From South Denver, drive west on US 285 (Hampden Avenue) for roughly 25 miles. Turn right onto South Turkey Creek Road and pull into the Meyer Ranch Park parking lot.

The Ride

Meyer Ranch Park takes its name from Norman F. and Ethel E. Meyer, former owners of the park site. Purchasing the land in 1950, the Meyers operated a successful grazing and haying business until 1986 when the land was acquired by Jefferson County Open Space.

Long before the Meyers moved in, the land was owned by Louis Ramboz, who purchased it from its original homesteader, Duncan McIntyre, in 1883. While Ramboz worked his ranch primarily for hay, timber, and cattle until 1912, legend suggests

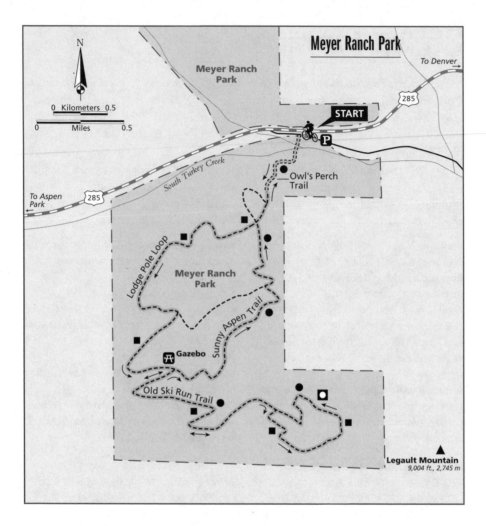

that in the late 1880s he leased parts of his ranch to the P. T. Barnum Circus as the winter quarters for circus animals. While remodeling the house in 1955, Norman Meyer stumbled across a very curious wooden board. Inscribed in the board were the words, CIRCUS TOWN, 1889.

Riders begin by climbing through lush meadows that display a variety of wildflowers including columbine, shooting star, and wood lily. After connecting with the Lodge Pole Loop Trail, riders continue climbing through evergreen and aspen forests along soft and smooth singletrack. The Sunny Aspen Trail challenges even the most accomplished of riders with moderately technical sections that include steep terrain and waterbars.

Riders continue on the Old Ski Run Trail, which passes through a portion of the park that was once used as a ski hill in the 1940s. In an ironic twist of the old telemark maxim, "Earn your turns," the climbing continues along the Old Ski Run Trail over wide, smooth singletrack and through mixed conifer and aspen forests.

The switchbacks that lie on the loop of the Old Ski Run Trail are moderately tight and offer a challenge before the trail begins its descent on smooth and fast singletrack. Shortly after passing the point where the Old Ski Run Trail forked to create its loop, a switchback lies in ambush of riders that are speeding too fast.

The remaining descent offers little in the way of moguls. Riders can make short work of their speedy descents back to their vehicles.

Miles and Directions

0.0 Begin climbing in a westerly direction on the wide doubletrack of the Owl's Perch Trail.

0.1 After passing the rest room, the Owl's Perch Trail will fork. Bear left onto the singletrack of the Owl's Perch Trail and climb into a mixed conifer and aspen forest.

0.3 The Owl's Perch Trail intersects with the Lodge Pole Loop Trail. Bear right onto the Lodge Pole Loop Trail, heading in a westerly direction.

0.9 The Lodge Pole Loop Trail intersects with the Sunny Aspen Trail. Bear right onto the Sunny Aspen Trail and continue climbing in a southerly direction.

1.2 The Sunny Aspen Trail intersects with the Old Ski Run Trail by a gazebo. Bear right onto the Old Ski Run Trail, continuing your climb in a southerly direction.

2.0 The Old Ski Run Trail forks, creating a loop of itself. Bear right at the fork, climbing in a counterclockwise direction.

2.4 Arrive at a point where the Old Ski Run Trail meets a worn footpath. Here, you can bear right and ride up the technically and physically challenging path or leave your bikes aside and walk up the short spur to rock outcroppings providing a bit of a view. After taking in the view, continue descending along the Old Ski Run Trail.

2.6 Arrive at the fork where the Old Ski Run Trail creates a loop of itself. Continue your descent along the Old Ski Run Trail, heading in a westerly direction.

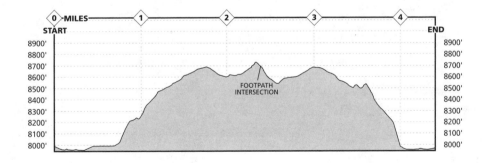

3.4 Reach the intersection where the Old Ski Run Trail intersected with the Sunny Aspen Trail by the gazebo. Bear right here, continuing your descent on the Sunny Aspen Trail.

3.9 The Sunny Aspen Trail intersects with the Lodge Pole Loop Trail. Bear right, continuing on the Lodge Pole Loop Trail, descending in a northerly direction.

4.1 The Lodge Pole Loop Trail intersects with the Owl's Perch Trail. Bear right onto the Owl's Perch Trail and return toward the start.

4.4 Arrive at your vehicle.

Ride Information

Local Information

Conifer Chamber of Commerce, 26437 Conifer Road, Conifer 80433; (303) 838-0178

Local Events and Attractions

Colorado Trail, 470-mile trail from Denver to Durango

Restaurants

Coney Dog Stand, Conifer; (303) 838-4210

◀ *Cruising through an old ski run trail.*

37 Coyote Song Trail

The Coyote Song Trail offers an easy and short ride through wide-open meadows below the Rocky Mountain foothills. The route travels along wide singletrack as it passes intriguing red rock formations. After connecting with a paved bike path, riders descend on a dirt road. From the dirt road, riders connect to the Lyons Back singletrack that crosses a low-lying ridge of Lyons Hogback. From the ridge top it's a moderately rocky descent to the wide singletrack that returns you to your vehicle. When combined with the riding in Deer Creek Canyon (Ride 38), located just up the road, riders can extend their route to more than 14 miles.

Start: The Coyote Song trailhead on the north side of Deer Creek Canyon Road

Distance: 4.6-mile lariat

Approximate riding time: Advanced riders, 15–20 minutes; intermediate riders, 30–45 minutes

Aerobic level: Physically easy due to the trail's relatively short length and insignificant elevation gain

Technical difficulty: Technically easy with some rougher, rockier riding along the singletrack of the hogback

Terrain: Singletrack, dirt road, paved bike path for mostly smooth riding through meadows

and over a hogback, passing red rock formations along the Rocky Mountain foothills

Schedule: March–November

Maps: DeLorme *Colorado Atlas & Gazetteer*, page 40; USGS: Indian Hills, CO

Nearest town: Littleton

Other trail users: Hikers

Canine compatibility: Dog-friendly, although trail passes through coyote country and provides no water

Trail contact: Jefferson County Open Space, Evergreen; (303) 271-5975

Finding the Trailhead: From Denver, drive west on Interstate 70 to Colorado Highway 470. Drive east on CO 470 to the Kipling Street exit. Exit southbound, and drive on South Kipling Street until it bears right (west) and becomes West Ute Avenue at a stop sign. Drive for 0.2 mile on West Ute Avenue before bearing right onto Deer Creek Canyon Road. Drive on Deer Creek Canyon Road for roughly 2.1 miles before bearing left into a pullout just before South Valley Road. The Coyote Song trailhead will be directly across from where you parked on Deer Creek Canyon Road.

The Ride

The Coyote Song Trail, as part of South Valley Park, is one of Jefferson County's latest land acquisitions. At the time of this writing, Jefferson County Open Space hadn't even produced any printed maps of the area. In fact, the maps found in the kiosks at the park's trailheads are conceptual plans. Because of its newness and the fact that the area is still under development, the Coyote Song Trail doesn't see too many users.

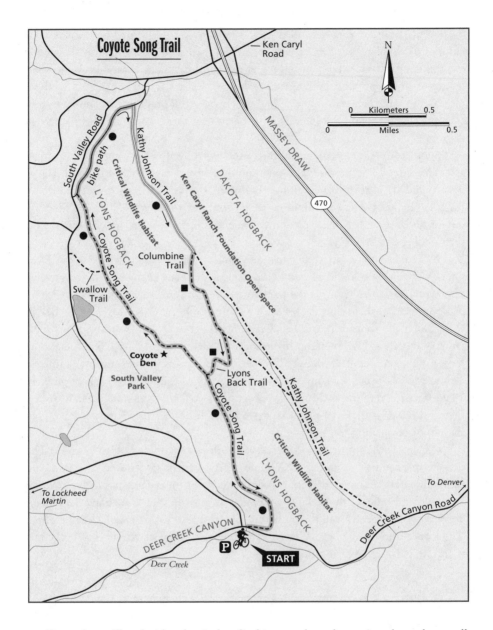

From the trailhead, riders begin by climbing moderately, passing through a small ridge of red rock formations. The trail continues over wide but sandy singletrack as it passes through meadows of piñon pine and scrub oak reminiscent of riding in Moab, Utah. Lending an air of authenticity to this Moab-like trail, these vertical red rock formations look like petrified whales breaching the surface of the earth. And in many ways, they are.

Seventy million years ago, these great sandstone ledges formed the beaches and sands of a vast inland sea. Over time, the sand and sediment left behind by the receding seas compressed and galvanized under extraordinary pressure and heat into solid masses of sandstone rock. Folding and faulting of Earth's crust gradually raised these monolithic submariners from their prehistoric ocean floor, prompting an appropriate name: the Fountain Formation. Some of the area formations slope as much as 90 degrees.

Among some of the more notorious outlaws that lived in the Deer Creek Canyon area, Horsethief Thompson was a onetime member of the Hole in the Wall Gang, which eluded authorities many times by hiding out with friends on the land now occupied by Lockheed Martin. In fact, tales continue to circulate around a mysterious cache of loot that many old-time residents still believe lies hidden in the area surrounding Lockheed Martin.

Horsethief Thompson wasn't the only one of ill repute to frequent the Deer Creek Canyon area. So did alleged cannibal Alferd Packer. Having served a seventeen-year sentence at the state penitentiary for making a meal of his prospecting companions near Breckenridge, Packer settled in to the sleepy little town of Critchell in 1901, along the south fork of Deer Creek. Working as a hired hand on many local ranches and always maintaining his innocence, many of his Deer Creek neighbors took a liking to him. Having died in 1907, Packer now lies resting in a Littleton cemetery. Bishop Frank Hamilton Rice led a party of followers to Packer's grave in 1940. Rice's ceremony included an exorcism of Packard's sins, after which casting them onto a goat tied to a nearby tree—and to Bishop Frank Hamilton Rice goes the honor of creating the term "scapegoat."

Nearing a mile into your ride, you may notice a coyote den off to your left. The den lies in a batch of scrub oak. Oftentimes, particularly between April and June, you can glimpse coyotes and their pups sitting outside of their den, identifiable by their rust-colored bodies with markings of white and gray on their throat and belly. Their vocalizations range in sound from short yips to barks to extended clear howling. These vocalizations sing a song that call members of the pack together as well communicate pack member locations.

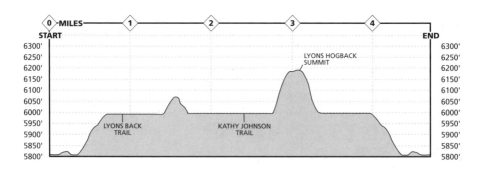

Walking it down the set of stone stairs of the Lyons Hogback.

Generally, coyotes keep to themselves and are shy around humans. However, on rare occasions, coyotes have been known to approach people and attack unattended pets. Should you see a coyote, it's best to just relax and enjoy the wildlife from a distance; however, if it comes near, speak in a loud and authoritative voice. Because coyotes are opportunistic hunters, never allow your pets to go unattended and never move toward a coyote. Should the coyote continue its approach, try throwing sticks and rocks to scare the animal away.

After connecting with the Kathy Johnson Trail, riders enter the Ken-Caryl Ranch Foundation Open Space. The Kathy Johnson Trail runs through the valley of the Dakota and Lyons Hogbacks. Riders then connect with the Columbine Trail and climb to the top of the Lyons Hogback through oak thickets. The ridge of the hogbacks separates the Ken-Caryl Ranch Foundation Open Space from the Jefferson County Open Space–South Valley Park.

As this area hosts a critical wildlife habitat, rare plants, archaeological sites, and nesting falcons, only the trail is open to public access, so take care when crossing over it.

The Lyons Back Trail descends from the ridge of the hogback over imbedded granite and a set of stone stairs. After a short and fast descent over rocks and through sandy patches, connect with the Coyote Song Trail and return to your vehicle.

Miles and Directions

0.0 Begin riding in a northeasterly direction on the smooth, wide singletrack of the Coyote Song Trail. The trail immediately crosses over the ridge of some red rock formations. Caution: These rocks are closed to all public use.

0.4 The trail forks; bear right here, following a brown trail marker sign.

0.9 The Coyote Song Trail intersects with the Lyons Back Trail on the right. Continue heading north on the Coyote Song Trail. You'll eventually loop around and over the Lyons Hogback to this junction to return to your vehicle. (FYI: After passing the Lyons Back Trail intersection, you'll notice Lockheed Martin [advanced technology systems/aerospace] to your left.)

1.1 The Coyote Song intersects with the Swallow Trail to the left. Continue riding on the Coyote Song Trail.

1.3 The Coyote Song Trail reaches the northern terminus of the park at South Valley Road. Bear right onto the paved bike path and descend along South Valley Road.

1.9 The South Valley Road bike path intersects with the Kathy Johnson Trail on the right. Bear right onto the gravel road of the Kathy Johnson Trail.

2.4 The Kathy Johnson Trail intersects with the Columbine Trail to the right. Bear right onto the Columbine Trail, climbing up the Lyons Hogback. **Option:** At this point, you may choose to descend on the Kathy Johnson Trail, which will deliver you roughly 1 mile south of your vehicle on Deer Creek Canyon Road.

2.9 The Columbine Trail intersects with the Pass Trail and becomes the Lyons Back Trail. Bear right here and continue on the Pass/Lyons Back Trail, heading underneath a set of power lines.

3.2 Arrive at the summit of the Lyons Hogback and the boundaries of the Ken-Caryl Ranch Foundation Open Space and the Jefferson County Open Space. From here, continue descending along the Lyons Back Trail.

3.5 The Lyons Back Trail intersects with the Coyote Song Trail. Bear left onto the Coyote Song Trail and retrace your path to the trailhead.

4.6 Arrive at your vehicle.

Ride Information

Trail Information

Colorado Division of Wildlife, Denver; (303) 297-1192

Denver Parks and Recreation, Parks Division; (303) 964-2512

Jefferson County Open Space, ranger staff; (303) 904-0249

Ken-Caryl Parks and Open Space information, (303) 979-1876 ext. 129

Local Information

Denver Metro Chamber of Commerce, 1445 Market Street, Denver 80202; (303) 534-8500

Local Events and Attractions

Chatfield State Park, Littleton; (303) 791-7275

Deer Creek Canyon Park (Ride 38)

38 Deer Creek Canyon Park

Mountain bikers can access great singletrack trails in Deer Creek Canyon Park. The park encompasses 1,881 acres and 10.6 miles of trails. While the Meadowlark, Golden Eagle, and Homesteader Trails are reserved for hikers only, that still leaves roughly 7.5 miles of trails for bikers. When combined with the Coyote Song Trail (Ride 37), located just down the road, riders can extend their route to more than 14 miles. The park offers some challenging terrain: loose, football-size rocks, steep climbs, and exposed areas. But it also offers fast descents on hard-packed terrain through ponderosa forests. In short, it's a great ride for intermediate to more advanced riders, offering views of the foothills' hogbacks and the Denver skyline.

Start: The Plymouth Creek Trail trailhead off Grizzly Drive
Distance: 9.6-mile double lariat
Approximate riding time: Advanced riders, 1.5 hours; intermediate riders, 2–2.5 hours
Aerobic level: Physically moderate due to the challenging climb to Red Mesa. Some sections are physically challenging, particularly the climbing that is required at the trail's outset.
Technical difficulty: Technically moderate to challenging due to the steeper and rockier sections both when climbing and descending
Terrain: Singletrack and doubletrack over loose sand and rock. While much of this trail is exposed, riders do enter into thick stands of ponderosa pine as they gain elevation.
Schedule: May–October
Maps: DeLorme *Colorado Atlas & Gazetteer*, page 40; USGS: Indian Hills, CO; Jefferson County Open Space Deer Creek Canyon Park map
Nearest town: Littleton
Other trail users: Hikers and horseback riders
Canine compatibility: Dog-friendly
Trail contact: Jefferson County Open Space, Evergreen; (303) 271-5975

Finding the Trailhead: From Denver, drive west on Interstate 70 to Colorado Highway 470. Drive east on CO 470 to the Kipling Street exit. Exit southbound, and drive on South Kipling Street until it bears right (west) and becomes West Ute Avenue at a stop sign. Drive for 0.2 mile on West Ute Avenue before bearing right onto Deer Creek Canyon Road. Drive on Deer Creek Canyon Road for roughly 3 miles before bearing left onto Grizzly Drive. Drive on Grizzly Drive for 0.4 mile before bearing right into the parking lot. Park in spaces provided at the Deer Creek Canyon Park trailhead.

The Ride

The area surrounding Deer Creek Canyon Park once served as holdup and hideout to a variety of characters as colorful as the nearby sandstone is red. Deer Creek Canyon Park and its surrounding mesas or tabletops were originally a campground for the Arapaho and Ute Indians. These nomadic tribes would spend their winters here, scouting out over the eastern plains looking for elk and buffalo as well as for raiding marauders.

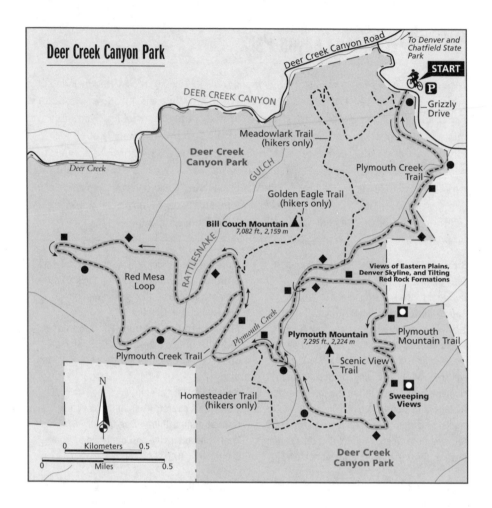

Deer Creek Canyon Park

To Denver and Chatfield State Park

START

Grizzly Drive

Deer Creek Canyon Road

DEER CREEK CANYON

Meadowlark Trail (hikers only)

Deer Creek Canyon Park

GULCH

Deer Creek

Plymouth Creek Trail

Golden Eagle Trail (hikers only)

Bill Couch Mountain 7,082 ft., 2,159 m

RATTLESNAKE

Red Mesa Loop

Views of Eastern Plains, Denver Skyline, and Tilting Red Rock Formations

Plymouth Creek

Plymouth Creek Trail

Plymouth Mountain 7,295 ft., 2,224 m

Plymouth Mountain Trail

Scenic View Trail

Homesteader Trail (hikers only)

Sweeping Views

N

Kilometers 0.5

Miles 0.5

Deer Creek Canyon Park

From the trailhead, riders descend a short, sinuous track before starting their climb. The climb comes soon enough, offering switchbacks over wide singletrack strewn with waterbars. After passing the intersection for the hikers-only Meadowlark Trail, riders have to negotiate a physically challenging and technically moderate hill climb before the trail becomes a smoother doubletrack. At this point, riders pass through a cool riparian area of mixed vegetation and conifers. Adding to the lushness of this section are the wild raspberries that grow trailside.

Connecting to the Plymouth Mountain Trail, the route travels along narrow but smooth singletrack beneath the shade of an aspen and ponderosa pine forest. As the Plymouth Mountain Trail veers south, continuing its climb of Plymouth Mountain, riders are greeted with views of the eastern plains, the Denver skyline, and tilting sandstone red rocks. Plymouth Mountain takes its name from John Williamson. Hailing from Plymouth, England, Williamson originally homesteaded this area in 1872.

Just to the southwest of Plymouth Mountain lies Sampson Mountain, named after the African-American minister who discovered gold there in 1874. Legend has it that Jesse James favored Sampson Mountain as one of his hideouts. While cooling off after a train robbery, James stumbled upon the Mielke family who had been living on Sampson Mountain for some time. James reportedly gave Mr. Mielke a gold nugget for his hospitality. Who knows? James may have been the impetus behind Woody Guthrie's "Pretty Boy Floyd," a song about another "misunderstood" rebel. In the song, Guthrie captures a similar sentiment in the line: "I must tell you of a stranger that come to beg a meal and underneath the napkin left a thousand dollar bill."

From the sweeping views that Plymouth Mountain offers, riders continue climbing over a number of switchbacks that lead in a southerly direction. After passing the intersection with the Homesteader Trail, riders are rewarded with a fast descent. It is short-lived, however, as riders will climb once again, this time on the Plymouth Creek Trail.

From the Plymouth Creek Trail, riders link to the Red Mesa Loop, which extends to the park's western boundary. The initial climb up Red Mesa traverses thick forests and open meadows that reach farther west into Rattlesnake Gulch and the old Couch Ranch.

A lawyer with an education from Oxford University, Sam Couch owned more than 600 acres near Dutch Creek. Although living in the lap of luxury for the times, Couch and his family were always on edge for fear of warring Indians. Being an educated man, and a lawyer to boot, he suggested that his wife schmooze up to nearby Ute Indian Chief Colorow by feeding him homemade biscuits and honey whenever he was in the area. Knowing well that you can catch more flies with honey than you can with vinegar, the Couches were able to avoid the tribe's warpath.

Not all of the white settlers in the Deer Creek area would be as lucky. One story describes the tragedy of a family whose members were each scalped and butchered near their Riverside Acres home and then left hanging from nearby trees. The site of this brutal attack now lies buried just east of here under the weight of the Chatfield Dam.

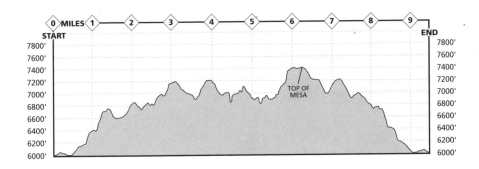

Looking east onto the eastern plains from Plymouth Mountain Trail.

From the top of the mesa, riders descend rapidly over prime singletrack and through mixed conifer forests. The descent along the Plymouth Creek Trail is quite rocky and sandy, so check your speed, as other trail users may be coming up. There are also a few sandy switchbacks that don't present themselves until you're right above them, so ride within your limits when returning to your vehicle.

Miles and Directions

0.0 Begin riding in a southerly direction on the Plymouth Creek Trail.

1.1 The Plymouth Creek Trail intersects with the Meadowlark Trail to your right. Continue climbing on the Plymouth Creek Trail. The Meadowlark Trail is a hikers-only trail.

1.7 The Plymouth Creek Trail intersects with the Plymouth Mountain Trail to the left. Bear left onto the Plymouth Mountain Trail, continuing in an easterly direction as you continue climbing.

3.3 The Plymouth Mountain Trail levels off onto doubletrack as it starts heading in a northwesterly direction.

3.5 The Plymouth Mountain Trail intersects with the multiuse Scenic View Trail on the right, and shortly thereafter, the hikers-only Homesteader Trail on the left. Continue riding in a northwesterly direction along the Plymouth Mountain Trail. **Option:** riders can choose to ride the 0.4 mile to the top of the Scenic View Trail where they are offered 360-degree views. There is one steep section to this trail.

3.9 The Plymouth Mountain Trail intersects with the Plymouth Creek Trail. Bear left here, continuing on the Plymouth Creek Trail and climbing in a northwesterly direction.

4.1 The Plymouth Creek Trail intersects with the Homesteader Trail. Continue on the Plymouth Creek Trail.

4.6 The Plymouth Creek Trail intersects with the Red Mesa Loop. Continue straight, along the Red Mesa Loop, riding the loop in a counterclockwise direction.

4.8 The Red Mesa Loop intersects with the hikers-only Golden Eagle Trail to the right. Continue climbing along the Red Mesa Loop.

6.2 Reach the top of the mesa and begin descending.

7.2 The Red Mesa Loop finishes its loop and again intersects with the Plymouth Creek Trail. Bear right at this point onto the Plymouth Creek Trail and return the way you came.

7.8 The Plymouth Creek Trail intersects with the Plymouth Mountain Trail. Bear left here, continuing on the Plymouth Creek Trail in a northerly direction.

8.2 The Plymouth Creek Trail again intersects with the Plymouth Mountain Trail on the right. Bear left here, continuing on the Plymouth Creek Trail toward the start.

9.6 Arrive at your vehicle.

Ride Information

Local Information

Denver Metro Chamber of Commerce, 1445 Market Street, Denver 80202; (303) 534-8500

Local Events and Attractions

Chatfield State Park, Littleton; (303) 791-7275

Coyote Song Trail (Ride 37)

39 Waterton Canyon

Waterton Canyon is a favorite trail among Denver–area residents. As such, it may be crowded during the weekends. The trail begins on a wide, dirt service road as it travels through the canyon. Following the South Platte River, this section of the trail offers a mellow cruise, a great family ride. The trail, however, becomes increasingly more difficult, with steeper climbs and moderate switchbacks, as riders near the beginning of the 470-mile Colorado Trail.

Start: Trailhead of the Colorado Trail in Waterton Canyon

Distance: 17.5-mile lariat with innumerable options off the 470-mile Colorado trail. (Note: If you do decide to continue on the Colorado Trail, special arrangements for your return must be considered, as these routes will not lead you back to your vehicle at the mouth of Waterton Canyon.)

Approximate riding time: Advanced riders, 1.5 hours; intermediate riders, 2–2.5 hours

Aerobic level: Physically moderate. Although there isn't any significant elevation gain, there are a number of tougher and steeper climbs.

Technical difficulty: Technically moderate. The first 6 miles offer an easy, scenic ride along the South Platte River on an improved dirt road. The singletrack of the Roxborough Connection offers some tight ascending switchbacks, with sudden tight twists along the trail on the descent.

Terrain: Singletrack, doubletrack, and improved dirt road; the single- and doubletrack offer a variety of terrain: sand, rocks, and softened forest growth

Schedule: Open daily, 4:00 A.M. to 9:00 P.M. year-round (Roxborough Connection may only be available May–October)

Maps: DeLorme *Colorado Atlas & Gazetteer,* page 50; USGS: Kassler, CO; Platte Canyon, CO; Trails Illustrated: #135, Deckers & Rampart Range, CO; Waterton Canyon Map, Denver Water

Nearest town: Littleton

Other trail users: Horseback riders, anglers, campers, hikers, and picnickers

Canine compatibility: Dog-unfriendly. Dogs are not allowed in the canyon for two reasons: they may contaminate drinking water, and they may disturb the resident herd of bighorn sheep in the canyon.

Trail contact: Pike National Forest, South Platte Ranger District, Morrison; (303) 275-5610

Finding the Trailhead: From Denver, take Interstate 25 south to exit 207B. Exit at 207B, and drive south on U.S. Highway 85, which will Y shortly after the exit; stay to your left. Take US 85 south for 10 miles until reaching Colorado Highway 470. Veer right onto CO 470, heading west. Drive west on CO 470 for a few miles before exiting at Wadsworth Boulevard. Following signs for Waterton Canyon, bear left, driving under CO 470, and pick up CO 121 south. Drive south on CO 121 for roughly 4.5 miles before turning left into Waterton Canyon State Park. The parking lot will be on your left.

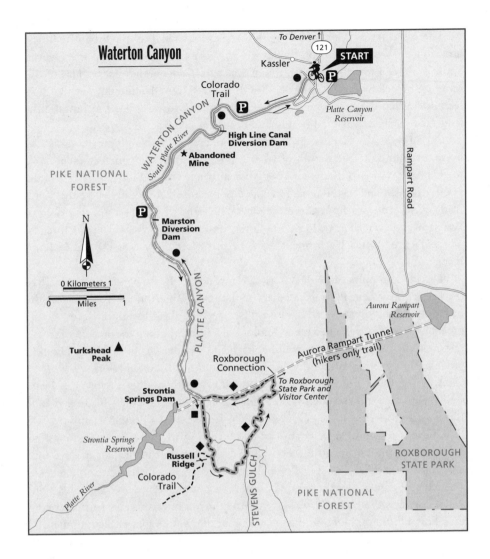

Waterton Canyon

To Denver
121
START
Kassler
Platte Canyon Reservoir
Colorado Trail
WATERTON CANYON
South Platte River
High Line Canal Diversion Dam
★ Abandoned Mine
PIKE NATIONAL FOREST
Rampart Road
N
Marston Diversion Dam
0 Kilometers 1
0 Miles 1
PLATTE CANYON
Aurora Rampart Reservoir
Turkshead Peak
Roxborough Connection
Aurora Rampart Tunnel (hikers only trail)
Strontia Springs Dam
To Roxborough State Park and Visitor Center
Strontia Springs Reservoir
Russell Ridge
ROXBOROUGH STATE PARK
Colorado Trail
Platte River
STEVENS GULCH
PIKE NATIONAL FOREST

The Ride

If you're looking for proof of Denver's metropolis status, you need only look to the Denver Broncos, the Colorado Rockies, the Denver Nuggets, and the Colorado Avalanche—but even that wouldn't present the whole picture. Consider the $4.3 billion Denver International Airport, the $76 million refurbished Central Library, and the yearly loss of 90,000 acres of farmland to development, and you've got one heck of a megalopolis. But what distinguishes Denver from other large U.S. cities isn't its sports teams or the fact that its airport rests on a site larger than Manhattan, but rather that it's only minutes away from some of the sweetest stretches of single-track in all of Colorado.

The easternmost trailhead of the 470-mile Colorado Trail sits on an improved dirt road in Waterton Canyon. Following the former railroad bed of the Denver, South Park, & Pacific Railroad through Waterton Canyon, the first 6 miles of this route are a mellow cruise along the South Platte River—admittedly, not the most technical. What the first 6 miles through Waterton Canyon lack in technical challenge, they deliver in natural beauty and historical significance.

On July 6, 1820, Stephen H. Long (remembered in the naming of Longs Peak) led an expedition to the mouth of what is now Waterton Canyon. As a member of the US Army Corps of Engineers, Long was instructed to find the headwaters of the Platte, Arkansas, and Red Rivers. His expedition camped at the site where the South Platte River emerges from the mountains. His camp would become the town of Waterton and even later the location of the Denver Union Water Company, forebear of the Denver Water Department—the largest water district in the entire Front Range.

The initial 6 miles through Waterton Canyon are a hydrologist's dream. In 1912 the Kassler Treatment Plant, located at the mouth of Waterton Canyon, became the first English slow-sand water filtration plant west of the Mississippi River. At the time, this system was the newest technological advancement in the area of water filtration. Only two other towns could boast being equipped with this latest filtration process: Albany, New York, and Ashland, Wisconsin (on Lake Superior).

About 3 miles from the trailhead and the mouth of the canyon, the Platte Canyon Intake Dam and the Marston Diversion Dam route South Platte and Blue River water to Marston Reservoir. At mile 6.1, the Strontia Springs Dam skies 243 feet above the South Platte stream bed and diverts water into a 3.4-mile-long tunnel under the mountains to the Foothills Water Treatment Plant. This massive tunnel project, and others like it in Colorado, is necessary because the state only receives 14 inches of annual precipitation. An even larger tunnel (23 miles long and 10 feet wide) connects the South Platte River with a Dillon reservoir. This particular conduit, bored through the Front Range, is one of the world's longest such tunnels.

As you head east from the Strontia Springs Dam, the road begins to climb. Within a mile, the Colorado Trail's singletrack begins to your left. From here the trail

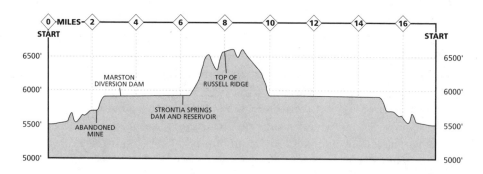

Riders converge at the junction of the Colorado Trail and Roxborough State Park Loop atop Russell Ridge.

rises out of the canyon to Russell Ridge (6,560 feet). The singletrack to this point offers a moderately challenging climb to the top. Among this section's highlights are smooth-running singletrack, thick ponderosa pine forests, and switchbacks (which deserve special attention). Intermediate riders can manage the switchbacks with careful balance and control, while advanced riders can spin their way to the top with minimal effort. The last switchback, which breaks right before summitting Russell Ridge, is beset with rocks. Keep spinning, don't forget to smile, and you'll make it with relative ease.

Atop the ridge, the Colorado Trail will continue southwest to Durango. To begin your return of the Waterton Canyon route, you'll have to turn off the Colorado Trail at this point and follow the sign marking Roxborough State Park.

The singletrack of this section of trail is sweet. Thick overgrowth at the section's beginning makes for very narrow and tight paths. The trail weaves its way through cool forests and offers riders a number of screams. One such scream comes at mile 8.2. The singletrack descent is steep and narrow as it hugs the slope of the ridge. For an added element of fear, a tree at the bottom welcomes any would-be tree-hugger. The trail winds through forests, over creeks, and through one meadow before delivering another tight spot at mile 10.8. A big, rocky drop-off invites you to take it down the center.

From here, ride for another mile using "The Force" as you go. The forest once again struggles to engulf the trail and impede visibility. Finishing the Roxborough

Loop leaves the rider with a feeling of pleasant amazement: How can such sweet singletrack be so close to a city? Arrive at the road where you started your ride. Bear right and top-ring it back to your vehicle.

Miles and Directions

0.0   Start at the parking lot of Waterton Canyon State Park. Ride back out of the parking lot and cross the road. The Colorado Trail sign marks the beginning of the ride into Waterton Canyon. Follow the trail around as it weaves itself onto the improved dirt road and into the canyon.

2.2   Pass an abandoned mine to your left.

3.3   Reach Marston Diversion Dam.

4.3   Cross Mill Gulch Bridge.

6.1   Reach Strontia Springs Dam and Reservoir. Beware the bighorn sheep that descend from the tall canyon walls, making their way to the Colorado Trail. A herd of 20–35 bighorn sheep lives in the canyon, remaining at low elevation all year, rather than typically traveling to higher elevation in the summer.

6.3   Reach the junction of the Roxborough Connection and the Colorado Trail. Here is where the route will return after the loop. For now, keep heading east, ascending straight on.

6.6   Reach the start of the Colorado Trail singletrack, on the left side of the road. From this point, the maintained dirt road is closed to public use.

8.0   Reach the top of Russell Ridge, the route's high point. At this point, the Colorado Trail continues heading southwest all the way to Durango. Instead, bear left (east) onto the singletrack marked by the Roxborough State Park sign.

10.3   Here the singletrack T's. Bearing right will lead you to the Roxborough State Park and Visitor Center—however, this section of trail is off-limits to bikes. Instead, bear left and head toward Waterton Canyon. This way will lead you back to the improved dirt road on which you began your ride, just above the Strontia Springs Dam in Waterton Canyon.

11.2   As you reach the improved dirt road of the Colorado Trail in Waterton Canyon, bear right and return to your vehicle the way you came.

17.5   Arrive at your vehicle.

Ride Information

Trail Information

Colorado Division of Wildlife, Denver; (303) 297-1192

U.S. Army Corps of Engineers, Omaha District, Tri-Lakes Project Office, Littleton; (303) 979-4120

Local Information

Denver Metro Chamber of Commerce, 1445 Market Street, Denver 80202; (303) 534-8500

Local Events and Attractions

Chatfield State Park, Littleton; (303) 791-7275

Roxborough State Park, Littleton; (303) 973-3959

Books

The Colorado Trail: The Official Guidebook by Randy Jacobs (Englewood, Colo.: Westcliffe Publishing, 2000)

In Addition

The Truck Stops Here—Any And All Bikes

"We bring the candy store to the kid's front door."
—*Don O'Connor, Any And All Bikes founder and owner*

Any And All Bikes (A³ Bikes) was the brainchild of Don O'Connor. In 1994, tired of the routine of his brick-and-mortar bike store, Don decided to sell out, buy an old truck, and convert it into a mobile bike shop. Don met Dan French at a Bike-to-Work function in 1995. Dan was so impressed with Don's success that he bought the newly converted truck from Don two weeks later. Shortly thereafter, Don converted another truck for himself, and the wheels of a new franchise were set in motion. Randy Wittmer came on-line in 1996 after seeing Don's truck parked outside Waterton Canyon.

Today, three fully stocked trucks compose the Any And All Bikes fleet. The trucks themselves are 25 feet long, 7 feet tall, 8 feet wide, and weighted to 10,000 pounds. Each truck includes roughly $50,000-worth of inventory: Bike frames and wheel sets hang from the ceiling, tools and various bike parts lie securely in Race Face storage units, and suspension forks and various other merchandise press against the walls. The trucks, while operating under the same business name, are individually owned and maintained.

Each truck's license plate speaks to this individuality: "Bike Man" (Don and his wife, Vi); "Bike Spa" (Dan); and "Bike Guy" (Randy). Operating their truck as a team, Don and Vi cover south Denver. Dan focuses his attentions in north Denver. Having run his own repair shop from his garage for a number of years, Dan provides a uniquely personalized neighborhood-oriented business. Randy works mostly in east Denver. Even with more than 20 other bike shops in the area, Randy admits, "There's more work in the Denver area than we can handle." Not surprisingly, almost all of their work is done by appointment.

In addition to working in area neighborhoods, Any And All Bikes also participates in corporate tune-ups, tuning up to 60 bikes daily for employees of MCI, Qwest, and ICT. But being mobile also offers opportunities to explore a variety of other business avenues, as "we each have our certain niche," Randy says.

Don and Vi have Colorado tours locked up. A³ Bikes has been the official technicians for Bicycle Tour of Colorado, Tour de Cure, and the MS 150. As a onetime motocross racer, Randy has focused his business efforts on Colorado's racing market, handling the HandleBar & Grill's racing team (see In Addition: HandleBar & Grill, following Ride 30), the Morgul-Bismark Vitamin Cottage Race Team, and the

The Any And All Bikes fleet and crew (from left) Randy Wittmer, Don and Vi O'Connor, and Dan French.

triathlon team of Team Hustler. He also served as mechanic for the Pizza Hut/Costa Rica Racing Pro Team during the 2001 World Championships in Vail.

These varied niches serve to complement the business as a whole. "It's really nice to have all that experience under one roof and to be able to feed off that," Randy acknowledges. Needless to say, Any And All Bikes caters to any and all clientele. Customers need only understand their own needs in choosing which of the three trucks to patronize. By providing same-day delivery and one-on-one attention and by encouraging customers to ask questions while their bikes are being worked on, A³ Bikes serves as a resource not only for speedy service but also as a repository of information.

Of course, luring people inside the trucks by way of education is cloaked with a certain degree of business acumen. It's the educated customer that ends up purchasing the merchandise within. Although Any And All Bikes does nearly 20,000 tune-ups a year, each competitively priced at $29.95, the business is more than a service shop. By offering custom bikes, selling frames, and carrying $700 wheel sets, A³ Bikes is a complete bike store with each truck responsible for roughly $500,000 in annual revenues. And all signs point to increased numbers in the future, given A³ Bikes' lack of competition.

The May 2000 issue of *Bicycle Retailer Magazine* reported, "Fred Clements, the National Bicycle Dealers Association's executive director, knows of no other mobile shop like it." According to Don, "we're the only ones in the country doing this." There are, however, headaches involved with running a mobile bike shop business: having to be on two ends of town at the same time during heavy traffic for instance. Dan, however, offers a solution to this logistical nightmare when he suggests to "make sure you're working on a bike during rush hour" and not driving.

Perhaps the key to Any And All Bikes' success has less to do with its apparent lack of competition than with the fact that each of the owners started this thing for the same reason: love for biking. For Randy and the others, "success is loving what you do and doing what you love."

Don and Vi O'Connor
2436 West Harvard Avenue
Denver, CO 80219
phone: (303) 995–3731
fax: (303) 742–7984
www.anyandallbikes.com

Dan French
phone: (800) 708–5058

Randy Wittmer
12A South Nome Street
Aurora, CO 80012
phone: (303) 363–7568
pager: (800) 813–0988
e-mail: aaabikes@home.com

40 Reynolds Park

Reynolds Park is an oftentimes-overlooked riding area for those on the Front Range. Its inconspicuous hideout along Foxton Road secludes it from more well-known area rides. However, this, as well as its diversity of terrain and its fine singletrack, makes this area worth riding. Along the trail riders climb to panoramic views of Rampart Range and Pikes Peak, then they descend over moderately technical rocky and sloping terrain. Hill climbers will appreciate the grueling initial ascent along the Elkhorn and Raven's Roost Trails. A second climb occurs roughly midway through the ride. While not as long as the first climb, its late arrival does challenge anyone's lung capacity.

Start: The Reynolds north trailhead on County Road 97

Distance: 5.6-mile loop with an out-and-back spur

Approximate riding time: Advanced riders, 45 minutes; intermediate riders, 1–1.5 hours

Aerobic level: Physically moderate to challenging due to the long and steep climbing along Raven's Roost, as well as the Hummingbird Trail

Technical difficulty: Technically moderate with some more challenging rocky and big drop-off sections along Oxen Draw Trail, as well as some precipitously sloping sandy terrain along Hummingbird Trail

Terrain: Singletrack and doubletrack that roll through open meadows and dense forests and open to expansive views

Schedule: June–October

Maps: DeLorme *Colorado Atlas & Gazetteer*, page 50; Jefferson County Open Space Reynolds Park map; USGS: Pine and Platte Canyon, CO; Trails Illustrated: #135, Deckers-Rampart Range, CO

Nearest town: Conifer

Other trail users: Hikers, picnickers, anglers, and horseback riders

Canine compatibility: Dog-friendly

Trail contact: Jefferson County Open Space, Evergreen; (303) 271-5975

Finding the Trailhead: From North Denver, drive west on Interstate 70 to Colorado Highway 470. Drive south on CO 470 for roughly 5.8 miles before bearing right to head west on U.S. Highway 285 for roughly 15.4 miles. Just after passing through the town of Conifer, bear left onto Foxton Road (County Road 97). Drive south on Foxton Road for 5 miles before bearing right, after a brown Reynolds Park sign, into the north trailhead for Reynolds Park. Park in the spaces provided at the trailhead.

From South Denver, drive west on US 285 (Hampden Avenue), through the town of Conifer, for roughly 28.9 miles. Just after passing through Conifer, bear left onto Foxton Road (County Road 97). Drive south on Foxton Road for 5 miles before bearing right, after a brown Reynolds Park sign, into the north trailhead for Reynolds Park. Park in the spaces provided at the trailhead.

The Ride

Jefferson County acquired 1,100 acres of the park on May 28, 1975, after Mrs. Eva Dell Reynolds donated the land in memory of her husband, John A. Reynolds. Since

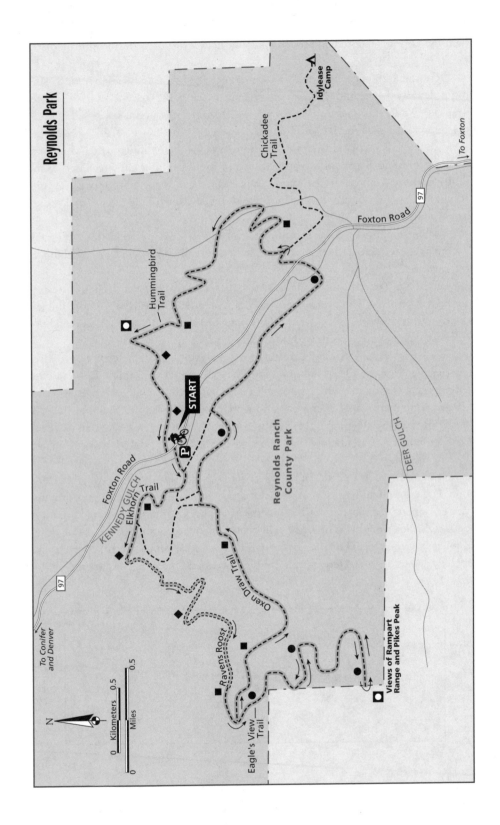

Reynolds Park

To Conifer and Denver

N

Kilometers
0   0.5

Miles
0   0.5

Foxton Road

KENNEDY GULCH

Elkhorn Trail

P

START

Hummingbird Trail

Oxen Draw Trail

Ravens Roost

Eagle's View Trail

Reynolds Ranch County Park

DEER GULCH

Views of Rampart Range and Pikes Peak

Chickadee Trail

Idylease Camp

Foxton Road

97

To Foxton

then the county acquired additional land and held a formal dedication of the park in 1977.

Now, the 1,260-acre Reynolds Park is jam-packed with trail riding variety. The route described here incorporates every trail in the park, save for the Chickadee Trail, a 0.5-mile trail that leads to the Idylease Camp. The camp takes its name from the dude ranch that the Reynolds family ran in this area from 1913 to 1942. The Idylease Dude Ranch welcomed guests from as far as the Atlantic coast and offered such amenities as you might expect: fishing, horseback riding, hiking. There were fourteen guest cabins on the ranch, with the main lodge also serving as the Reynolds's own residence. Today, the Idylease Dude Ranch lodge is the park manager's residence.

The initial climb up Elkorn Trail offers very steep terrain. Add to this numerous waterbars strewn across the trail, and you have a very physically challenging climb at the outset.

Once you connect with the Raven's Roost Trail, the route climbs steeply through mixed conifer forests over wide doubletrack. The Raven's Roost singletrack, however, rewards riders with a short but sweet dash across a south-sloping hillside to the trail's intersection with the Eagle's View Trail.

The Eagle's View Trail climbs steadily over sandy and rocky singletrack, as it skirts the perimeter of the Open Space boundary. After roughly 1.5 miles, the trail cuts through a forest mixed with ponderosa pine, blue spruce, Douglas fir, aspen, and Rocky Mountain maple over wide and smooth singletrack. The climbing here is steady over moderately sloping terrain on hard-packed singletrack. The trail switches back a number of times before delivering riders to a clearing and views of Rampart Range and Pikes Pike.

From your "eagle's perch," it's a fast and fun descent to the three-way intersection. The continued descent on the Oxen Draw Trail makes up for all the climbing you've done up to this point. The underbrush along the trail is thick, making for a beautiful ride through a ravine. The trail delivers tight, rocky singletrack as one nears 3 miles into the ride. The sand, loose rock, and waterbar drop-offs make for a quite technical and fun ride. Here, purple thistle flowers line the steep-sloping trail.

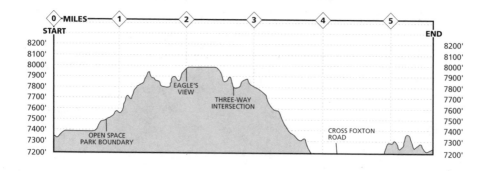

Taking a break at Eagle's View.

These flowers are quite pervasive in Colorado's open meadows, woodlands, and watery ravines. Some stand as tall as 8 feet high. The purple head of the thistle can be boiled or steamed and eaten like an artichoke. For those of you with a bent toward beers after the ride, you'll be happy to know that thistles benefit the liver.

The Songbird Trail offers riders some relief from the rocky technical descent of the Oxen Draw Trail. After connecting with the Songbird Trail, riders zip through a fast meadow over smooth singletrack to meet Foxton Road. But this smooth cruise soon ends, as riders cross the road and begin their second major climb of the day on the Hummingbird Trail.

Don't let the name of this trail fool you—it delivers a grunt of a climb over exposed and rocky singletrack terrain. Riders reach the high point as they near 5 miles into the ride. From here, riders can get a good look of the park and the surrounding area.

Reynolds Park and the area surrounding it was one of Colorado's original pioneering settlements and served as a communications portal for arriving pioneers throughout the west. In fact, pack trains traveling between Denver and Leadville made the park a frequent stop. Moreover, the Reynolds Ranch house once served as a way station for the Pony Express.

It seems fitting, then, that riders should mount their own makeshift ponies and descend from their lofty perch above the park. The descent along the Hummingbird Trail is quite challenging over tight, precipitously sloping, sandy and rocky single-track. The final swoop to Foxton Road comes up steep and fast, so take care on your approach.

Miles and Directions

0.0 Begin riding in a northwesterly direction on the Elkhorn Trail, passing the rest rooms on your right. The Elkhorn Trail briefly parallels Foxton Road.

0.1 Elkhorn Trail intersects with Oxen Draw Trail on your left. Continue heading straight on Elkhorn Trail.

0.2 Elkhorn Trail intersects with the Raven's Roost Trail. Bear right onto the Raven's Roost Trail, heading in a southwesterly direction.

0.8 Raven's Roost Trail meets the Open Space Park boundary. There is no public access beyond this point. From here, bear left onto the singletrack, continuing on the Raven's Roost Trail.

1.2 Raven's Roost Trail intersects with the Eagle's View Trail and the Oxen Draw Trail. Bear right here onto the Eagle's View Trail, climbing in a southerly direction.

2.0 Arrive at Eagle's View. Turn around to return to the three-way intersection of Eagle's View, Raven's Roost, and Oxen Draw Trails.

2.7 Arrive at the three-way intersection. Bear right, continuing east on the Oxen Draw Trail.

3.4 Oxen Draw Trail ends and intersects with the Elkhorn Trail. Continue straight on Elkhorn Trail, heading in an easterly direction.

3.7 Elkhorn Trail intersects with the Songbird Trail. Bear right onto the Songbird Trail.

4.2 The Songbird Trail intersects with Foxton Road and the Hummingbird Trail. Carefully cross Foxton Road and continue riding on the other side, climbing along the Hummingbird Trail.

4.3 The Hummingbird Trail intersects with the Chickadee Trail on the right. Continue climbing up the Hummingbird Trail.

5.6 Intersect Foxton Road, cross it, and return to your vehicle.

Ride Information

Local Information
Conifer Chamber of Commerce, 26437 Conifer Road, Conifer 80433; (303) 838-0178

Local Events and Attractions
Colorado Trail, 470-mile trail from Denver to Durango
Elkhorn Interpretive Trail, Reynolds Park

Restaurants
Coney Dog Stand, Conifer; (303) 838-4210

41 Kenosha to Georgia Pass

The Kenosha Pass to Georgia Pass ride is mack-daddy (to those over thirty, it's groovin'). On top of plush terrain and the rich groves of aspen, the trail includes awe-inspiring descents through hillside meadows and dense forests, as well as technical rocky and rooty climbs. Views from the top of Georgia Pass and the Continental Divide are breathtaking, including the entire South Park Valley below. The town of South Park, incidentally, was the inspiration for the quirky fictional town in Comedy Central's popular cartoon series *South Park*. South Park City, a restored mining town located in South Park, offers a glimpse into life of a nineteenth-century Colorado mining town.

Start: At the trailhead for the Colorado Trail atop Kenosha Pass on the west side of U.S. Highway 285

Distance: 23.8-mile out-and-back

Approximate riding time: Advanced riders, 3 hours; intermediate riders, 4 hours

Aerobic level: Physically moderate to challenging due to the higher elevations at which you're riding.

Technical difficulty: Technically moderate to challenging due to the abundance of exposed roots and rocks.

Terrain: Singletrack and doubletrack. Most of this route rolls over smooth, soft forest earth. There are, however, a few rougher sections of roots and rocks. Aspen and evergreen forests, high alpine valleys, and mountain passes form the backdrop to this incredible ride.

Fees and permits: $4.00 (fee subject to change)

Schedule: July–September

Maps: DeLorme *Colorado Atlas & Gazetteer*, pages 48–49; USGS: Jefferson, CO; Boreas Pass, CO; Trails Illustrated: #105, Bailey and #109, Breckenridge; Pike National Forest map

Nearest town: Fairplay

Other trail users: Hikers, bikepackers, horseback riders, and backpackers

Canine-compatibility: Dog-friendly

Trail contact: Pike National Forest, South Park Ranger District, Fairplay; (719) 836-2031

Finding the Trailhead: From North Denver, drive west on Interstate 70 to Colorado Highway 470. Drive south on CO 470 for roughly 5.8 miles before bearing right to head west on U.S. Highway 285 for roughly 47.5 miles to Kenosha Pass. Turn right (west) into the Kenosha Pass Picnic Ground area. Park in the available spaces by the brown Colorado Trail sign. Drinking water and toilet facilities are available.

From South Denver, drive west on US 285, passing through the town of Bailey at approximately 43 miles. Continue for another 19 miles to Kenosha Pass (10,001 feet). Once atop Kenosha Pass, turn right (west) into the Kenosha Pass Picnic Ground. Park in the available spaces by the brown Colorado Trail sign. Drinking water and toilet facilities are available.

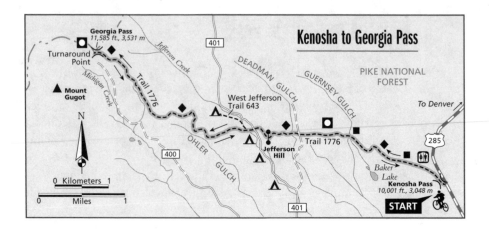

The Ride

Situated at the western end of the Pike National Forest, the trail begins atop the 10,001-foot Kenosha Pass and continues to the 11,585-foot Georgia Pass, the Continental Divide. Green and gold Q-tipped aspens crowd the trail along its westerly route like bristles in a mountainous brush, lending a special quality found only in Colorado's highest places.

As home to this kind of Colorado quality, the Pike National Forest enjoys an appropriately respectable history. After the private Front Range timber stores were savagely depleted by the mining and railroad industries in the late 1800s, cutters turned to scouring public lands to obtain their valuable timber. As a result, large tracts of public forestland were rubbed out along the Front Range. In response to growing concerns for Colorado's depleting natural resources, Congress passed an act in 1891 delegating President Benjamin Harrison the authority to create timber reserves. These reserves, forebears to our national forests, were large tracts of forestland that were set aside and protected from further depletion.

The first mile of the trail climbs moderately over very smooth terrain. Riders are coddled between a feeling of peaceful quietude descending from the thick canopy above and the snap, crackle, and pop of a tire's first meeting with a fallen pine needle below. The first technical section arrives within the first 2 miles. After descending very rapidly through a meadow and into an aspen grove, the trail switches back sharply to the left and over a group of large rocks, adding a nice wake-up call to the drowsily smooth singletrack. After roughly 2.4 miles, the singletrack exits the forest and opens up onto a hillside meadow awash with wildflowers. In view are the Continental Divide and Mount Gugot (13,370 feet), both straight ahead. Georgia Pass (11,585 feet) lies to the northwest, while the entire South Park Valley opens to the south.

The South Park Valley is an expansive 900-square-mile island in a sea of rolling mountains. In its center lies the small town of South Park. After gold was discovered here in 1859, eager prospectors flocked to the South Park Valley in droves. Within months, the unblemished valley floor became freckled with the mining camps of Tarryall, Leavick, Eureka, and Buckskin Joe. With increased development and trade, these rough-and-tumble mining camps metamorphosed into flourishing communities until all the gold was gone. With no gold to dig, miners found little reason to stay, and the mining camps, in turn, crumbled. These camps and the spirit that fueled their development had all but been forgotten until 1957.

In 1957 the South Park City restoration project was conceived. By 1959, with 34 original buildings housing more than 60,000 artifacts, South Park, the one-time boomtown of the late 1800s, was again a functioning town. The year also marked the centennial anniversary of Colorado's first gold rush. The restored mining camp of South Park City features the industries that made life in nineteenth-century Colorado livable. This re-creation of a Colorado boomtown invites you to take a step back in time and listen for the slightly out-of-tune piano heard from Rache's Place. Farther up the street you'll notice the Simpkins General Store, the Garo School, and Merriam's City Drug Store. Complete with all the early-day tinctures, remedies, and poultices, Merriam's may provide temporary relief from the pains of climbing to Georgia Pass.

After crossing Deadman Gulch, the trail becomes very narrow as it runs its course over large exposed roots. As you begin the last 6-mile push to Georgia Pass, the route climbs steadily. Upon reaching Forest Service Road 400, bear left and pedal to Georgia Pass. The descent from Georgia Pass to Jefferson Creek Road is fast and rocky. After crossing Deadman Gulch in the opposite direction, begin a tough climb through the meadow to the gate. From the gate, it's a fast and smooth descent through clustered aspens to the floor of South Park Valley.

The final 1.5 miles to Kenosha Pass and your vehicle are perhaps the most exhilarating. Smooth-running singletrack through quiet stands of aspen and pine offer the weary rider a certain peace-in-motion. The trail's narrow width, its smooth running

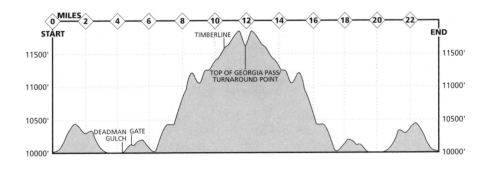

South Park City.

course, and the close-standing trunks of pine and aspen enfold the rider into the forest's high society. Riders silently track their tires into the soft belly of the earth, revealing unto no one but themselves and the surrounding forest, the simple pleasures shared by two.

Miles and Directions

0.0 Start at the Colorado Trail 1776 trailhead atop Kenosha Pass. Begin riding through serene groves of aspen and pine on smooth and hard-packed singletrack.

2.5 Cross Guernsey Creek and continue riding on the singletrack.

4.3 Cross Deadman Gulch and continue riding in a westerly direction, negotiating through a tough root singletrack section as it winds its way up a hillside marked by a miniature forest of pine saplings.

5.1 Pass through a gate, closing it behind you, and continue riding through a moderately technical rocky singletrack section.

5.8 Descend through lush forests of pine and aspen before arriving at FR 401 (Jefferson Creek Road). Cross FR 401 and Jefferson Creek, continuing on the Colorado Trail to Georgia Pass. Just after crossing Jefferson Creek, ride to where the singletrack intersects with a doubletrack. Bear right onto this doubletrack, following signs for the Colorado Trail and Georgia Pass.

6.0 Notice the continuation of the Colorado Trail singletrack bearing left into the pine forest. A sign on the right reads WEST JEFFERSON TRAIL 643, JEFFERSON CREEK CAMPGROUND AND GEORGIA PASS VIA TRAIL 643. Continue to follow signs for the Colorado Trail and Georgia Pass, veering left onto the singletrack. At this point, you're about 6 miles from Georgia Pass.

7.7 The Colorado Trail intersects with the Michigan Creek Road Trail. Continue on the Colorado Trail in a northerly direction, passing the Michigan Creek Road Trail on your left (west).

10.5 Near the timberline, with views of Mount Gugot and Bald Mountain immediately to your left. Continue climbing over tundralike terrain to Georgia Pass. Since the area is treeless, cairns mark the path of travel.

11.9 Arrive at Forest Road 400. Bear left and ride to the top of Georgia Pass. Turn around here and retrace your tracks back to your vehicle.

23.8 Arrive back at your vehicle.

Ride Information

Local Information

Park County Tourism Office, 501 Main Street, P.O. Box 1373, Fairplay 80440; (719) 836-4279

Local Events and Attractions

Fairplay Beach Recreation Area, Fairplay; (719) 836-4279

Forest Service Mountain Bike Trails, Fairplay; (719) 836-4279

South Park City Museum, Fairplay; (719) 836-2387

Organizations

Colorado Trail Foundation, Lakewood; (303) 526-0898; www.coloradotrail.org

Books

The Colorado Trail: The Official Guidebook by Randy Jacobs (Englewood, Colo.: Westcliffe Publishing, 2000)

42 Kenosha Pass to Lost Creek Wilderness

The stretch of the Colorado Trail that extends from the top of Kenosha Pass to the Lost Creek Wilderness Area is one of the most prime fall foliage rides. Aside from riding through thick stands of aspen, the trail opens out onto views of the entire South Park Valley and Tarryall Mountains, where innumerable stands of aspen dot the landscape. The trail rolls over hard-packed and sometimes sandy singletrack through forests and meadowlands before ending at the Lost Creek Wilderness Area where no bikes are allowed. While not offering the elevation gain, nor the 360-degree views of its west side cousin (Kenosha to Georgia Pass, Ride 41), the Kenosha Pass to the Lost Creek Wilderness Area stretch offers a colorful ride guaranteed to satisfy.

Start: The trailhead for the Colorado Trail atop Kenosha Pass on the east side of U.S. Highway 285

Distance: 13.2-mile out-and-back

Approximate riding time: Advanced riders, 2 hours; intermediate riders, 2.5–3 hours

Aerobic level: Physically moderate to challenging due to some extended hill climbs at elevations exceeding 10,000 feet

Technical difficulty: Technically moderate to challenging in spots due to some steeper, rockier sections

Terrain: Singletrack that rolls through mixed conifer forests, aspen glens, and meadows; rocks and a good deal of roots line the trail

Fees and permits: $4.00 (fee subject to change)

Schedule: July–October

Maps: DeLorme *Colorado Atlas & Gazetteer,* page 49; USGS: Jefferson, Mount Logan, and Observatory Rock, CO; Trails Illustrated: #105, Tarryall Mountains and Kenosha Pass; Pike National Forest map

Nearest town: Fairplay

Other trail users: Hikers, horseback riders, and backpackers

Canine compatibility: Dog-friendly, although the trail atop Kenosha Pass that leads to the wetland is off-limits to dogs and other pets

Trail contact: Pike National Forest, South Park Ranger District, Fairplay; (719) 836-2031

Finding the Trailhead: From North Denver, drive west on Interstate 70 to Colorado Highway 470. Drive south on CO 470 for roughly 5.8 miles before bearing right to head west on US 285

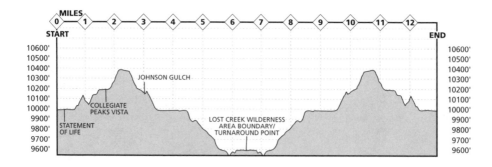

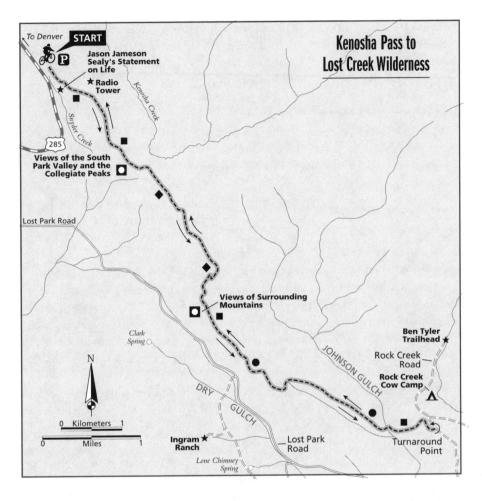

Kenosha Pass to
Lost Creek Wilderness

for roughly 47.5 miles to Kenosha Pass. Turn left (east) into the Kenosha Pass Picnic Ground area. Park in the available spaces by the brown Colorado Trail sign. Drinking water and toilet facilities are available.

From South Denver, drive west on US 285, passing through the town of Bailey at approximately 43 miles. Continue for another 19 miles to Kenosha Pass (10,001 feet). Once atop Kenosha Pass, turn left (east) into the Kenosha Pass Picnic Ground. Park in the available spaces by the brown Colorado Trail sign. Drinking water and toilet facilities are available.

The Ride

The nomadic tribes of the Ute Indians often crossed Kenosha Pass in their search for bison, elk, deer, and other large game that flourished in the South Park Valley. With the discovery of gold in 1859, towns like Fairplay, Leadville, and Tarryall sprang up like soldiers called to attention. As is often the case in how mountain bike trails evolve, the Kenosha Pass Road used the already worn hunting path made years earlier by the Utes as a toll road and stage line that serviced the mining camps in the area. Needless to say, the race for transportation to and from the mining towns in the interior Rockies became a heated battle.

For now though, let's fire our own jets and start riding. Soon after beginning the trail, riders enter a large grove of aspen trees. As you ride through the aspens, you can't help but feel like you're riding through one of Bev Doolittle's whimsical or mystical paintings, straddling a mountain bike in lieu of a horse. Soon, the Tarryall Mountains and the entire South Park Valley explode into view before the trail starts climbing moderately.

After being lost in the illusion of a Bev Doolittle painting, riders awake to face the physical and technical challenge of climbing over very steep terrain of loose rock and sand. After roughly 2.5 miles of riding, however, the trail begins to descend over loose and rocky terrain before letting out onto an open meadow. As the trail wears on, the route becomes increasingly more physically and technically challenging.

Here football-size rocks and tentacle-like roots threaten your progress, as the expansive views of the Tarryall Mountains tempt you to lift your eyes from the ground and take in all that you can from the horizon. From here it's a speedy descent through Johnson Gulch. This descent through aspen glens and hillside meadows is as good as any singletrack descent you're likely to come across and is in a word, fantastic.

After crossing the creek, riders climb for roughly one-half mile before reaching the Lost Creek Wilderness Area boundary. The Lost Creek Wilderness Area covers roughly 120,152 acres and received protective wilderness status in 1980. Riders, by now, should be familiar with the fact that bikes are not allowed in wilderness areas. This, however, shouldn't be discouraging news. Rather, we riders should be encouraged by the fact that other kinds of recreational opportunities still abound. After all, the Wilderness Act of 1964 states that wilderness areas offer "outstanding opportunities for solitude or a primitive and unconfined type of recreation." In a sense, wilderness areas allow us to get back to our recreational roots.

From the Lost Creek Wilderness Area boundary, riders turn around and follow their path back to their vehicles.

Miles and Directions

0.0 Begin riding on the singletrack of the Colorado Trail, heading in a southeasterly direction.

0.3 Arrive at Jason Jameson Sealy's Statement on Life.

1.7 Arrive at a vista of the South Park Valley and the Collegiate Peaks.

Doubletrack through aspens along the aspen-lined trail. ▶

3.0 Continue descending through Johnson Gulch, heading in a southeasterly direction.

6.0 Descend to cross the creek and arrive at a cattle-grazing area. Continue climbing on the other side of the creek.

6.6 Arrive at the Lost Creek Wilderness Area boundary. Turn around to return the way you came.

13.2 Arrive at your vehicle.

Ride Information

Local Information

Park County Tourism Office, 501 Main Street, P.O. Box 1373, Fairplay 80440; (719) 836-4279

Local Events and Attractions

Fairplay Beach Recreation Area, Fairplay; (719) 836-4279

Forest Service Mountain Bike Trails, Fairplay; (719) 836-4279

South Park City Museum, Fairplay; (719) 836-2387

Wetlands Trail, located atop the east side of Kenosha Pass. The trail follows an old railroad bed to a wetlands viewing area and an overlook with incredible views of the South Park Valley. No pets are allowed on this trail.

Organizations

Colorado Trail Foundation, Lakewood; (303) 526-0898; www.coloradotrail.org

Books

The Colorado Trail: The Official Guidebook by Randy Jacobs (Englewood, Colo.: Westcliffe Publishing, 2000)

43 Pine Valley Ranch to Buffalo Creek Mountain Bike Recreation Area

Pine Valley Ranch Park serves as an excellent access point into the northern sector of Buffalo Creek Mountain Bike Recreation Area. Delivering the cool, rushing waters of the North Fork of the South Platte River, picnic tables, rest rooms, potable water, and 5.2 miles of trails, Pine Valley Ranch Park offers riders a pleasant oasis in the otherwise more-crowded Buffalo Creek Area. The park is truly one of Jefferson County's most beautiful. The route described here incorporates two trails found in Pine Valley Ranch Park and combines them with six trails in the Buffalo Creek Mountain Bike Recreation Area, making for a 13.4-mile loop. In general, the single-track here is well groomed and well marked.

Start: The Pine Valley Ranch Park

Distance: 13.4-mile loop

Approximate riding time: Advanced riders, 1.5–2 hours; intermediate riders, 2–3 hours

Aerobic level: Physically moderate due to the lesser degrees of elevation gain. The trail also alternates its ascents and descents.

Technical difficulty: Technically easy, as the trail rolls over consistently smooth gravel single-track. Sections do require some technical skills, however, as the trail also includes rocky and sloping terrain.

Terrain: Singletrack and doubletrack that roll over hard-packed trails and loose granite-rock singletrack, and through burned sections of the Pike National Forest caused by the Hi Meadow Fire of 2000

Schedule: May–October

Maps: DeLorme *Colorado Atlas & Gazetteer*, page 49; USGS: Pine, CO; Trails Illustrated: #105, Tarryall Mountains and Kenosha Pass, CO; Buffalo Creek Recreation Area map; Pine Valley Ranch Park map

Nearest town: Pine Junction

Other trail users: Hikers, horseback riders, anglers, and picnickers

Canine compatibility: Dog-friendly

Trail contact: Pike National Forest, South Park Ranger District, Fairplay; (719) 836-2031

Finding the Trailhead: From North Denver, drive west on Interstate 70 to Colorado Highway 470. Drive south on CO 470 for roughly 5.8 miles before bearing right to head west on U.S. Highway 285 for roughly 21.7 miles. Turn left onto Pine Valley Road (Road 126) at the light in Pine Junction. Drive on Pine Valley Road for 6 miles before turning right onto Crystal Lake Road, following the sign for Pine Valley Ranch Park. Drive on Crystal Lake Road for 0.6 mile before entering the park. Parking spaces are available.

From South Denver, take US 285 west to Conifer. At the light in Pine Junction, make a left onto Pine Valley Road (Road 126). Drive on Pine Valley Road for 6 miles before turning right onto Crystal Lake Road, following the sign for Pine Valley Ranch Park. Drive on Crystal Lake Road for 0.6 mile before entering the park. Parking spaces are available.

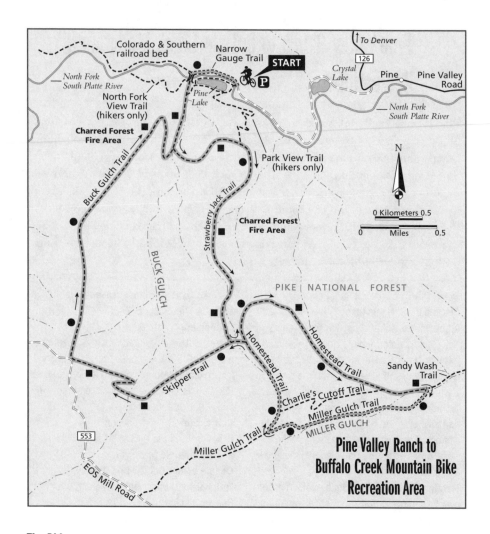

The Ride

Part of what makes Pine Valley Ranch Park one of the more exquisite Jefferson County Open Space Parks is the historic Pine Valley Lodge. Nestled in the timbers above the parking lot, the historic lodge incorporates native rock and white spruce into its exterior and interior construction.

The lodge was the brainchild of William A. Baehr, who bought Pine Valley Ranch in 1925. Inspired by the natural surroundings, noted Denver architect J. B. Benedict designed the lodge to reflect the manor homes found in Germany's Black Forest.

Known as the "Baehrden of the Rockies," the lodge includes intricate wrought iron detailing and wood highlighted with pyrographic etchings. These etchings serve as a haunting foreshadowing of what this valley would later have to endure.

Riders begin their route heading west on the Narrow Gauge Trail that parallels the North Fork of the South Platte River. Before Baehr's arrival, Charlie Eggert ran an ice company here. Eggert's ice company bought the land in 1908 and started producing ice by diverting water from the North Fork of the South Platte River into area man-made lakes. The ice was then cut into large blocks and transported to Denver via the Colorado & Southern Railroad (CSR). Today, the Narrow Gauge Trail follows the CSR's railroad bed.

After intersecting with the Buck Gulch Trail, riders climb moderately over wide singletrack dusted with loose granite rock to the Strawberry Jack Trail.

The Strawberry Jack Trail provides riders their first look into the fire-scarred remains of the Pike National Forest. Backed by winds in excess of 60 mph, the Hi Meadow Fire ripped through this area in 2000. Because it was a wind-driven fire, the blaze traveled quickly, scorching all in its path with high-intensity heat. Fortunately, many of the trees' root systems were saved. Thus, the nutrient-rich soils that naturally occur after a blaze such as this will eventually enable the trees and underbrush to recover. Indeed, some of the area's vegetation has already begun to flourish, as is evidenced in the vegetation along the Strawberry Jack Trail.

Nevertheless, the tree and vegetation loss brought on by the Hi Meadow Fire made this area particularly prone to flooding. Parts of the Strawberry Jack Trail can get quite sandy and rutted after heavy rains. The loss of much of the forest canopy, along with its underbrush, has made this trail particularly hot and dry.

Once they intersect with the Homestead Trail, riders travel over narrower singletrack as it passes through a large boulder field. The Homestead Trail descends quickly over granite-gravel singletrack. This gravel has a curious ball-bearing effect, so check your speed. Nearing 5 miles into your ride and after negotiating moderately rocky and root-filled terrain, the Homestead Trail delivers riders to a pleasant riparian section of the route.

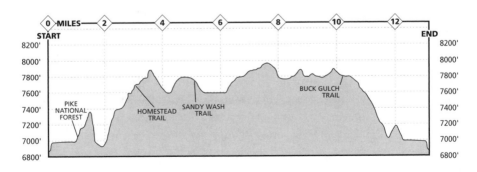

The pack heads home via the Miller Gulch Trail.

Riders soon connect with the unmarked Miller Gulch Trail then climb gradually on wide doubletrack. Luckily, after 1 mile a Miller Gulch Trail sign does appear on the right, relieving any route uncertainty.

After its second intersection with Charlie's Cutoff Trail, the Homestead Trail descends swiftly over smooth doubletrack and through a variety of meadows before returning riders to its intersection with the Strawberry Jack and Skipper Trails.

The Skipper Trail descends to Buck Creek via moderate switchbacks before rising up from it again. This is possibly the sweetest section of trail. From the creek, riders have to negotiate over physically challenging and technically moderate terrain, as the trail rising from the creek bed is rutted and sandy.

Although the descent on the Buck Gulch Trail is very fast, the water diversion ditches that stretch across the trail can provide both good bunny-hop potential and bum-blasting potential. The trail switches back a few times along a north-facing, slippery slope before arriving at its intersection with the Strawberry Jack Trail. The descent along Buck Gulch has a particularly spooky air to it, as you can literally smell the charred trees whose trunks are still scarred with soot from the Hi Meadow Fire.

The blaze began in the Hi Meadow section of the Burland Ranchettes subdivision near the town of Bailey on Monday, June 12, and lasted for eight days. For four of those days, the Hi Meadow Fire released as much energy every half-hour as one hydrogen bomb. Flames soared 150 feet high. At first, the fire was believed to have been started by a lightning strike. Further investigation revealed its cause to be an errant campfire. In all, the Hi Meadow Fire consumed 10,500 acres and destroyed 51 homes and 7 other structures. Property damage, combined with suppression and rehabilitation costs, amounted to more than $15 million. While the Strawberry Jack, Miller Gulch, and Buck Gulch Trails were temporarily closed during rehabilitation efforts, they have now all been reopened and are in surprisingly good shape.

Leaving the charred remains of the past to heal itself, riders continue their descent along the Buck Gulch Trail to its intersection with the cool-running waters of the South Platte River. From this intersection, it's an easy flow back to your vehicle.

Miles and Directions

0.0 Descend from the parking lot, pass the rest rooms, and begin riding in a westerly direction on the doubletrack, multiuse Narrow Gauge Trail.

0.3 The Narrow Gauge Trail intersects with the North Fork View Trail and the Buck Gulch Trail. Cross over the river via the bridge and continue riding straight in a southerly direction on the singletrack of the Buck Gulch Trail.

0.8 The Buck Gulch Trail (Trail 772) enters into the Pike National Forest and intersects with the Strawberry Jack Trail (Trail 710). Bear left onto the Strawberry Jack Trail, crossing a creek, and continue climbing more arduously in a southeasterly direction.

1.4 The Strawberry Jack Trail intersects with the hikers-only Park View Trail to the left. Continue riding in a southerly direction along the Strawberry Jack Trail. The Park View Trail descends to Pine Valley Ranch Park.

3.0 The Strawberry Jack Trail intersects with the Skipper and Homestead Trails. Bear left (east) onto the Homestead Trail and continue riding on plush singletrack.

4.6 The Homestead Trail intersects with the Charlie's Cutoff Trail on the right. Continue riding on the Homestead Trail as it makes its descent to the Sandy Wash Trail. **Option:** Riders wanting to shorten the loop of their ride by 3.4 miles can bear right onto the Charlie's Cutoff Trail, avoiding all of the Miller Gulch Trail.

5.1 The Homestead Trail leads into the Sandy Wash Trail. Continue riding on the Sandy Wash Trail.

5.8 After a short and moderately technical climb, the Sandy Wash Trail reaches its high point and intersects with the Miller Gulch Trail on the right. At this point, the Miller Gulch Trail is unmarked and goes off in a westerly direction, while the Sandy Wash Trail continues its descent in a southeasterly direction. Bear sharply to the right here, switchbacking above the route that you had been following along the Sandy Wash Trail, and continue on the unmarked, wide doubletrack of the Miller Gulch Trail, heading in a westerly direction.

6.7 The Miller Gulch Trail curves to the right, as riders pass a brown Miller Gulch Trail sign on the right. Welcome evidence of being on the correct trail.

7.9 The Miller Gulch Trail intersects with the Homestead Trail (Trail 728) on the right. Bear right here onto the Homestead Trail, and continue riding in a northerly direction.

8.0 The Homestead Trail intersects with Charlie's Cutoff Trail on the right. Continue straight here on the Homestead Trail.

8.8 The Homestead Trail intersects with the Strawberry Jack and Skipper Trails. Bear left here, choosing the Skipper Trail.

10.2 The Skipper Trail intersects with Service Road 553 and the Buck Gulch Trail. There is no sign for the Buck Gulch Trail at this intersection, but there will be a sign reading PINE VALLEY that points in a northerly direction. Bear right onto the Buck Gulch Trail by the PINE VALLEY sign and descend in a northerly direction.

12.6 The Buck Gulch Trail intersects with the Strawberry Jack Trail. At this point, continue your northerly descent along the Buck Gulch Trail back to the trailhead.

13.4 Arrive at your vehicle.

Ride Information

Trail Information
Jefferson County Open Space Trails Hotline, Evergreen; (303) 271-5975

Local Information
Conifer Chamber of Commerce, 26437 Conifer Road, Conifer 80433; (303) 838-0178

Local Events and Attractions
Colorado Trail, 470-mile trail from Denver to Durango
Denver Firefighters Museum, Denver; (303) 392-1436

Restaurants
Coney Dog Stand, Conifer; (303) 838-4210

Organizations
Front Range Mountain Bike Patrol, frmp@mindspring.com

Books
The Colorado Trail: The Official Guidebook by Randy Jacobs (Englewood, Colo.: Westcliffe Publishing, 2000)

44 Baldy Trail to Gashouse Gulch Trail

The Buffalo Creek Mountain Bike Recreation Area includes a network of outstanding singletrack within an hour's drive of Denver. Most of the riding rolls through thick forests over smooth and tacky singletrack. Some sandy sections appear along the way, but they don't last long. Charred trees mark the path of a forest fire that devastated much of this area. Despite the burn scars, the Buffalo Creek Mountain Bike Recreation Area remains a mountain biker's playground. A variety of campsites dot the region in case you want to turn your day ride into an overnighter.

Start: Junction of FR 550 and FR 543

Distance: 7.7-mile loop with options to connect to a host of other singletrack trails

Approximate riding time: Advanced riders, 45–60 minutes; intermediate riders, 1.5 hours.

Aerobic level: Physically easy to moderate due to short mileage but some moderate climbing

Technical difficulty: Technically easy to moderate due to occasional sandy and rocky sections

Terrain: Improved dirt roads, doubletrack, and singletrack. The terrain consists of mostly smooth-running singletrack, but there are a number of sandy patches to ride through, particularly at the route's onset. Two small rocky sections along the Gashouse Gulch Trail offer a challenging ride.

Schedule: May–October

Maps: DeLorme *Colorado Atlas & Gazetteer*, pages 49 and 50; USGS: Green Mountain, CO; Trails Illustrated: #135, Deckers & Rampart Range, CO; Buffalo Creek Recreation Area map

Nearest town: Buffalo Creek

Other trail users: Anglers, hikers, campers, and picnickers

Canine compatibility: Dog-friendly

Trail contact: Pike National Forest, South Platte Ranger District, Morrison; (303) 275-5610

Finding the Trailhead:

From North Denver, drive west on Interstate 70 to Colorado Highway 470. Drive south on CO 470 for roughly 5.8 miles before bearing right to head west on U.S. Highway 285 for roughly 21.7 miles. Turn left onto Pine Valley Road (Road 126) at the light in Pine Junction. Drive on Pine Valley Road for 13.9 miles. Turn right onto Forest Road (FR) 550, roughly 4 miles past the town of Buffalo Creek. Once on FR 550, drive for another 5 miles before parking your vehicle at the junction of FR 550 and FR 543. Park on the right side, along Buffalo Creek. There is additional parking at the nearby Meadows Group Campground. The ride begins on FR 543 after crossing Buffalo Creek.

From South Denver, take US 285 west to Pine Junction. At the light in Pine Junction, make a left onto Pine Valley Road (Road 126). Drive on Pine Valley Road for 13.9 miles. Turn right onto FR 550, roughly 4 miles past the town of Buffalo Creek. Once on FR 550, drive for another 5 miles before parking your vehicle at the junction of FR 550 and FR 543. Park on the right side, along Buffalo Creek. There is additional parking at the nearby Meadows Group Campground. The ride begins on FR 543 after crossing Buffalo Creek.

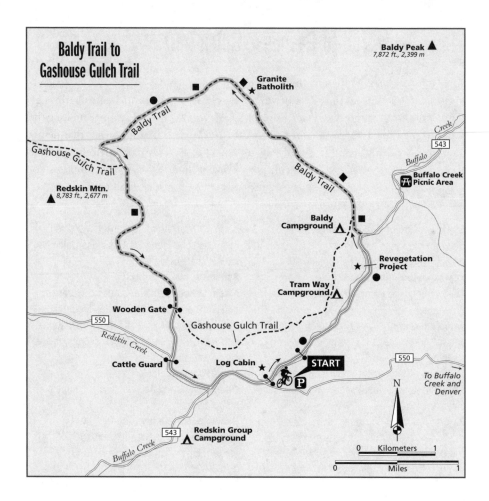

Baldy Trail to Gashouse Gulch Trail

Baldy Peak ▲
7,872 ft., 2,399 m

Granite ★
Batholith

Baldy Trail

Creek

543

Buffalo

Gashouse Gulch Trail

Redskin Mtn. ▲
8,783 ft., 2,677 m

Baldy Trail

Buffalo Creek
Picnic Area

Baldy
Campground ▲

Revegetation
Project ★

Tram Way
Campground ▲

Wooden Gate

Gashouse Gulch Trail

550

Redskin Creek

Cattle Guard

Log Cabin ★

START

P

550

To Buffalo
Creek and
Denver

N

543

Redskin Group
Campground ▲

Buffalo Creek

0   Kilometers   1

0   Miles   1

The Ride

Just 30 miles southwest of Denver lies a mini metro–mountain biking mecca. Commonly referred to as the "Buffalo Creek Mountain Bike Recreation Area," this part of the Pike National Forest provides a vast network of fine singletrack. Along with being one of several put-ins for the 470-mile Colorado Trail, the Buffalo Creek Mountain Bike Recreation Area is also home to the Baldy and Gashouse Gulch trails. Acclaimed for its smooth and easily negotiable singletrack, the 7.7-mile Baldy to Gashouse Gulch route provides as much satisfying sweetness as a short stack of flapjacks on a breezy camper's morning.

Within the first 0.5 mile, the route delivers with a fast and cool descent on FR 543, following Buffalo Creek downstream. After a mile, you come upon the chilling remains of a once-thriving forest. Thrown from your mountain biking reverie, the bitter reality of nature's destructive and regenerative forces is brought immediately to bear. Before you lies the charred remains of the 1996 Buffalo Creek forest fire.

On Saturday, May 18, 1996, a campfire left for dead atop Gashouse Gulch turned itself into a wind-whipped wildfire. Within hours, the flames had grown from the confines of a rock-lined fire pit to a 10,000-acre furnace. Ten miles long and 2 miles wide, the fire raged for five days and destroyed 12,000 acres at a cost of $2.8 million. The effects of such an inferno take on a whole new reality when one follows its devastating path. Beginning at mile 1.5, the Baldy Trail weaves its singletrack course in between the standing corpses of ponderosa pine. As the Baldy Trail scratches its sandy way to higher ground, staccato islands of roundleaf bluebell (*campanula rotundifolia*) and mullein (*verbascum thapsus*) reaffirm nature's recuperative powers.

Portions of this route's 7.7 miles remain remarkably unscathed by fire and are full of life. After 2 miles into the ride, the trail enters a wonderful ponderosa pine forest and climbs gradually. The singletrack narrows, and the forest through which you're riding opens up a bit. The trees here seem taller and less crowded—a welcome contrast to the soot-caked skeletons that introduced your ride.

As you near the summit and the junction of Baldy and Gashouse Gulch Trails, the singletrack exits the forest and crosses a huge rock face. Pushing its way up into overlying metamorphic rocks, this granite batholith remains as a tremendous intrusion of molten magma. Continue your fire-ride by scaling this formerly molten magma, then veer to the left. By mile 3.7, the forest has been overtaken by boulders. A natural grotto to your left provides a dry respite from the area's sudden and regular thunderstorms.

From this point, the trail takes you over grassy knolls and through meadows and flat-surfaced forests. While the Gashouse Gulch Trail began as a dirt road, it eventually disintegrates into a rough-looking doubletrack before connecting to a singletrack trail leading off to the left. The Gashouse Gulch singletrack offers fast descents, tight switchbacks, creek-crossings, and one very technical rocky section at mile 5.8. Pass through the wooden gate, and enjoy a fast ride on the road to FR 550, hitting as many jumps as possible. From there, FR 550 takes you back to your vehicle.

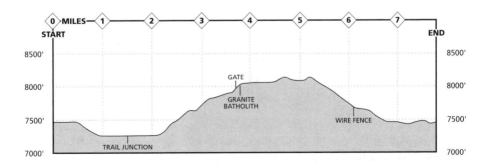

Racing out of the scorched forest.

Miles and Directions

0.0 Start at the gate at FR 543. Go under the gate and begin your ride, with Buffalo Creek to your right. A beautiful alpine log home will be to your left. Fashioned after the Euro-style log homes of old, this private residence backs up to a collection of enormous rocks.

0.4 Go around another gate and cross Buffalo Creek a second time.

1.3 Arrive at the sandy bottom. A revegetation project along the banks of Buffalo Creek will be to your left. Following FR 543 downstream for approximately 50 yards past this project, you'll notice a large sandy area to your left. Strewn across this area will be four large rocks imbedded in the sand. Veer left off of FR 543, riding between these rocks and continue through the sand heading into the burned forest. The singletrack will begin to your left shortly thereafter marked by the Gashouse Gulch trail sign.

1.5 Junction of the Gashouse Gulch and Baldy Trails. Veer right onto Baldy Trail.

2.3 A fallen pine tree obstructs the trail. Carefully walk your bike under it and continue your ride. Be aware of blowdowns.

3.7 Cross wire gate. The area here is distinct for its large rock formations—a great place to mix bouldering in with your day of riding. If you scurry to the tops of these boulders to your right, you'll be treated to a killer view of Baldy Peak.

4.5 Junction of Gashouse Gulch and Baldy Trails. Gashouse Gulch will lead both to the right and to the left. Take the left route. At this point the trail will become a rough-looking dirt road.

5.1 The rough doubletrack/dirt road will intersect with a singletrack veering off to the left. Veer left onto this singletrack.

6.1 Cross another wire fence.

6.8 Arrive at FR 550. Veer left onto FR 550, crossing the cattle guard at 6.9 miles.

7.2 FR 550 intersects with FR 543 to your right. Bear left, continuing on FR 550.

7.7 You return to your vehicle.

Ride Information

Trail Information
Pike and San Isabel National Forests, Pueblo; (719) 523-6591

Local Information
Conifer Chamber of Commerce, 26437 Conifer Road, Conifer 80433; (303) 838-0178

Local Events and Attractions
Colorado Trail, 470-mile trail from Denver to Durango
Denver Firefighters Museum, Denver; (303) 392-1436

Restaurants
Coney Dog Stand, Conifer; (303) 838-4210

Organizations
Front Range Mountain Bike Patrol, frmp@mindspring.com

Books
The Colorado Trail: The Official Guidebook by Randy Jacobs (Englewood, Colo.: Westcliffe Publishing, 2000)

Honorable Mentions

Denver Region

Five more rides in the Denver region deserve mention, even though they didn't make the "A" list. They may be a bit out of the way or more heavily traveled, but they still deserve your attention when considering a destination.

L Kingston Peak Loop

The Kingston Peak Loop is a popular four-by-four vehicle route that doesn't deter cyclists from making it a popular high-mountain ride. Beginning in the old mining town of Alice, the route travels to 12,000 feet, as it makes its loop around 12,147-foot Kingston Peak. Be advised, however, that a good deal of this route travels above timberline, so it's best to get an early start on the day.

Some riders may appreciate the loop's proximity to St. Mary's Glacier. At 11,000 feet high, St. Mary's Glacier provides a permanent ten-acre snowfield, offering year-round skiing and snowboarding. For the adventurous type, you can complement a day's riding in the saddle with a day's riding in the snow.

To reach the Kingston Peak Loop, drive west on Interstate 70 and take exit 238 (Fall River Road). Bear right onto Fall River Road and drive for roughly 9 miles. Pass Alice Road on your left and drive for another 0.5 mile before parking in the dirt pullout area on the left side of the road near an old chair lift. Return to Alice Road and begin riding toward the town of Alice.

For more information on the Kingston Peak Loop, contact the Roosevelt National Forest at (303) 444–6600.

M South Platte River Greenway

As one of the first greenway systems in America, downtown Denver's South Platte River Greenway is truly a success story. This 30-mile paved bike path follows the South Platte River from Chatfield State Park through Denver to the river's confluence with Clear Creek. The river runs for 10.5 miles through the downtown, residential, and industrial neighborhoods of Denver.

Since its inception, the South Platte River Greenway Foundation has created 150 miles of trails, boat launches, chutes, and parks in four counties and nine municipalities, and it has served as an example for more than a dozen greenways across the nation.

For more information, contact the Greenway Foundation, South Platte River Commission at www.greenwayfoundation.org.

N Cherry Creek Singletrack

The Cherry Creek Singletrack is a hidden jewel of a trail in an otherwise urbanized landscape. The trail parallels Cherry Creek, as well as the paved Cherry Creek Bike Path, from Colorado Boulevard to the Highline Canal. The paved bike path extends for 15 miles. The trail may be closed periodically due to flooding during the spring runoff season. The singletrack itself offers narrow and rocky sections that sometimes fall steeply to the creek. Should any sections be too challenging to risk riding, riders can bail to the paved bike path, which is always, for the most part, close at hand. This trail is ideal for the family whose preferences are split between riding on pavement or riding on dirt. For the urban jungle swinger who hasn't yet traded in his mountain bike for a bus pass, this trail offers some tasty singletrack that pierces directly through the heart of Denver—and isn't that incentive enough?

From downtown Denver, drive south on Speer Boulevard for roughly 4.3 miles, crossing University Avenue, to the Cherry Creek Mall. Park behind the south side of the mall and pick up the Cherry Creek Bike Path.

For more information, contact the Bicycle Program City of Denver, (303) 640–BIKE (2453) or DRCOG Pedestrian Bicycle Committee, (303) 455–1000.

O Chatfield Reservoir State Park

Chatfield Reservoir State Park offers riders a mellow cruise on its multiuse trails, many of which are wheelchair-accessible. The 24 miles of trails crisscross throughout the park.

The reservoir is primarily a haven for Denver urbanites, accommodating more than 1.5 million visitors a year. As such, you might expect it to deliver a multitudinous variety of recreational activities. And it does.

As one of the most complete parks in all of Colorado, Chatfield Reservoir State Park offers the metro area 5,600 acres of land and 1,450 acres of water. The park is popular for horseback riding, hiking, boating, swimming, fishing, camping, picnicking, and bird-watching.

For more information contact Chatfield State Park, (303) 791–7275.

To get to Chatfield Reservoir State Park, drive south on Wadsworth Boulevard (Colorado Highway 121) past Colorado Highway 470, and turn left into the park at the Deer Creek entrance. You can also reach the park by driving south on Santa Fe Boulevard and turning right (west) onto Titan Road. Drive about 3 miles on Titan Road before turning right again (north) onto Roxborough Park Road, entering the park via the Plum Creek entrance.

P Castlewood Canyon State Park

In a sport that has become so identified with the mountains that you can't speak its name without first saying "mountain," Castlewood Canyon State Park serves as a reminder that mountain biking need not take place in the mountains.

Castlewood Canyon State Park stands as a mountain biking monument to Denver's hinterlands, the sprawling grasslands of Colorado's eastern plains. Although providing views of 14,110-foot Pikes Peak to the south and 14,255-foot Longs Peak to the north, the routes that pass through Castlewood Canyon State Park course through prairie grasses and past juniper and piñon trees.

One such route is the Castlewood Canyon Loop, a route that follows a dirt road through the park for more than 25 miles. While the loop is long, it isn't tough, as there are no significant elevation gains. The route begins in Castle Rock and travels south on Gilbert Street before connecting with Castlewood Canyon Road (County Road 51) through the park. Once through the park, riders connect with CO 86 and return to Castle Rock.

Located in the Black Forest of central Colorado, east of Castle Rock, Castlewood Canyon State Park has as its centerpiece the century-old Castlewood Canyon Dam. In 1890 Cherry Creek, the creek that runs through the canyon, was dammed for irrigation. When the dam broke on August 3, 1933, the subsequent flooding claimed two lives and caused $1 million in damages. What remained, however, was an exquisite canyon with unique ruins. Where the reservoir once lay behind the dam now is an open prairie, displaying Douglas fir and ponderosa pine trees. The many cliffs, bluffs, and overlooks make for incredible photo opportunities and invite the skilled rock climber.

There are also a number of scenic hiking trails that descend to the bottom of the canyon and those that traverse its rim. The park also offers a visitor center.

To reach Castlewood Canyon State Park, drive south from Denver on I–25 to exit 181 in Castle Rock. Bear right onto Colorado Highway 83. Drive south on CO 83 for 7 miles to the main entrance, roughly 5 miles past the intersection with Colorado Highway 86. The entrance is on the right (west).

For more information, contact Castlewood Canyon State Park at (303) 688–5242. Also, contact Colorado State Parks at (303) 866–3437.

Colorado Springs Region

Colorado Springs is surround by majestic mountain beauty, a beauty that didn't go unnoticed when Katharine Lee Bates was inspired to compose "America the Beautiful" while standing atop Pikes Peak more than a century ago. Perhaps that is why Pikes Peak has become known as America's Mountain.

But while Colorado Springs sits at the foot of Pikes Peak, there are a variety of other spectacular geological points of interest. The Garden of the Gods is a free, city-owned park comprised of spectacular, 300-million-year-old, red sandstone formations that can be seen jutting toward the sky from many places in and around Colorado Springs. Early Native Americans believed the Garden of the Gods to be just that and so considered it a sacred place. The Cave of the Winds is another natural wonder. This cave system began to form more than 200 million years ago deep within the Williams Canyon limestone, a rare geological formation that occurs nowhere else in the world. It wasn't until 1881 that two young brothers on a church outing discovered the caves, which are encrusted with colorful stalactites, stalagmites, and flowstone curtains. Also nearby are the Manitou Cliff Dwellings. Ancestral Puebloans lived in these dwellings between 1100 and 1300 A.D. and crafted some of this country's finest early pottery. Needless to say, these Ancestral Puebloans, along with native Ute, Cheyenne, Kiowa, and Arapaho Indians, were the earliest known residents of the Colorado Springs area. While many of these tribes were hostile toward one another, they all laid down their weapons upon entering the sacred grounds of the nearby Manitou Springs and the Garden of the Gods.

General William Jackson Palmer, a Civil War general from Pennsylvania, founded the city of Colorado Springs in 1871 as a tourist destination. To service the tourist industry, Palmer also founded the Denver & Rio Grande Railroad in that same year. He envisioned Colorado Springs becoming a world-class resort destination and went so far as to nickname the new town "Little London." But it was gold, not tourism, that attracted miners to the area, settling the mining town of Cripple Creek in 1890, just west of Colorado Springs. By 1900 Colorado Springs was the leading mining exchange center of the world and received a new nickname—"City of Millionaires"—and for good reason. By 1904 Colorado Springs was home to thirty-five of the country's one hundred millionaires from gold mined in Cripple Creek. But Palmer would have his day yet. Following the end of the gold rush in 1903, Colorado Springs' sunny conditions and dry, mild climate attracted many visitors and still continue to do so.

Today, tourism is Colorado Springs' third largest industry, employing more than 14,000 people and contributing more than $800 million to the local economy. More than 6 million people visit Colorado Springs each year. With a population of 350,000, Colorado Springs is Colorado's second-largest city next to Denver. The Springs, as it is commonly referred to, offers residents and tourists alike incredible outdoor recreational opportunities. Nearby Pikes Peak, North and South Cheyenne Canyon Park, Manitou Springs, and Woodland Park offer outdoor enthusiasts a varied assortment of bike-riding opportunities.

For more information on these areas, or on the greater Pikes Peak region, contact the Colorado Springs Convention and Visitors Bureau at (800) DO–VISIT or the Pikes Peak Country Attractions Association at (800) 525–2250.

45 Raspberry Chautauqua Mountain Trail

The Raspberry Chautauqua Mountain Trail is a gem that relatively few riders have come to appreciate. (It is perhaps more commonly known as the Limbaugh Canyon Loop to most residents of Monument and the rest of the Colorado Springs area.) The beginning of the ride described here includes a steady climb up Mount Herman Road to the intersection with the Raspberry Chautauqua Mountain Trail. Aside from a moderate warm-up to the day ahead, the road offers views of Elephant Rock, Monument Rock, and the U.S. Air Force Academy. Once the road intersects with the singletrack, the Raspberry Chautauqua Mountain Trail weaves a sinuous path through Limbaugh Canyon and skirts Chautauqua Mountain. The trail can be quite technical in spots, offering tight singletrack, steep grades, and large rock drop-offs. While the trail is mostly hidden in dense tree cover, there is one section (Inspiration Point) that offers riders views of the town of Monument and the Palmer Lake area.

Start: Red Rocks Drive where you parked your vehicle
Distance: 9.7-mile loop
Approximate riding time: Advanced riders, 1.5 hours; intermediate riders, 2 hours
Aerobic level: Physically moderate, due to sustained climbs on Mount Herman Road
Technical difficulty: Technically moderate to challenging, due to the tight and rocky singletrack
Terrain: Dirt road and singletrack, which is tight and technical and runs over large rocks and through dried creek beds and open meadows

Schedule: May–October
Maps: DeLorme *Colorado Atlas & Gazetteer,* page 50; USGS: Palmer Lake, CO; Trails Illustrated: #137, Pikes Peak–Cañon City, CO; Monument/Palmer Lake Trails Map
Nearest town: Monument
Other trail users: Hikers and campers
Canine compatibility: Dog-unfriendly, due to the vehicular traffic along this route
Trail contact: Pike National Forest, South Platte Ranger District, Morrison; (303) 275-5610

Finding the Trailhead: From Colorado Springs, drive north on Interstate 25 for 19.5 miles then take exit 161 for Monument and Palmer Lake. At the end of the ramp by the stoplight, bear left onto Colorado Highway 105 and drive west crossing over I-25. This road becomes Second Street. Pass straight through a stoplight and continue driving west on Second Street for roughly 1 mile to Mitchell Avenue at a T intersection. Bear left onto Mitchell, following signs for Monument Fire Center, Mount Herman Road, and Forest Road 320, and drive roughly half a mile before bearing right onto Mount Herman Road. Drive 2.4 miles on Mount Herman then bear right onto Red Rocks Drive. Immediately bear right again into the parking lot pullout.

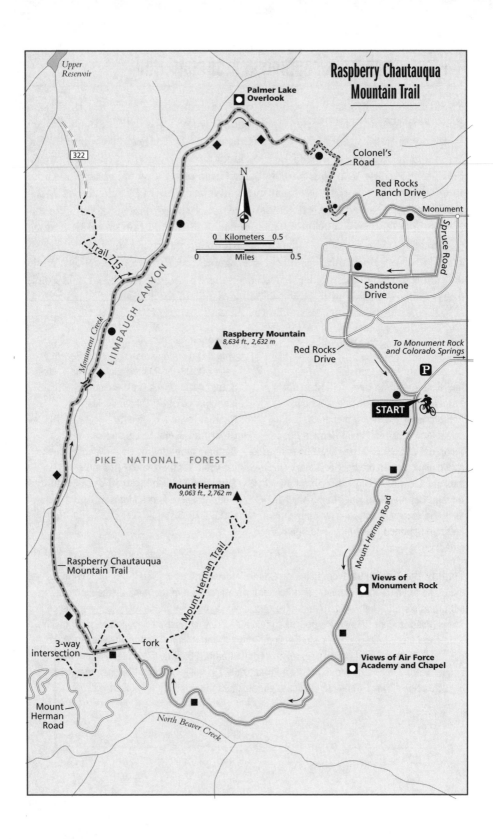

Raspberry Chautauqua Mountain Trail

Upper Reservoir

Palmer Lake Overlook

Colonel's Road

Red Rocks Ranch Drive

Monument

322

Trail 715

Spruce Road

N

0 Kilometers 0.5

0 Miles 0.5

Sandstone Drive

Monument Creek

LIIMBAUGH CANYON

Raspberry Mountain
8,634 ft., 2,632 m

Red Rocks Drive

To Monument Rock and Colorado Springs

P

START

PIKE NATIONAL FOREST

Mount Herman
9,063 ft., 2,762 m

Mount Herman Trail

Raspberry Chautauqua Mountain Trail

Views of Monument Rock

Mount Herman Road

3-way intersection

fork

Views of Air Force Academy and Chapel

Mount Herman Road

North Beaver Creek

The Ride

Shortly after leaving your vehicle on Red Rocks Road, you'll begin climbing up Mount Herman Road. This is a popular thoroughfare for weekend enthusiasts and offers residents of Monument an immediate access point to the mountains. Founded in 1879, the town of Monument is one of Colorado's oldest established communities. For more than a hundred years, Monument's showpiece building has been the Estemere Estate.

Dr. William Finley Thompson built the Estemere Estate in 1887. Originally from Baltimore, Thompson began construction of the 5,700-square-foot Victorian mansion during the area's "Ambitious 80s" period. And with six fireplaces and eighteen rooms, some of which are dedicated solely to billiards and chess, this mansion is quite ambitious even by today's standards. For all the mansion's amenities, Dr. Thompson was certainly not a homebody. Indeed, he may have been one of Colorado's earliest commuters, as he regularly commuted to Denver via the Denver & Rio Grande (D&RG) Railroad to practice dentistry.

Continue riding up Mount Herman Road through fields of scrub oak before reaching the higher elevations with Douglas fir and ponderosa pine. As you ride, you may notice the bald spot atop Mount Herman. The mountain's premature root loss was caused by a wildfire that spread across its crown in the late 1980s. The road continues through much of the fire's path, distinguishable if not by the sometimes barren and burned scrub oak fields then most certainly by the Monument Fire Center that lies just off to your left.

As you start gaining elevation on the road, you may notice Elephant Rock to the northeast. Located in the town of Castle Rock, Elephant Rock is home to the annual Compass Bank Elephant Rock Cycling Festival. The festival draws hundreds of cycling enthusiasts each year and offers a variety of road and off-road cycling events and races to all ages and abilities. In 2002 a new $6 million Events Center was constructed in the Douglas County Fairgrounds roughly half a mile southeast of Castle Rock. The Events Center is home to the festival's start, finish, and Party at the Rock post-ride picnic and cycling exposition.

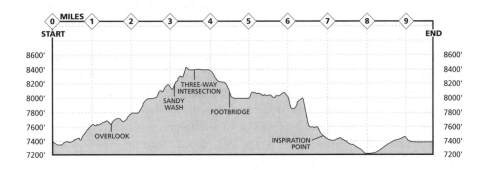

Monument Rock.

Higher still along the road, you may catch a glimpse of the Air Force Academy to the south, noticeable by its distinctively pointed-roofed chapel. Designed by Walter Netsch in 1954 and constructed in 1963, the modern expressionist Air Force Academy Chapel's seventeen silvery aluminum spires stand more than 150 feet tall. The chapel was designed to resemble a phalanx of fighter jets shooting up into the sky.

Once you intersect with the Raspberry Chautauqua Mountain Trail, continue climbing over marble-size Pikes Peak granite through dense forests of ponderosa pine and Douglas fir. Upon reaching the fork and the dried creek bed, bear left to climb the final push before arriving at the three-way intersection and the continuation of the Raspberry Chautauqua Mountain Trail.

The trail's continuation is marked by a bullet-riddled NO MOTORCYCLES sign on your right. From here, the trail is fast and rutted as it descends through tall stands of aspens to Monument Creek and through Limbaugh Canyon. Raspberry Mountain lies to the east, while Chautauqua Mountain lies to the northwest. Once crossing the creek, however, your ride mellows a bit as it runs through open meadows and intermittent stands of aspen. After about 5.5 miles into your ride, the trail travels along precipitously sloping terrain to your right. The trail here is quite narrow and rocky.

Your technical descent is rewarded, however, upon reaching a beautiful overlook of Palmer Lake at roughly 7 miles into your ride.

Leading an army expedition through the Rocky Mountains in 1835, Colonel Henry Dodge originally named it Summit Lake. The lake would be renamed Divide Lake before receiving its present name in honor of General William Palmer, who began building the D&RG Railroad in 1871. Palmer Lake is located on the Palmer Divide, where a watershed drainage separates the waters of the Platte River to the north and the Arkansas River to the south. In 1872 Palmer Lake served as a water supply for the steam engines of the D&RG Railroad. Ice houses at the south end of the lake also supplied ice for the railroad's dining cars. In 1882 the lake was enlarged to its present-day size of ten acres, and a boathouse, park, fountain, and covered pavilion were added to attract tourists to the area.

From the overlook, you'll dive into your final descent on steep singletrack to Colonel's Road before riding through Red Rocks Ranch and returning to your vehicle.

Miles and Directions

- **0.0** Start by bearing left from Red Rocks Drive to Mount Herman Road.
- **0.1** Red Rocks Drive intersects with Mount Herman Road. Bear right onto the dirt Mount Herman Road and begin climbing in a southerly direction.
- **1.5** Arrive at an overlook with views of Monument Rock to the north and the Air Force Academy to the south.
- **3.0** Mount Herman Road intersects with the Raspberry Chautauqua Mountain Trail (715, a.k.a. Limbaugh Canyon Loop Trail) on your right, marked by a NO SHOOTING sign. Bear right onto the Raspberry Chautauqua Mountain Trail and begin climbing on hard-packed singletrack and heading in a northerly direction.
- **3.1** The trail will fork at a sandy wash and dried creek bed. Bear left here and continue climbing toward the three-way intersection and the continuation of the Raspberry Chautauqua Mountain Trail. (Bearing right and choosing to ride up the dried creek bed delivers a grueling 0.4-mile climb through sandy and rutted terrain to a saddle where there are some interesting rock formations. Bearing left at the saddle will eventually lead to the three-way intersection and the continuation of the Raspberry Chautauqua Mountain Trail.)
- **3.6** Arrive at the three-way intersection and the continuation of the Raspberry Chautauqua Mountain Trail, marked by a bullet-riddled NO MOTORCYCLES sign on your right. Continue straight here onto the Raspberry Chautauqua Mountain Trail through Limbaugh Canyon.
- **4.5** Cross Monument Creek via a footbridge and portage your bike over some larger boulders.
- **6.9** Arrive at an overlook (Inspiration Point) with views of Palmer Lake. Continue descending on the Raspberry Chautauqua Mountain Trail.
- **7.3** The Raspberry Chautauqua Mountain Trail will intersect with an old watershed access road. Bear left here onto the road and pass through the aluminum fence.

7.4 The old watershed access road will intersect with Colonel's Road at a T intersection; bear right onto Colonel's Road and pass beyond a metal link gate. After the gate, Colonel's Road turns into Red Rocks Ranch Drive. Bear left onto Red Rocks Ranch Drive and descend through the Red Rocks Ranch area.

8.4 As Red Rocks Ranch Drive intersects with the paved Spruce Road, turn right onto Spruce and begin climbing.

8.6 Spruce Road intersects with Sandstone Drive. Bear right onto Sandstone Drive.

9.0 Sandstone Drive intersects with Red Rocks Drive at a four-way stop. Bear left onto Red Rocks Drive.

9.7 Arrive at your vehicle.

Ride Information

Local Information

Palmer Lake Tourist Information, P.O. Box 208, 42 Valley Crescent Road, Palmer Lake 80133; (719) 481-2953

Local Events and Attractions

Compass Bank Elephant Rock Cycling Festival, May–June, Castle Rock; www.elephantrock ride.com

Estemere Estate, Palmer Lake; (719) 481-0651

Palmer Lake, (719) 481-2953

Santa Fe Regional Trail, a 14-mile trail that runs south from Monument to the U.S. Air Force Academy

U.S. Air Force Academy, Colorado Springs; (719) 333-1110

46 Lovell Gulch Trail

Resembling the shape of a lollipop, the Lovell Gulch Trail is a popular ride located in the heart of Woodland Park. This trail offers a scenic route through a large, open valley and some of the area's best views of Pikes Peak. Camping is permitted at undeveloped sites along the trail. Climbing out of Lovell Gulch offers a moderate workout, but one well worth the effort as you intersect with the Rampart Range Road and the beginning of a screaming descent beneath power lines. The trail is well marked by National Forest trail signs.

Start: The Lovell Gulch trailhead
Distance: 5.5-mile lariat
Approximate riding time: Advanced riders, 30 minutes; intermediate riders, 45–60 minutes
Aerobic level: Easy to moderate due to lack of any significant elevation gains. The climb through Lovell Gulch, however, is physically moderate.
Technical difficulty: Technically easy to moderate due to the trail's predominantly smooth terrain; some sections of rock, loose sand, and roots, particularly after passing the interesting rock formations on the left just under 2 miles into your ride
Terrain: Singletrack and doubletrack over mostly smooth terrain through mixed conifer forests. There are some rockier and sandier sections, with one stream-crossing. Parts of the trail, like many trails in the Colorado Springs area, are covered in Pikes Peak granite.
Schedule: April–November
Maps: DeLorme *Colorado Atlas & Gazetteer*, page 50; USGS: Mount Deception, CO; Pike National Forest; Trails Illustrated: #137, Pikes Peak–Cañon City, CO
Nearest town: Woodland Park
Other trail users: Hikers and horseback riders
Canine compatibility: Dog-friendly
Trail contact: Pike and San Isabel National Forests, Pikes Peak Ranger District, Colorado Springs; (719) 636–1602

Finding the Trailhead: From Colorado Springs, drive west on U.S. Highway 24 for 17.7 miles before bearing right onto Baldwin Road in Woodland Park. Baldwin Road will run behind McDonald's and eventually turn into Rampart Range Road after passing Woodland Park High School on your right. Drive on Baldwin Road for 2 miles then turn left into the Lovell Gulch trailhead, next to the City Road Maintenance Building. Park in the designated parking lot by the trailhead.

The Ride

The first mile climbs gradually over smooth singletrack and through aspen and lodgepole pine forests. As you ride north out of Woodland Park along the edge of the timber, you'll pass private residences on your right. There are a number of campsites along the way as well.

Just under a mile into your ride, you'll pedal through thicker stands of aspen and ponderosa pine over soft and smooth singletrack. Here the trail can be very quiet

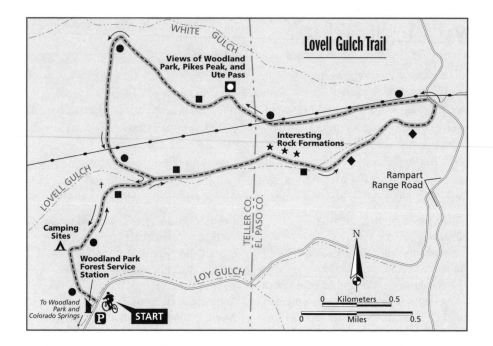

and calming. If you look carefully, you might spy a cross standing roughly 60 feet from the trail on the left. But that might be the only thing that is "left" in these parts.

Just 20 miles east of Woodland Park, in Colorado Springs, more than eighty national conservative Christian ministries have located their headquarters. Among the largest of these ministries is Focus on the Family, headed by Dr. James Dobson. Focus on the Family conducts popular Community Impact Seminars nationwide. These seminars typically attract between 400 and 600 people and are held in fundamentalist churches across the country. But for now, you are far from any church— or are you? Upon closer inspection, you notice that the cross is white, topped with a crown of barbed wire, and has nails hammered into its south, east, and west points, unmistakably representative of the wounds of Jesus Christ's crucifixion. Underneath the nails lie scraps of white paper containing handwritten notes, reportedly written by area schoolchildren.

After passing the cross at 0.7 mile, the trail narrows considerably. While narrow, the trail isn't particularly straight, but it's fun nevertheless. Vegetation gets thicker the closer you get to the stream at the bottom of Lovell Gulch. Once you cross the stream, the trail forks where a sign describes the loop ahead as being 3.75 miles around. The sign marks the beginning of the loop. From here, the trail climbs moderately, as it travels in an easterly direction upstream through the narrow valley of Lovell Gulch. The trail isn't too technical and travels over smooth singletrack. As you pass the interesting rock formations to your left just under 2 miles into your ride, you face the trail's first moderately technical climb, a nice challenging break from your otherwise mellow ride. The section delivers loose rocks and exposed roots.

Soon thereafter, you'll reach another physically and technically challenging section of exposed roots, deep ruts, and steep terrain. Your hard work pays off, however, as you intersect with Rampart Range Road. Coming to the top of the ridge, at the trail's junction with Rampart Range Road, the trail loops back to the west. Riding along the ridgeline, you are offered spectacular views of Pikes Peak, along with a thrilling descent beneath towering power lines over smooth singletrack.

Just under 3 miles into the ride, the trail once again leads into a mixed conifer and aspen forest along wider singletrack. By 3.4 miles, you'll climb a short but moderate hill under a thick canopy to the top of a grassy knoll where you can enjoy views of Woodland Park, Pikes Peak, and Ute Pass. From this point on the trail, it's easy to see how Woodland Park got its name: from the area's thickly wooded hills and valleys. The above-timberline crown of Pikes Peak stands in bold relief against seas of forest green and sky blue.

A Ute legend offers an explanation for the origins of Pikes Peak. It is said that the Great Spirit poured snow and ice through a funnel in the sky to form the Great Peak. Using the mountaintop as a stepping stone to retreat from the heavens to Earth, the Great Spirit poked holes with his fingers into the mountainside in which the plants and trees could grow. The Great Spirit's daughter would later be taken by a giant grizzly bear; their offspring became the Ute Indian Nation, first residents of Woodland Park. While Woodland Park, the town, had only been incorporated in 1891, the area has played host to the Ute Indians for more than one thousand years. The Ute Indians, the only tribe indigenous to Colorado and one of the few tribes never to have been conquered by another civilization in battle, would regularly pass through Woodland Park along the Ute Pass Trail, one of the oldest Native American thoroughfares in the country.

Ute Indians believed the Great Spirit of Manitou resided in the town of Manitou Springs, as evidenced by his blowing bubbles in the mineral springs. Beginning below the town, Ute Pass led northwest into the mountains to the town of South Park, from where Ute Indians would regularly transport salt. These early residents

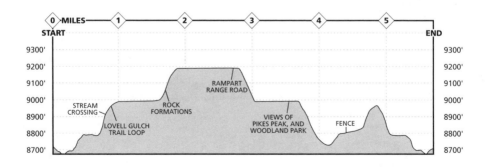

View of Pike's Peak.

knew well that Ute Pass was a well-established bison trail. Later, Ute Pass Trail became a wagon road before the Colorado Midland Railway laid its tracks to service the mountain mining operations farther west. The trail leads up and over Ute Pass, which skirts the north side of Pikes Peak and climbs 3,000 feet to the summit of the divide at 9,165 feet.

From the knoll, it's a quick descent on smooth and steep singletrack. The trail runs speedily under tall stands of aspen to rejoin the stream. From the stream it's a mellow cruise back to your vehicle.

Miles and Directions

0.0 Start by passing through the gate and descending down the wide doubletrack, heading in a northwesterly direction to the singletrack on the right.

0.5 Pass under power lines.

0.8 Cross a small stream and reach the beginning of the loop by the Lovell Gulch Trail Loop sign. Bear right, riding the loop in a counterclockwise direction and following the trail upstream in an easterly direction.

1.7 Pass some interesting rock formations to your left.

2.4 The Lovell Gulch Trail will intersect with Rampart Range Road beneath high power lines. Bear left under these power lines and continue riding on the singletrack in a westerly direction.

3.6 Reach the top of a grassy knoll, where you are offered the route's best views of Pikes Peak and the town of Woodland Park.

4.4 The trail meets a private fence line and parallels the fence.

4.6 Return to the beginning of the loop. Bear right. Cross the stream and return the way you came.

5.5 Reach your vehicle.

Ride Information

Local Information

Woodland Park Chamber of Commerce, 210 West Midland Avenue, Woodland Park 80866; (719) 687-9885; www.woodland-park-co.org

Local Events and Attractions

Crystola Canyon, off US 24 behind the Crystola Inn

Florissant Fossil Beds National Monument, $2.00–$4.00 admission, Florissant; (719) 748-3252 (fees subject to change)

Garden of the Gods, free admission, Colorado Springs; (719) 634-6666

Ute Pass Cultural Center and Historical Society, Midland; (719) 687-5284

Restaurants

The Donut Mill, Woodland Park; (719) 687-9793

Grandmother's Kitchen, Woodland Park; (719) 687-3118

Tres Hombres, Woodland Park; (719) 687-0625

47 Rampart Reservoir Shoreline Loop

The Rampart Reservoir Shoreline Loop offers mountain bikers of any ability the chance to test their skills on a variety of terrain. From sand to gravel to rocks and soft forest earth, the loop delivers it all. Within a stone's throw of the reservoir and under the watchful eye of Pikes Peak, this trail follows the shoreline all the way around, providing opportunities for fishing and picnicking. A favorite among locals, the Rampart Reservoir Shoreline Loop can get crowded on the weekends. It's best that mountain bikers ride the trail in a clockwise direction, so as not to come upon riders unexpectedly around the many tight and rocky curves.

Start: Trailhead of the Rampart Reservoir Shoreline Loop
Distance: 15.3-mile lariat
Approximate riding time: Advanced riders, 1.5 hours; intermediate riders 2–2.5 hours
Aerobic level: Physically moderate, due to a modest elevation gain
Technical difficulty: Technically moderate to difficult due to a few tight rocky sections.
Terrain: Improved dirt road and singletrack. The singletrack is covered in Pikes Peak granite, pebblelike rocks that absorb water, keeping trails in good shape during wet weather. These rocks are like ball bearings under your tires, making it tough to get out of steeper climbs.

Schedule: April–November
Maps: DeLorme *Colorado Atlas & Gazetteer*, page 62; USGS: Woodland Park and Cascade; Trails Illustrated: #137, Pikes Peak–Cañon City, CO; Team Telecycle map; Selected Colorado Hiking Trails: Pikes Peak Series
Nearest town: Woodland Park
Other trail users: Hikers, anglers, picnickers, boaters, horseback riders, campers, and seasonal ski tour groups.
Canine compatibility: Dog-friendly
Trail contact: Pike and San Isabel National Forests, Pikes Peak Ranger District, Colorado Springs; (719) 636-1602

Finding the Trailhead: From Colorado Springs, take Interstate 25 north to exit 141. After exiting, continue heading west on U.S. Highway 24 for 17.8 miles to the WELCOME TO WOODLAND PARK sign on your right. Turn right onto Baldwin Road, taking you behind McDonald's. Passing Woodland Park High School on your right, Baldwin Road will become Rampart Range Road. After 2.9 miles from when you turned onto Baldwin Road, Rampart Range Road will fork; take the right fork then turn right again onto the dirt road and the continuation of Rampart Range Road at 4.4 miles, following signs to the reservoir. Having driven 6.8 miles from when you turned onto Baldwin, the trailhead will be on your left. Pull into the lot for the Rampart Reservoir Shoreline Loop and begin your ride beyond the wooden gate.

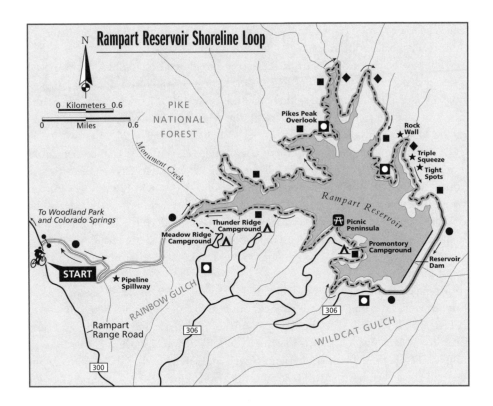

The Ride

Due in large part to the eye-catching pink granite pebbles blanketing this trail's 12-mile stretch of singletrack, the Rampart Reservoir Trail is a popular mountain biking ride among Colorado Springs riders. This trail's singletrack is made of the same stuff as Pikes Peak—namely, Pikes Peak granite. The rock consists of interlocking crystals of glasslike quartz, flat-surfaced white and pink feldspar, and a dash of black flaky mica.

Aside from its aesthetic appeal, Pikes Peak granite absorbs a great deal of water. For this reason, the Rampart Reservoir Trail sheds water easily, staying dry and in good shape, even after the wettest of weather. This feature allows the loop to remain active nearly twice the measly three-month, prime-time window Colorado typically affords mountain bikers. But Pikes Peak granite isn't necessarily always working in the mountain biker's best interest.

Its pebbly form acts as a kind of geological ball bearing. A collection of these pesky pink pebbles can throw even sequoia-like limbs into a tizzy. With the Rampart Reservoir's many roller coaster dips, up and around protruding boulders, and in and out of a variety of creek beds, the Pikes Peak granite singletrack does make for a physically challenging ride.

The ride begins at the Rampart Reservoir Shoreline Loop trailhead. As you cross the wooden gate, the trail begins with a fast, easterly 1.5-mile run through stands of quaking aspen to the pipeline spillway and the bridge. Bear left and continue on the north side of the spillway. On your right, the spillway brings water from mountain runoff to Rampart Reservoir.

After 4 miles, you cross Monument Creek and confront huge granite formations along the banks of the reservoir. For all you lounge lizards, here's a great place to take your rest and bask in pleasant warmth. Just beyond these rocks is a thick evergreen forest, complete with coiling roots and moist earth. This section quickly fades as the trail dries and leads into a tricky rocky section before offering a beautiful view of Pikes Peak. Part of the Rampart Reservoir Trail's appeal is its flirtatious skirting around huge boulders and through tight rocky sections. Pick your lines carefully and watch the noggin.

By mile 8.4 the trail leads to what local riders call The Dip. Large boulders lie in front of you as the trail descends to meet the banks of the reservoir. When the water is high, you'll have to take the left spur of the singletrack, traversing up and over these rocks. If the water level is low, after carefully negotiating the tight rocky section just before these boulders, lift your bicycle and scramble over the rocks to rejoin the trail above. Just beyond this section is the Triple Squeeze. These tight rocky sections keep you honest on a trail as user-friendly as this. Once you reach the dam, absorbing views of Pikes Peak await. Be careful here, as vehicles readily use this road.

As a holding tank, Rampart Reservoir supplies Colorado Springs with water via a 12-foot wide tunnel. A Swedish engineering firm bored Rampart Reservoir's shaft and its connecting tunnel. They bet city planners that the shaft and the tunnel would connect within 1 inch of specifications. The Swedes hit it right on the nose—an impressive display of engineering acuity if you consider the 20 miles the tunnel had to travel.

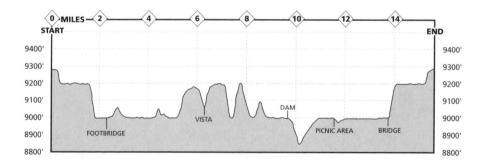

After rejoining the Rampart Reservoir singletrack just beyond the Wildcat Wayside Pike National Forest sign, continue through the ponderosa pine forest. Cross a stone culvert before arriving at Picnic Peninsula—a picnic area offering tables, water spigots, and shoreline views. Continue on the singletrack, veering right as it passes in front of the picnic table with the large boulder backdrop. This area contains many offshoots from the main trail. Know that the shoreline loop generally runs the course of the land contour through here. Passing through Picnic Peninsula, you're rewarded with a fast and smooth singletrack descent to the bridge. Veer left by the bridge and return to your vehicles.

Miles and Directions

0.0 Start at the trailhead located to the left of the parking lot. Go through the wooden gate and begin riding on the fast-descending Rampart Reservoir Shoreline Road to the spillway.

0.7 Reach the spillway and bear left over it. Continue riding downstream, now with the spillway on your right.

1.5 Reach a footbridge. This footbridge also marks the point to which you'll be returning. Pass the bridge and keep heading straight—we're going clockwise. (You have the option of riding the trail in a clockwise or counterclockwise direction, but there are three good reasons to ride the trail clockwise. 1) Logic and courtesy dictate that you travel in a clockwise direction, so as to avoid colliding with other trail users around the many blind curves. 2) It's more rideable in a clockwise direction. 3) Your drive train will usually be hanging downhill if ridden in a clockwise direction, minimizing the chances of damaging it.)

1.7 The singletrack begins.

2.3 Reach a marshy area. Cross this marshy area via footbridge.

5.4 Encounter technical, rocky section. The middle line offers the best results. This trail does have some tight rocky sections, so pick your lines carefully.

6.3 Beautiful place to take your rest and a view of Pikes Peak.

6.8 The trail divides here, leading into another marshy, forested area. The tendency is to follow the trail to the left, which will soon thereafter lead into a meadow, ultimately dead-ending. Instead, bear right, scouting out the trail, and cross the creek.

8.4 Reach the Dip. Here a rock wall blocks immediate passage. You'll have to portage your bicycle up and around this wall.

9.7 Reach the dam. Cross it and pick up the singletrack on the other side.

10.4 Come to the sign, WILDCAT WAYSIDE (PIKE NATIONAL FOREST). The singletrack trail continues 10 yards past the sign, on the right, just beyond the parked cars. At this point, you can take the road back to your vehicle. Although far less technical, this option does add some mileage to your ride, as well as a significant amount of climbing. Bear right onto the singletrack. Note that this section of the trail has a higher level of foot traffic, so be cautious.

11.6 Reach a sweet picnic spot, offering picnic tables and water spigots. Here the trail will Y. A hiking trail will veer to the left and split the two picnic tables, as the Rampart Reservoir Loop Trail keeps to the right, passing the picnic table with the large boulder behind it.

13.8 Reach the bridge. Bear left and climb back up the road the way you came.

15.3 Arrive back at your vehicle.

Ride Information

Local Information

Woodland Park Chamber of Commerce, 210 West Midland Avenue, Woodland Park 80866; (719) 687-9885; www.woodland-park-co.org

Local Events and Attractions

Florissant Fossil Beds National Monument, $2.00-$4.00 admission, Florissant; (719) 748-3252 (fees subject to change)

Garden of the Gods, free admission, Colorado Springs; (719) 634-6666

Mountain Bike Tours

Challenge Unlimited, Colorado Springs; (719) 633-6399 or (800) 798-5954

Restaurants

The Donut Mill, Woodland Park; (719) 687-9793

Grandmother's Kitchen, Woodland Park; (719) 687-3118

Tres Hombres, Woodland Park; (719) 687-0625

48 Waldo Canyon Trail

The Waldo Canyon Trail, although primarily a hiker's trail, does invite gonzo-minded mountain bikers to strut their stuff. What makes this trail particularly appealing to tough riders is its steep climbs out of creek beds and its fast and rocky descent—added to this is the variety of terrain Waldo Canyon delivers. Views from its highest point include Pikes Peak, Colorado Springs, and NORAD (North American Aerospace Defense Command). Its location right beside U.S. Highway 24 makes for a speedy assault of the trail for those in transit. For those of you whose riding mentality is one fry short of a Happy Meal, try tackling the stairs on your return.

Start: Trailhead to Waldo Canyon

Distance: 7-mile lariat

Approximate riding time: Advanced riders, 1 hour; intermediate riders, 1.5–2 hours

Aerobic level: Physically challenging due to the variety of climbing and portaging of your bicycle over rocky creeks

Technical difficulty: Technically moderate to challenging due to the many rocky sections and big drop-offs

Terrain: Singletrack that covers a variety of different terrain: various kinds of rock surfaces, hard-packed dirt, wet forest earth, large roots, Pikes Peak granite

Schedule: May–October

Maps: DeLorme *Colorado Atlas & Gazetteer*, page 62; USGS: Woodland Park and Cascade, CO; Trails Illustrated map: #137, Pikes Peak–Cañon City, CO

Nearest town: Colorado Springs

Other trail users: Campers, but this trail is primarily used by hikers—a good reason to stay clear of the mountain bike riding in this area on the weekends

Canine compatibility: Dog-friendly

Trail contact: Pike and San Isabel National Forests, Pikes Peak Ranger District, Colorado Springs; (719) 636-1602

Finding the Trailhead: From Colorado Springs, take Interstate 25 to exit 141 and US 24 west. Drive west on US 24 for 7.8 miles before reaching the turnoff for Waldo Canyon to your right. Park your vehicle here. You'll have to portage your bicycle up a set of stairs to the registration box and the trailhead before beginning your ride.

From Woodland Park, starting from the intersection of US 24 and Baldwin Road, head east on US 24 toward Colorado Springs. At 9.9 miles, you'll arrive at the turnoff for the Waldo Canyon trailhead on your left. The trailhead will be to the north side of US 24, so you'll have to cross US 24's westbound traffic. (Should you miss this opportunity to cross US 24's westbound traffic, another turnoff will be to your left. Stay in the left lane and turn left at 11 miles, now backtracking westbound on US 24. Drive for 1.1 miles and bear right into the Waldo Canyon parking lot.)

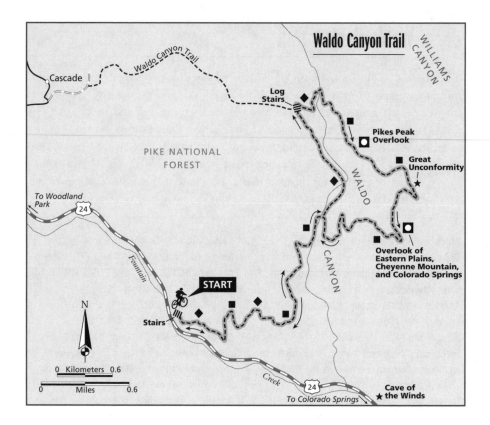

The Ride

At its worst, Waldo Canyon is a crowded thoroughfare for weekend hikers. At its best, it's a grunt of a climb to some of the area's best unobstructed views of Pikes Peak. The tireless mountain biker is rewarded with a singletrack descent of titillating switchbacks, past a veritable smorgasbord of geological timetables and drop-offs.

To help maintain and operate the district system trails, a donation of $1.00 is asked of every user and is collected at the bottom of the wooden stairs leading to the trail's registration box and the start of your ride.

If not paralyzed with quizzical angst, wondering why you just carried yourself and your bike up these steep wooden steps, begin riding up the switchbacks. The trail parallels US 24 for roughly a mile then climbs steadily, your tires relentlessly spinning through the ball-bearing–like Pikes Peak granite that blankets the trail. On a softer note, patches of lavender mullein *(Verbascum thapsus)* and roundleaf bluebell *(Campanula rotundifolia)* stand alongside these unrelenting granite pebbles. Each spring and summer these wildflowers passively assert Waldo Canyon's soft beauty among the harshness of semiarid sand and rock. As the trail turns away from the highway, you're given your last look at civilization for a while. Views of the city of Colorado Springs vanish as you descend farther into this sun-splashed foothill oasis.

Riding through tall stands of leafy greens, surrounded by the smell of summer camp, you descend into a cool meadow area, complete with campfire rings. If you plan to camp and need a campfire, it's best that you use these rings, so as not to scorch the earth any more than necessary. Once you arrive at the WALDO CANYON LOOP, 3½ MILES sign, bear left. In so doing, you'll be riding the loop in a clockwise direction, choosing to climb in the shade rather than in the more exposed areas of Waldo Canyon. From here the work begins.

A mile of steep climbing awaits you. The large rocks, knotty tree roots, and creek-crossings make it a grunt by anyone's standards—a true trial rider's dream. By mile 2.5, the trail Ys before sending you up another set of wooden stairs. This time, the stairs are a bit more manageable, as long as you hug the left side—anyone less than advanced might find this difficult to ride. Bear right at another Waldo Canyon sign and continue ascending through the ponderosa and fir forest. Areas of this trail are severely loaded with rocks, so be aware on the approach. By the third mile the trail levels out and offers incredible views of 14,110-foot Pikes Peak along the east rim of Waldo Canyon.

By mile 3.4 you come upon an example of the "Great Unconformity"—a term coined by the "Father of Geology" James Hutton. The Great Unconformity refers to a break in the geologic record in which two kinds of rock are found in abnormal succession. In this case, Precambrian metamorphic rock (granite) sits directly beneath Pennsylvanian red sandstone, with no sign between of the Ordovician, Silurian, Devonian, or Mississippian periods. With 500 million years of time apparently lost, a crucial piece in Earth's geological jigsaw puzzle remains missing. Possible explanations for this mysterious absence are severe erosion, folding, and faulting.

From the site of the Great Unconformity, the trail traverses the sun-exposed hills above Williams Canyon before snaking its way back down into Waldo Canyon. Williams Canyon cuts through the hillside in which the Cave of the Winds is

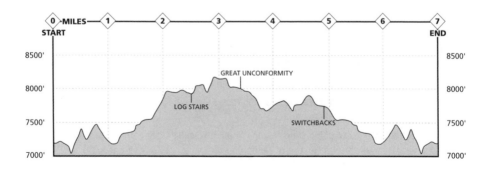

located. Colorado's only limestone cavern developed as a tourist attraction, Cave of the Winds deposits its dissolved limestone along the roadside leading through Williams Canyon. Cave of the Winds is a dazzling network of rooms and passageways encrusted with limestone stalactites, stalagmites, and flowstone curtains. In 1881 two young brothers, picnicking with their church, decided to explore the area, discovering a 200-million-year-old geological phenomenon. Today, Cave of the Winds is one of Colorado's leading attractions. The cave is open year-round (10:00 A.M. to 5:00 P.M. in the winter and 9:00 A.M. to 9:00 P.M. in the summer), offering a variety of tours, for the casual walker or the hard-core spelunker, and an outstanding laser-light show.

Riding high above Williams Canyon, the trail passes gorgeous views of the eastern plains, Colorado Springs, and the hollowed-out Cheyenne Mountain—home to NORAD (North American Aerospace Defense Command). The underground city housing NORAD monitors foreign aircraft, missiles, and space systems that could threaten U.S. security. Aside from the vast array of antennae protruding from its scalp, Cheyenne Mountain is virtually indistinguishable from any other mountain in Colorado. The trail from this point is packed with dirt and thick with overgrowth as it begins its descent back into Waldo Canyon.

This descent is fast and fun as it travels over a variety of terrain, keeping you on your toes if not putting you on your noggin. Manitou limestone–sprinkled switchbacks, precipitously sloping Sawatch sandstone, crowded Peerless (better known as "Fearless") dolomite sections, and carvable Pikes Peak granite turns—all challenge the standards of your ANSI and SNELL headgear. Riders are afforded a crash-course in geology as a host of interpretive signs explains the pedigree of each of these sections.

By mile 5.3 you arrive at a tributary of Fountain Creek and the WALDO CANYON LOOP, 3½ MILES sign. Bear left and return to your vehicle. After a short climb out of this valley, the descent to your vehicle is sweet and fast, offering blind corners and a number of rocks. You'll arrive at the trail register at 7 miles. If you're feeling lucky, try doing the stairs down to the parking lot.

Miles and Directions

- **0.0** Start at the registration tower and box at the top of the stairs.
- **0.1** Waldo Canyon Trail will bear left. To the right will be an overlook of US 24 and a description of the composition of Pikes Peak granite.
- **0.8** Cross the ridge and begin descending into a clearing.
- **1.6** Arrive at a brown sign reading WALDO CANYON LOOP, 3½ MILES. Bear left here. You'll return to this spot after completing the loop.
- **2.5** Reach the second set of log stairs leading to an intersection with another trail. Veer right, as the left route will lead you out of Waldo Canyon and to the town of Cascade.

3.4 Here's a good example of the Great Unconformity.

4.9 Begin your switchback descent.

5.3 Arrive at the creek and the Waldo Canyon sign.

7.0 Arrive back at the trail registration tower and box.

Ride Information

Local Information

Woodland Park Chamber of Commerce, 210 West Midland Avenue, Woodland Park 80866; (719) 687-9885; www.woodland-park-co.org

Local Events and Attractions

Cave of the Winds, Manitou Springs; (719) 685-4444

Florissant Fossil Beds National Monument, $2.00–$4.00 admission, Florissant; (719) 748-3252 (fees subject to change)

Garden of the Gods, free admission, Colorado Springs; (719) 634-6666

Mountain Bike Tours

Challenge Unlimited, Colorado Springs; (719) 633-6399 or (800) 798-5954

Restaurants

The Donut Mill, Woodland Park; (719) 687-9793

Grandmother's Kitchen, Woodland Park; (719) 687-3118

Tres Hombres, Woodland Park; (719) 687-0625

49 Captain Jack's Trail

I don't think Billy Joel had this trail in mind when he wrote "Captain Jack will get you high tonight. Just a little push and you'll be smiling," but the words still apply, if not the original meaning. A bit of pushing to reach the top is all it takes for you to be smiling—on the way down. This trail is certainly one of Colorado Springs' best, offering a good climb and a fast, and somewhat technical, descent. Area riders divide Captain Jack's Trail into Upper and Lower sections. While either one of the sections can be ridden as one, complete ride, this description combines both sections, which, as any rider in Colorado Springs will tell you, is what you should do anyway. High Drive Road divides the two sections of Captain Jack's Trail.

Start: Captain Jack's trailhead
Distance: 7.2-mile loop
Approximate riding time: Advanced riders, 1 hour; intermediate riders, 1.5-2 hours
Aerobic level: Physically moderate due to some longer climbs at higher elevations
Technical difficulty: Technically moderate to challenging due to some tighter, rockier sections over steep and precipitously sloping terrain
Terrain: Singletrack and dirt road that leads through a rocky canyon over sometimes tight and rocky terrain

Schedule: North Cheyenne Canyon Park is open May 1–November 1, 5:00 A.M.–11:00 P.M. and November 1–May 1, 5:00 A.M.–9:00 P.M.
Maps: DeLorme Colorado Atlas & Gazetteer, page 62; USGS: Manitou Springs, CO; Trails Illustrated: #137, Pikes Peak–Cañon City, CO
Nearest town: Colorado Springs
Other trail users: Hikers and motorcyclists
Canine compatibility: Dog-unfriendly due to the preponderance of vehicular travel both on the singletrack and on Gold Camp Road
Trail contact: Pike and San Isabel National Forests, Pikes Peak Ranger District, Colorado Springs; (719) 636-1602

Finding the Trailhead: From Colorado Springs, drive west on Interstate 24 from its intersection with I-25 for 1.5 miles then bear left onto Twenty-first Street, heading up the hill, and drive for 0.8 mile. Turn right at the stop light onto Lower Gold Camp Road and continue for 1.2 miles before arriving at a four-way stop intersection. Here Lower Gold Camp Road turns into Gold Camp Road. Drive through the intersection and continue driving on Gold Camp Road for 4.2 miles. The road will turn to dirt as you enter North Cheyenne Park. Continue on the dirt Gold Camp Road for roughly 2 miles before turning right into the parking lot, just before the first tunnel.

The Ride

Begin by riding through North Cheyenne Canyon Park on the dirt Gold Camp Road. Views of the eastern plains and Colorado Springs lie to your left, as you pass through the first of two tunnels. Gold Camp Road climbs gradually and offers a comfortable warm-up to the climbing that lies ahead. Be advised that there is vehicular

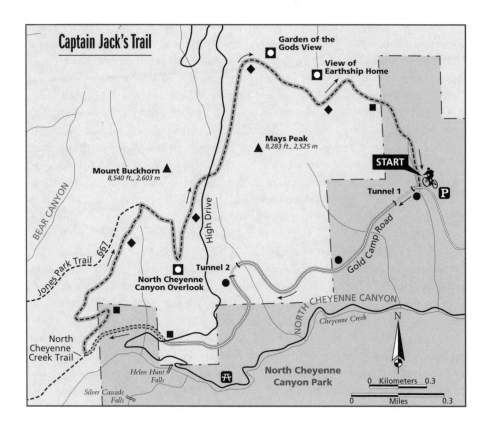

Captain Jack's Trail

Garden of the Gods View

View of Earthship Home

Mays Peak
8,283 ft., 2,525 m

Mount Buckhorn ▲
8,540 ft., 2,603 m

START

Tunnel 1

P

High Drive

BEAR CANYON

Jones Park Trail 667

Tunnel 2

North Cheyenne
Canyon Overlook

Gold Camp Road

NORTH CHEYENNE CANYON

Cheyenne Creek

N

North
Cheyenne
Creek Trail

Helen Hunt
Falls

Silver Cascade
Falls

North Cheyenne
Canyon Park

0   Kilometers   0.3

0   Miles   0.3

traffic on Gold Camp Road, so be careful. In the early 1900s, Gold Camp Road served as a rail bed for the narrow gauge Colorado Springs & Cripple Creek District Railway Company (CS&CCD) whose trains carried gold ore mined in Cripple Creek to Colorado Springs. The CS&CCD, or "Short Line" as it had become known, ran nearly 46 miles between Colorado Springs and the Cripple Creek–Victor Mining District. The rails long since gone, all that is left for you to do is to marvel at this century-old engineering achievement and to ride to the beginning of the singletrack and the beginning of your own personal, physical achievement.

Having passed through the parking lot, you connect with the trail's singletrack (some refer to this singletrack as the beginning of the Buckhorn Trail, while others refer to it as Upper Captain Jack's Trail). This marks the beginning of a moderately tough climb over a saddle where Upper Captain Jack's Trail intersects with the Jones Park Trail (alternately known as the Buckhorn Trail). Leading to this saddle, the trail switches back over smooth, but narrow singletrack that falls precipitously to the right. After riding for roughly 3.5 miles, ponderosa pine give way to taller stands of Douglas fir as you continue grunting your way to the saddle.

While the saddle offers good reason to rest and wait for straggling riders, it doesn't offer much in the way of views. For the overlook reward, continue riding on Upper Captain Jack's to a beautiful North Cheyenne Canyon Park overlook to your right. Here, enjoy the views of Mount Baldy and the North American Aerospace Defense Command (NORAD) inside Cheyenne Mountain. The NORAD buildings inside Cheyenne Mountain are supported by 1,319 springs, each weighing half a ton, which protect the delicate electronic equipment inside from shock. NORAD is tasked to maintain aerospace warning and control initiatives for North America. That means, if UFOs, or some such other threatening aircraft, were to attack us, NORAD would come to our defense and save us from certain ruin. According to NORAD, the "defense" includes a "network of ground-based radars and fighters to detect, intercept, and if necessary, engage any air-breathing threat to the continent. These fighters consist of U.S. F-15s and F-16s, and Canadian CF-18s."

So as not to be mistaken as a grounded UFO, descend from this overlook over fast and technical terrain. The trail combines granite-laden singletrack with a narrow and sloping surface. This section of trail includes some of the more technical sections of the entire route. Be sure to keep an eye out for motorcyclists on their way up as you race down to meet with High Drive Road.

Once you intersect and cross High Drive Road, continue your ride on Lower Captain Jack's Trail, which parallels High Drive Road to the north before bearing in a more easterly direction. The singletrack on this section of trail can be quite fast and sinuous, offering beautiful views of the Garden of the Gods after 5.5 miles into your ride. The Garden of the Gods offers an impressive array of red and white sandstone that has been shaped into tall spires by the slow, erosive elements of wind and water. While these rocks are the same as the upturned red sandstones between Denver (Red Rocks Amphitheater) and Colorado Springs, they are also larger and more impressive than anywhere else along the Front Range.

From this same viewpoint, if you look carefully enough, you might notice an interesting-looking home. To the northwest sits an earth ship, built in the spirit of renewable and sustainable living. Earth ships typically are passive solar homes made

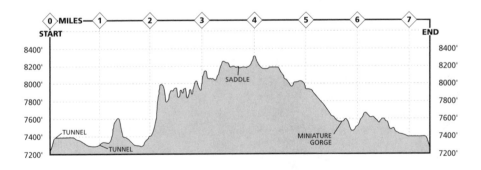

Checking out the view from the Cheyenne Mountain Overlook.

of natural and recycled materials. Aside from their environmentally friendly construction, another benefit to earth ships includes an off-grid home that incurs low to no utility bills. From this viewpoint, ride through a very narrow, steep, and high-walled section of trail. Like riding through a 15-foot-long miniature gorge, the terrain is technical and tight. It's a good idea not to meet with an oncoming motorcycle through this section of trail, as the steep, high walls offer no shoulder. Here, jungle rules apply: gross tonnage wins. After passing through this mini-gorge, you'll ride another short grunt to another easterly overlook before descending the rest of the way to your vehicle.

There are a variety of other trail options in this general vicinity. One such trail is called the Chutes. It begins across Gold Camp Road and the parking lot to Captain Jack's Trail and descends on technical and fast terrain back to town.

Miles and Directions

0.0 From the parking lot of the Captain Jack's trailhead, bear right onto the dirt Gold Camp Road and begin climbing through North Cheyenne Canyon, heading in a southwesterly direction.

0.1 Pass through the first tunnel.

1.0 Pass through the second tunnel.

1.7 Gold Camp Road intersects with High Drive Road, by the second parking lot on your right. Bear right into the parking lot and intersect with the Upper Captain Jack's Trail wide doubletrack in the northwest corner of the parking lot.

2.4 The wide doubletrack will intersect with the continuation of the Upper Captain Jack's Trail on the right. Bear right onto the narrow singletrack and continue climbing in an easterly direction on the Upper Captain Jack Trail.

3.7 Reach a saddle and the intersection of the Upper Captain Jack's Trail and the Jones Park Trail on the left. Bear right, continuing on the Upper Captain Jack's Trail and heading in an easterly direction.

4.6 Upper Captain Jack's Trail intersects with High Drive Road, which divides Upper Captain Jack's Trail from Lower Captain Jack's Trail. Cross High Drive Road and continue riding on Lower Captain Jack's Trail.

5.7 Pass through the trail's miniature gorge.

7.2 Arrive at your vehicle.

Ride Information

Local Information

Woodland Park Chamber of Commerce, 210 West Midland Avenue, Woodland Park 80866; (719) 687-9885; www.woodland-park-co.org

Local Events and Attractions

Florissant Fossil Beds National Monument, $2.00-$4.00 admission, Florissant; (719) 748-3252 (fees subject to change)

Garden of the Gods, free admission, Colorado Springs; (719) 634-6666

Helen Hunt Falls Visitor Center, Memorial Day through Labor Day, 9:00 A.M.–5:00 P.M., North Cheyenne Canyon Park, Colorado Springs; (719) 633-5701

Starsmore Discovery Center, April 1 through November, 9:00 A.M.–5:00 P.M., North Cheyenne Canyon Park, Colorado Springs; (719) 578-6146

50 Shelf Road

The Shelf Road is a historic stagecoach toll road that connects Cañon City with the gold-mining camps of Cripple Creek and Victor. The Shelf travels precipitously along the limestone cliffs of Helena Canyon then descends into the canyon to run through incredibly tall red-rock walls. Here is a mellow ride that offers a lot of spinning. It's a cool ride to combine with a day of gambling in the town of Cripple Creek. The Banks-Shelf Road area is also world-renowned for its rock climbing. For those who want something a little more laid-back than Cripple Creek, make tracks to Victor, a traditional turn-of-the-twentieth-century mining town that doesn't allow gambling. Bighorn sheep abound within Helena Canyon and most often can be spotted drinking from Fourmile Creek at dusk. Helena Canyon is a "hard hat" zone, meaning loose rock will occasionally give in to gravity. The return from Cripple Creek or Victor is fast, offering a number of blind curves and washboard sections of road, with the last push to the Banks-Shelf Road parking area one burley climb.

Start: The Banks-Shelf Road parking area; take the right fork (Shelf Road)

Distance: 27.2-mile out-and-back

Approximate riding time: Advanced riders, 3.5 hours; intermediate riders, 4.5–5 hours

Aerobic level: Physically easy to moderate due to some degree of climbing

Technical difficulty: Technically easy with no major obstacles

Terrain: Shelf Road Trail follows an old wagon and stagecoach toll road; aside from the occasional washboard effect, the road is relatively smooth; at times it is very exposed

Schedule: April–October

Maps: DeLorme *Colorado Atlas & Gazetteer*, page 62; USGS: Cooper Mountain, CO; Cripple Creek South, CO; Trails Illustrated: #137, Pikes Peak-Cañon City, CO

Nearest town: Cripple Creek

Other trail users: Horseback riders, hikers, four-wheelers, bighorn sheep viewers, climbers, and gamblers

Canine compatibility: Dog-unfriendly due to vehicular traffic on Shelf Road

Trail contact: Bureau of Land Management, Royal Gorge Resource Area, Cañon City; (719) 269-8538

Finding the Trailhead: From Colorado Springs, drive south on Interstate 25 for 45 miles to Pueblo. In Pueblo, drive west on U.S. Highway 50 to Cañon City. Make a right onto Dozier Avenue near the Wal-Mart. (If you're coming from the west, make a left onto Dozier.) After 0.5 mile, Dozier turns west and becomes Central. Continuing on Central (Dozier), drive west for 1.6 miles then turn right onto Fields Avenue. It turns into a dirt road at 11.6 miles. Continue on Fields for another 2.3 miles before arriving at the Banks—a limestone cliff area located near the beginning of Shelf Road and known internationally for its incredible sport climbing. Park here and begin your ride, taking the right fork (Shelf Road).

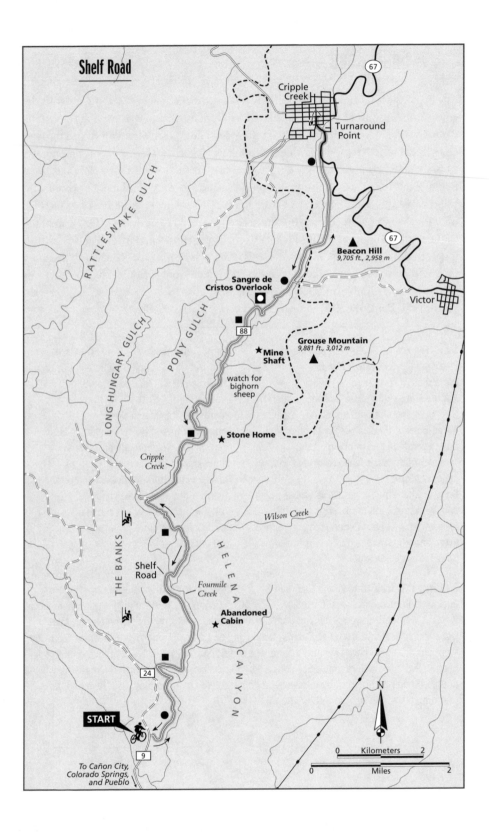

Shelf Road

Cripple Creek

Turnaround Point

Beacon Hill
9,705 ft., 2,958 m

Victor

Sangre de Cristos Overlook

Grouse Mountain
9,881 ft., 3,012 m

★ Mine Shaft

watch for bighorn sheep

★ Stone Home

Cripple Creek

Wilson Creek

Shelf Road

Fourmile Creek

★ Abandoned Cabin

START

To Cañon City, Colorado Springs, and Pueblo

RATTLESNAKE GULCH

LONG HUNGARY GULCH

PONY GULCH

THE BANKS

HELENA CANYON

N

Kilometers
0   2

Miles
0   2

The Ride

As part of the National Scenic Byway of Colorado's Gold Belt Tour and the Bureau of Land Management's designated National Backcountry Byway system, Shelf Road recalls much of the Old West. Originally built in 1892 as a wagon and stagecoach toll road, Shelf Road connected the Arkansas River Valley community of Cañon City with the turn-of-the-twentieth-century gold camps of Cripple Creek and Victor. Today the road offers the relaxed mountain biker a chance to experience Colorado history from the seat of his or her mountain bike.

Colorado in the 1890s was home to America's last great gold rush. Towns such as Cripple Creek, Victor, Florence, McCourt, Adelaide, and Wilbur (towns included within the Cripple Creek Mining District) all shared in the spoils that gold could afford. Gold offered these towns a chance to make a name for themselves—or, as in the case of Cripple Creek, a new name. When Bob Womack discovered gold in October of 1890 in a high-country cow pasture west of Pikes Peak, the town of Poverty Gulch officially changed its name to Cripple Creek.

Throughout its gold-mining days, Cripple Creek enjoyed a standard of living never before seen in Colorado. By 1893 Cripple Creek had unearthed $3 million in gold ore. That figure grew to $59 million by 1899, and by the end of the gold rush (circa 1903), area gold mines within the Cripple Creek Mining District had produced $432 million—making it the fourth-largest gold-producing camp in the world.

Cripple Creek established itself as a social center as well. Grand opera houses were built where a variety of musicians performed. Jack Dempsey drew huge crowds to his boxing bouts in town. Even President Teddy Roosevelt visited Cripple Creek, and while squatting and rubbing elbows with fellow miners, panned for gold.

Today, Cripple Creek continues to grow by offering limited-stakes gambling. Other than housing an estimated 2,200 new jobs, many of Cripple Creek's original brick buildings now merely serve as vintage facades to the glittering casinos within. Though meant to maintain the city's National Historic District designation, Cripple Creek casinos can't help but lend an element of gross excess. Their buzzing bells,

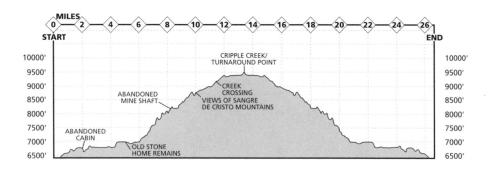

neon lights, and reeling pace all but erase any semblance of Cripple Creek's Old West charm.

Six miles from Cripple Creek lies the gold-mining town of Victor. Known as the City of Mines, Victor is the heart of the great Cripple Creek Mining District and, by point of pride, remains true to its roots. Its century-old streets offer quiet, non-gambling relief from Cripple Creek, while retaining much of the area's 1890s authenticity. The original brick buildings, built by residents after a fire destroyed their town in 1898, still stand. Even the hillsides are dotted with original miners' homes, visual echoes recalling the town's illustrious past.

Connecting Colorado's past with its present is Shelf Road. Six hundred feet above Fourmile Creek, Shelf Road cuts through Helena Canyon's limestone cliff walls. The initial 4 miles is perhaps the most dramatic section of the entire route. If you fear heights or are prone to vertigo, this section could be difficult. Shelf Road skirts dangerously above Helena Canyon, oftentimes offering only a car width's margin of error.

As you descend to the canyon floor and the banks of Fourmile Creek, a feeling of peace overcomes you as the exposed road gives way to hosts of juniper, legions of scrub oak, and a spattering of lush cottonwoods. Behind you remain the limestone crags whose allure has attracted many a rock climber. From here, one begins the extended 10-mile push to Cripple Creek. Shelf Road gradually climbs as it winds its way across and back Fourmile Creek.

By mile 6, the steeper part of the climbing begins and leads you through forests of lodgepole pine by mile 8. These elegant and slender tree trunks were used by American Indians as poles for their teepees, hence the name. Like smoke from a fire ring, your eyes are drawn upward to the tips of these trees and onward toward the tops of the canyon walls.

After passing a number of abandoned mines between miles 10 and 11.4, Shelf Road forks at mile 11.8. Victor is to the right, and Cripple Creek, to the left. Here remnants of the El Paso Mine remain. After veering left, your solitary bicycle ride quickly fades as you become absorbed in the bustle of Cripple Creek. Veer left once again onto Colorado 67 at mile 13.3 and you come to downtown Cripple Creek, home to the largest population of free-roving donkeys—some the direct descendants of those used during Cripple Creek's gold-mining glory.

Your return trip is fast and bumpy. Be cautious of your speed, as the descent on Shelf Road offers many tight turns. The many washboards are sure to test your shocks, and for those without shocks, your patience. Enjoy the ride.

Miles and Directions

0.0 Start at the Banks-Shelf Road parking area. Take the right fork and begin climbing up Shelf Road.

2.0 Riding along the steep limestone walls of Helena Canyon, you'll notice an old abandoned cabin from the late 1800s on the canyon floor.

4.0 Shelf Road eventually widens and leads into the floor of Helena Canyon, affording additional parking to climbers and those who would like to forgo the initial, narrow descent to the canyon bottom. (The crags behind you offer great climbing opportunities and can be accessed via a variety of foot trails.)

5.0 The remains of an old stone home are on your right.

8.1 Come to an old abandoned mine shaft to your right.

10.0 Take in the beautiful vista of the Sangre de Cristo Mountains off to the west.

11.4 Cross Cripple Creek.

11.8 Shelf Road forks. Here signs to the town of Cripple Creek point to the left fork, while signs for Victor point to the right fork. Take the left fork and ride toward Cripple Creek. Pass the Scenic Byway sign, marked by a Colorado columbine.

13.3 Shelf Road connects to CO 67. At the stop sign, bear left onto CO 67 and ride into Cripple Creek.

13.6 Reach the corner of Second Street and Bennett Avenue, downtown Cripple Creek. Turn around here and return the way you came.

27.2 Arrive at your vehicle.

Ride Information

Local Information

Cañon City Chamber of Commerce, 403 Royal Gorge Boulevard, Cañon City 81212; (719) 275-2331

Cripple Creek Chamber of Commerce, P.O. Box 650, Cripple Creek 80813; (719) 689-2169 or (800) 526-8777

Local Events and Attractions

Donkey Derby Days, last full weekend in June with donkey races, greased pigs, and fun, Cripple Creek; (719) 689-2169

Fiddlers on the Arkansas, July, Cañon City; (719) 276-3225

Gold Belt Tour, year-round, Cañon City; (719) 275-2331

Gold Rush Days, third weekend in July, Victor; (719) 689-3553 or (719) 689-3211

Limited-stakes gambling, with slot machines, poker, and blackjack tables, Cripple Creek; (719) 689-2169 or (800) 526-8777

Books

A Mountain Bike Tour Guide for Cañon City, Colorado by Carol Boody (Mountain Bike Tour Guides, 1989)

Honorable Mentions

Colorado Springs Region

Five more rides in the Colorado Springs area deserve mention, even though they didn't make the "A" list. They may be a bit out of the way or more heavily traveled, but they still deserve your consideration when choosing a destination.

Q Ute Valley Park

Ute Valley Park offers a short network of singletrack trails within one of Colorado Springs' city parks. The area is a great trail for beginners taking to the trail for the first time. Ute Valley Park packs a lot into a little space, offering a great combination of fast and wide trails and sometimes more technical terrain. Popular among bikers and hikers alike, Ute Valley Park offers open meadows and interesting rock formations. Due to the park's limited trail lengths, you would best be served by riding laps around the park. Otherwise, the entire park can be ridden well within 30 minutes.

The park is open May 1–November 1, 5:00 A.M.–11:00 P.M., and November 1– May 1, 5:00 A.M.–8:00 P.M.

To reach Ute Valley Park from Colorado Springs, drive west on Woodmen Road, which will become Rockrimmon Road. Follow Rockrimmon Road for roughly 1.5 miles before bearing right onto Vindicator. Drive on Vindicator for 0.75 mile to the parking lot and trailhead.

R Palmer Park

A great and huge city park in the middle of downtown Colorado Springs, Palmer Park offers a vast network of interconnected trails. While there are some maps available for the park, they are not very accurate or easy to read. It's best that you go to Palmer Park, at least for your first time, and explore. Otherwise, go with someone who knows the area.

The trail is mostly singletrack, with some dirt road and doubletrack, over hard packed dirt and rocky terrain, as it courses through scrub oak, piñon pine, and ponderosa pine trees and yucca plants. Watch out for hikers and horseback riders, as this is a very popular trail. You're offered incredible views of Pikes Peak.

To reach Palmer Park from north of Colorado Springs, drive south from the town of Castle Rock on Interstate 25 and take exit 150 at Academy Boulevard (CO 83). Drive south on Academy for roughly 7 miles before bearing right onto Maizeland Road. Drive 0.2 mile on Maizeland before taking your next right into the park and onto Paseo. Paseo Road splits the park in half and runs through to Mark Reyner Stables on the other side of the park.

To reach Palmer Park from downtown Colorado Springs, drive east on Platte Avenue for roughly 5.5 miles before bearing left onto Academy Boulevard. Drive north on Academy Boulevard for 1.9 miles before bearing left onto Maizeland Road. Drive on Maizeland for 0.2 mile before making your next right into the park.

Park your vehicle and begin riding.

The park is open May 1–November 1, 5:00 A.M.–11:00 P.M., and November 1–May 1, 5:00 A.M.–9:00 P.M. No alcoholic beverages allowed. Dogs must be on leash. Park in designated areas only. No vehicles off roadways. No illegal dumping, golfing, or excessive noise. No firearms. No camping. No wood burning or gathering.

S Garden of the Gods

The riding in the spectacular Garden of the Gods can be described as a bittersweet experience for mountain bikers. The Garden of the Gods is open to mountain biking in a very limited capacity but offers incredibly beautiful and stunning landscapes. The southeast corner of the park offers several trails that provide spectacular scenery, for example, Ute Trail. Riders can do a number of short, singletrack loops. Some of the trails can be narrow and sinuous in spots, making for a fun family ride.

To ride the Garden of the Gods is almost an afterthought, but one well worth considering. The 1,350-acre city-owned park delivers spectacular views of Pikes Peak framed by magnificent sandstone rock formations that are more than 300 million years old.

To reach the Garden of the Gods from Colorado Springs, drive west on the Garden of the Goads Road to Thirtieth Street. Bear left onto Thirtieth Street, and drive to the Garden of the Gods Visitors Center.

T Barr Trail

The Barr Trail is a Colorado Springs classic, but it's not for the weak or hungover. The Barr Trail combines a grueling 11-mile climb, over sometimes technically and physically challenging terrain, to the top of Pikes Peak (14,110 feet). It offers an impressive 4,000-foot elevation gain in just 6.5 miles. Most of the Barr Trail is in good shape with only a few unrideable sections, the most notable of which coming (as you might expect) just before reaching the summit. Not everyone reaches the summit, however, nor do they ever intend to.

Many riders choose to return after reaching Barr Camp, which is the midway point to the summit. People have made it somewhat a tradition to offer a donation to the caretaker of the camp. As traditions go, this is one that is worth the effort. Since the trail is very popular with hikers, riders should take care when descending.

To access the Barr Trail, drive west on US 24 to the Manitou Springs exit. Drive west on Manitou Avenue and turn left onto Ruxton.

∪ Section 16

Section 16 is part of Bear Creek Regional Park and offers a network of scenic trails with beautiful easterly views of Colorado Springs. Two trails that are accessible from Section 16 include Palmer Red Rock Loop (6 miles) and Forest Overlook (2 miles). The Palmer Red Rock Loop offers some steeper, technical sections, while the Forest Overlook Trail is a bit more reserved. Also accessible from Section 16 is the Intemann Trail, which travels to Manitou Springs.

To reach Section 16, drive west on I–24 from its intersection with I–25 for 1.5 miles. Turn left onto Twenty-first Street, heading up the hill for 0.8 mile. Bear right at the stop light onto Lower Gold Camp Road. Drive on Lower Gold Camp Road for 1.2 miles to a four-way-stop intersection. Here Lower Gold Camp Road turns into Gold Camp Road. Drive through the intersection and continue driving on Gold Camp Road for 0.8 mile before bearing right into the Section 16 parking lot.

Section 16 gets its name from the official U.S. term for land measurements. All of the land in this country is identified within a series of sections and townships. A section is one square mile in size and contains 640 acres of land. Townships consist of 36 sections. In 1876, the year Colorado became a state, the federal government deeded to Colorado all the section 16s and section 36s for the purpose of generating revenue for the state.

The El Paso County Park Department currently leases "Section 16." Income derived by the state from the lease or sale of Section 16 is deposited into a fund to support public schools. Presently, approximately three million acres of land throughout Colorado are under lease.

Appendix A: Map Resources

Arapaho and Roosevelt National Forests map, available at Arapaho and Roosevelt National Forests and Pawnee National Grassland, Forest Supervisor Office, Fort Collins; (970) 498–1100

Buffalo Creek Recreation Area map, available at Pike National Forest, South Park Ranger District, Fairplay; (719) 836–2031

Colorado Hiking Trails: Pikes Peak Series, available at Pike and San Isabel National Forests, Pikes Peak Ranger District, Colorado Springs; (719) 636–1602

Devil's Backbone Open Space trail map, available at the trailhead

Larimer County Parks and Open Lands map, available at the Larimer County Parks and Open Lands Department, Loveland; (970) 679–4570

Larimer County Parks Department Map: Horsetooth Mountain Park map, available at Horsetooth Mountain Park

Lory State Park: Colorado State Parks Maps, available at Lory State Park office, Bellevue; (970) 493–1623

Matthews/Winters Park Map: Jefferson County Open Space, available at the Village Walk trailhead

Monument/Palmer Lake Trails Map, available at the Balanced Rock Bike & Ski Shop, Monument; (719) 488–9007

Pike National Forest Map, available at Pike National Forest, South Park Ranger District, Fairplay; (719) 836–2031

Pine Valley Ranch Park map, available at the Pine Valley Ranch Visitors Center

Team Telecycle map, available at the Team Telecycle bicycle shop, Woodland Park; (719) 687–6165 or (800) 894–8961

White Ranch Park Map: Jefferson County Open Space, available at the trailhead

ZIA Maps, available at select mountain bike retailers and from ZIA Maps, Boulder; (800) 844–9391

Appendix B: Bicycle Clubs and Trail Groups

Alpine Snow Bicycle Association, 620 South Knox Court, Denver, CO 80218; (303) 935–8494

American Alpine Club, 710 Tenth Street, Golden, CO, 80401; (303) 384–0110

American Cycling Association, formerly the Bicycle Racing Association of Colorado (BRAC), P.O. Box 7129, Denver, CO 80204; (303) 458–5538 or www.americancycling.org

American Trails, P.O. Box 200787, Denver, CO 80220; (303) 321–6606

Bicycle Colorado, P.O. Box 698, Salida, CO 81201; (719) 530–0051

Boulder Area Trails Coalition (BATCO), P.O. Box 201, 1705 Fourteenth Street, Boulder, CO 80302; (303) 485–2162; www.bcn.boulder.co.us/batco/

Boulder Bicycle Commuters, 4820 Thunderbird Circle #108, Boulder, CO 80303; (303) 499–7466; e-mail dallured@indra.com

Boulder Off-Road Alliance, 1420 Alpine Avenue, P.O. Box 4954, Boulder, CO 80306; (303) 667–2467

Boulder Seniors on Bikes, 2431 Mapleton Avenue, Boulder, CO 80304; (303) 443–7623; (Wednesday and Friday road rides, May–October)

Colorado Bicycle Advisory Board, 4201 East Arkansas Avenue, Denver, CO 80222; (303) 757–9982

Colorado Bicycle Program, 4201 East Arkansas Avenue, Room 212, Denver, CO 80222; (303) 757–9982

Colorado Bicycle Racing Association for Seniors (COBRAS), 7963 South Vance Street, Littleton, CO 80128; (303) 866–3894

Colorado Heart Cycle Association, P.O. Box 100743, Denver, CO 80210; (303) 267–1112; www.heartcycle.org

Colorado Mountain Club, 710 Tenth Street, #200, Golden, CO 80401; (303) 279–3080

Colorado Springs Cycling Club, P.O. Box 49602, Colorado Springs, CO 80949-9602; (719) 594–6354; www.bikesprings.com; e-mail CSCC@bikesprings.com

Colorado Trail Foundation, P.O. Box 260876, Lakewood, CO 80226; (970) 526–0809

Continental Divide Trail Alliance, P.O. Box 628, Pine, CO 80470; (303) 838–3760 and (888) 909–CDTA (2382); www.cdtrail.org

Denver Bicycle Touring Club, P.O. Box 101301, Denver, CO 80250-1301; (303) 756–7240; www.dbtc.org

Front Range Mountain Bike Association, P.O. Box 1003, Englewood, CO 80150; (303) 674–4862

Highlands Ranch Cycling Club, 8413 South Painted Sky, Highlands Ranch, CO 80126; (303) 791–6792; www.highlandsranchcycling.com

International Mountain Bicycling Association (IMBA), P.O. Box 7578, Boulder, CO 80306; (303) 545–9011; www.imba.com

The Medicine Wheel, P.O. Box 685, Manitou Springs, CO 80829; (719) 228–3038; www.qrz.com/medicine.html

National Collegiate Cycling Association, One Olympic Plaza, Colorado Springs, CO 80909; (719) 578–4581; www.usacycling.org/ncaa2

National Off-Road Bicycling Association (NORBA), One Olympic Plaza, Colorado Springs, CO 80909; (719) 578–4717 or (719) 578–4581; www.usacycling.org

Pikes Peak Area Trails Coalition, 1426 North Hancock, Suite 4, Colorado Springs, CO 80903; (719) 635–4825

Rocky Mountain Cycling Club, P.O. Box 201, Wheat Ridge, CO 80034-0201; (303) 450–9056; www.rmccrides.com

Team Evergreen Bicycle Club Inc., P.O. Box 3804, Evergreen, CO 80439; (303) 674–6048; www.teamevergreen.org

Trails and Open Space Coalition, 1426 North Hancock, Suite 4, Colorado Springs, CO 80903; (719) 633–6884

United States Cycling Federation, One Olympic Plaza, Colorado Springs, CO 80909; (719) 578–4581; www.usacycling.org

USA Cycling Inc., One Olympic Plaza, Colorado Springs, CO 80909; (719) 578–4581; www.usacycling.org

Volunteers for Outdoor Colorado, 600 South Marion Parkway, Denver, CO 80209-2597; (303) 715–1010; www.voc.org

World Bicycle Polo Federation, P.O. Box 1039, Bailey, CO 80421; (303) 838–4878

Appendix C: Bicycle Camps and Clinics

Carpenter/Phinney Mountain Bike Camp, 2626 Baseline Road, P.O. Box 252, Boulder, CO 80302; (303) 442–2371

Dirt Camp, 3131 Endicott, Boulder, CO 80303; (303) 499–3178 or (800) 711–DIRT (3478)

About the Author

Writing for a variety of local and national outdoor and technical publications, Stephen Hlawaty still finds time to refuel his soul by mountain biking, back-country skiing, and backpacking with his wife, Amanda; son, Ethan; and their dog, Moab, in the mountains near their Livermore cabin. When he's not exploring Colorado's high country, he can often be found pickin' and slidin' on his Regal Reso. He is also the author of *Mountain Biking Colorado*.